Spaccio Della Bestia Trionfante. Or the Expulsion of the Triumphant Beast. Translated From the Italian of Jordano Bruno

SPACCIO

DELLA

BESTIA TRIONFANTE.

OR THE

EXPULSION

OF THE

TRIUMPHANT BEAST.

Tranſlated from the Italian
of Jordano Bruno.

LONDON

Printed in the Year 1713.

THE
Firſt DIALOGUE.

SOPHIA.
SAULINUS.
MERCURY.

Sophia. SO that if there was no Change in Bodies, no Variety in Matter, and no Viciſſitude in Beings, there would be nothing agreeable, nothing good, or nothing pleaſant.

Saul. You have demonſtrated this very well, *Sophia.*

Soph. We ſee that Pleaſure and Satisfaction conſiſts in nothing elſe but a certain Paſſage, Progreſs, or Motion from one State to another. 'Tis certain that the State of Hunger is irkſom and unpleaſant, and Satiety is a State of Sadneſs and Dulneſs: but

B   what

what is pleaſing in any of theſe, is a Change
from one to another.   The State of venereal
Ardor torments us; the State of quenched
Luſt ſaddens us , but that which gives us
ſatisfaction, is the paſſing from one to the
other of theſe States.   We can have no de-
light in any thing preſent, till we have been
fiiſt weary of what is paſt.   Labour pleaſes
us only a ſhort time after the State of Reſt:
and we find no pleaſure in Reſt, but only a
few minutes after the State of Wearineſs.

Saul. If the Caſe be ſo, then there is no
Pleaſure without a mixture of Pain , and a
Change from one State to another, partakes
of what pleaſes, and of what diſguſts us.

Soph. You ſay right.   To what I have already ſaid, I add, that ſometimes *Jupiter* (as if
he was weary of being *Jupiter)* diverts himſelf with Agriculture, ſometimes with Hunting, and ſometimes with War.   He is now
with the Gods, then with Men, and after-
waids with Beaſts.   Such as live in the Country take their Relaxation, Paſtime, and Di-
veiſions in the City; and ſuch as live in Cities, take their Pleaſures and Diverſions in the
Country.   Thoſe who are us'd to a ſeden-
tary Life, find great ſatisfaction in walking;
and thoſe who have much occaſion to uſe
their Feet, are no leſs pleas'd with Reſt.
He that has confin'd himſelf much to the
Houſe, is extremely pleas'd with the Fields:
and he that has been much in the Fields, is
no leſs pleas'd with reſting at home.   The
frequent

frequent repeating of the fame Difh, how delicious foever, makes us loath it at laft. So that the Change from one Extreme to another, with all the Intervals, moving from one Contrary to another by all the intermediate Spaces, is fure to bring Satisfaction: And in fine, we fee fo much Familiarity betwixt one Contrary and another, that they agree better with one another, than Like agrees with Like.

Saul. The Truth of this feems pretty clear to me, becaufe there is no occafion for the Exercife of Juftice where there is no Crime; there could be no Agreement, if there was not firft a Difagreement: that which is of a fpherical figure cannot receive or contain a Sphere, becaufe two Spheres can touch only in a Point: but a Body of a convex figure can reft in a Concave. And to apply this to Morality; a proud Man can never agree with a proud Man, nor a poor Man with a poor Man, nor a Mifer with a Mifer: but the firft of thefe loves a humble Man, the fecond a rich Man, and the third a liberal Man. And therefore if we confider this thing phyfically, mathematically, and morally, we fhall fee, that that Philofopher who found out the Coincidency of Contraries, was no mean Difcoverer; and that Sage who can affign the point of Coincidence, may be efteem'd a very able Practitioner. I am fatisfy'd therefore that whatever you have produc'd on this head is ftrictly true:

B 2 but

but I'd fain know, O *Sophia*, to what purpose, for what end you speak so.

Soph. What I would infer from this, is, That the Beginning, Middle, and End, the Birth, Growth, and Perfection of whatever we behold, is from Contraries, by Contraries, in Contraries, and to Contraries: And wheresoever Contrariety is, there is Action and Reaction; there is Motion, Diversity, Multitude, and Order, there are Degrees, Succession and Vicissitude. And therefore none who considers and reflects, will ever be discourag'd or lifted up with what he is, or hath for the present, how much soever the Qualifications and Fortune of others may appear good or bad, better or worse than his own. Thus I, with my divine Object, Truth (which has been so long banish'd, hid, born down, and overwhelm'd) have judg'd this Term, which is as it were the Beginning of my Return, Appearance, Exaltation and Magnificence, by the Appointment of Fate, so much the more to be regarded, by how much the greater have been the Contradictions and Oppositions.

Saul. Thus when one is to jump, and raise himself from the Earth with the greatest Nimbleness and Agility, he first bows his Body very much, and when one would leap over a Ditch with the greatest ease, and most effectually, he must gather force by going eight or ten paces back.

Soph.

Soph. And therefore I hope to find fo much more Succefs for the future, by the Grace of Fate, the worfe Succefs I have always had hitherto.

Saul. The more a Man is deprefs'd, and the lower he is in the Wheel of Fortune, he is fo much the nearer to that point, which makes the Wheel turn round, and mount up to the top: One that t'other day gave Laws to the World, to day muft lay his Head upon a Block. But pray, *Sophia,* pleafe to give me a more particular account of your De-fign.

Soph. The great Thunderer, *Jupiter,* after having enjoy'd Youth fo many Years, gave himfelf up to wild Ramblings, and took up all his time in the Affairs of Arms and Love: But now, being tam'd, he begins to decline in his Wantonnefs and Vices, and to lofe the Tafte of the Diverfions and Entertainments of Youth and Manhood.

Saul. The Poets fometimes introduc'd and defcrib'd the Gods after this manner, but Philofophers never did. *Jupiter* then, and the reft of the Gods grow old! Then it is not impoffible but they may have the River of *Acheron* to pafs.

Soph. Hold, *Saulinus,* don't take me from my Subject, but hear me to an end.

Saul. Go on then, and I will liften with the greateft attention, being firmly perfua-ded that nothing can flow from your mouth but what is grave and weighty: but I doubt

my

my Head will not be able to receive and retain what you fhall fay.

Soph. Never fear that. *Jupiter,* I fay, begins to advance in Years; and admits none into his Council, but fuch as have fnowy Heads, and furrow'd Brows; fuch as have Spectacles on their Nofes, Meal on their Chins, a Staff in their Hands, and Lead at their Feet : Such I mean, who have a juft Imagination, a due Thoughtfulnefs, and a retentive Memory in the Head; a quick Apprehenfion in the Forehead ; Prudence in the Eyes ; Sagacity in the Nofe, Attention in the Ears; Truth in the Tongue ; Sincerity in the Breaft ; regular Affections in the Heart ; Patience in the Shoulders; Forgetfulnefs of Affronts on their Back; Difcretion in the Stomach; Continency in their Loins ; Firmnefs and Conftancy in their Limbs; Uprightnefs in their Steps ; the Pentateuch of Decrees in the Left Hand; difcuffive Reafon, inftructive Knowledg, governing Juftice, commanding Authority, and executive Power in the Right Hand.

Saul. He is very well provided for Counfellors. But will it not be neceffary that he be firft well cleans'd and purg'd from his Pollutions ?

Soph. He does not now any more transform himfelf into Beafts. *Europa* does not horn him like a Bull: *Danae* does not lock him up like a Purfe of Gold: *Leda* does not feather him like a Swan: The Nymph *Afteria,* and the

Phrygian Boys don't bill him like an Eagle: *Dolida* does not turn him into a Serpent: *Mnemosyne* does not degrade him into a Shepherd: *Antiope* does not make a Half-Beast of him, by turning him into a Satyr: *Alcmena* does not transform him into *Amphytrion* For the Helm which turn'd and directed this Ship of the Metamorphosis, is now become so infirm, that it can scarce resist the Violence of the Waves, and 'tis likely that for want of Water 'tis run aground. The Sails are so full of Holes and Rents, that the Wind blows in vain to fill them. The Oars, in spite of contrary Winds, us'd to push the Vessel forwards; but now (let there be ever such a Calm, let the Field of *Neptune* be ever so smooth) in vain the Boatswain calls to pull, and hawl, and draw, for the Rowers are become like Men struck with a Palsy.

Saul. O! the grand Misfortune!

Soph. This is the reason why no-body now-a-days tells any more Stories of *Jupiter's* Carnality and Voluptuousness, for truly the good Father is given up to Devotion.

Saul. As he was, I suppose, who had so many Wives, so many Maids, and so many Concubines; after he was glutted, and cloy'd, and weary of them, he said, *VANITY OF VANITIES, ALL IS VANITY.*

Soph. He thinks of the Day of his Judgment: For the Term of six and thirty thousand Years, more or less, (as 'tis given out) is at hand. Then the Revolution of the

Year

Year of the World threatens that another *Celtus* will come and refume his antient Government. And by virtue of the Change made by the Trepidation of the Univerfe, as alfo by the Jumble, Confufion and Diforder of the Planets, he is afraid that Fate will difpofe and order the Hereditary Succeffion otherwife than it was in the foregoing great mundane Revolution, whatever prognofticating Aftrologers and other Diviners are pleas'd to fay to the contrary.

Saul. He is afraid then left fome more wary *Celfo* fhould come, who, to prevent all poffible future Mifchances, would take it in his head to banifh his Sons, after the example of *Prefter John,* to the Seraglio's of Mount *Amarat,* and perhaps further, for fear fome *Saturn* fhould take a fancy to geld him ; and for the greater fecurity defend himfelf with Steel-Breeches, and be fure never to lie down without Drawers of Diamond. And fo, any fuch Attempt failing of Succefs, he will fee a Bar put to all vexatious and troublefom Confequences ; and the Birth-Day of the Goddefs of *Cyprus,* the Fall of a limping *Saturn,* the exalting of *Jupiter,* the multiplying of Sons, and Son's Sons, Grandchildren and Grandchildren's Grandchildren, thro fo many Generations as down to our times and all future times within the term fet by Fate : all thefe things, I fay, will thus be prevented.

Nec iterum ad Trojam magnus mittetur Achilles.

Things being in this condition, and *Jupiter* beholding his Death as it were drawing near, in the ungrateful Register of feeble Strength, and weak Force ; he daily makes his warmest Devotions, and pours forth his most fervent Prayers to Fate, that in the Ages to come all things may happen according to his Wish.

Saul. You tell me amazing things, *Sophia.* Do you think that *Jove* is ignorant of the Nature and Temper of Fate, which by a proper and common Epithet, is intitled *Inexorable ?* And 'tis likely, that in his leisure hours (if Fate allows him any) he sometimes turns over a Poet, and we need not make any difficulty to suppose that *Seneca* the Tragedian has faln into his hands, who gives him this Lesson

> ————*Dum Fata finunt,*
> *Vivite læti. Properat cursu*
> *Vita citato, volucrique die*
> *Rota præcipitis vertitur anni.*
> *Duræ peragunt penfa forores,*
> *Nec sua retro fila revolvunt.*
> *At genus hominum fertur rapidis*
> *Obvia fatis, incerta fui.*
> *Stygias ultro quærimus undas.*

Soph. Altho this be the Nature and Dispofition of Fate, and altho *Jupiter* himself

knows

knows it is immovable, and that nothing can be, but that which muft and fhall be; yet he does not fail to run to his Deftiny by fuch means. Fate hath ordain'd Prayers for what cannot be obtain'd, as well as for what can be obtain'd ; and that tranfmigrating Minds may not be too much pain'd, it interpofes a Draught of the River *Lethe* in the time of the Change, that fo thro the benefit of Forgetfulnefs every one may be ftrongly difpos'd to preferve himfelf in his prefent ftate. Therefore Youths do not look back to the ftate of Infancy, Infants don't defire to return to their Mother's Bellies, and none of them all would wifh to be in the fame ftate in which he was before his prefent manner of Exiftence. A Hog would not die to be any other Creature than a Hog. A Horfe would not change his Nature for any other. *Jupiter* is mightily afraid, that by very preffing Neceffities he fhall ceafe to be *Jupiter*. But the Mercy and Grace of Fate will not change his State, without fwilling him in the Water of this River.

Saul. Is it fo then, O *Sophia?* Was ever the like heard, that this fame Deity muft pour out Prayers, and live in fear of Juftice ? I wonder'd why the Gods were fo afraid of breaking their Oaths, that they fwore by the *Stygian* Lake : but now I perceive it is becaufe of the Fees that the Gods themfelves are oblig'd to pay.

Soph.

Soph. You have hit it. He hath order'd his Smith, *Vulcan*, not to work on Holy-Days. He hath commanded *Bacchus* not to assemble his Court, and not to allow his Votaries to commit Debauches, except in the time of Carnaval, and the principal Feasts of the Year, and that only after Supper-time about Sun-setting; and not that neither, without his special and express Licence. *Momus*, who had spoken against the Gods, and (as they thought) censur'd their Slips too severely, and therefore was banish'd from their Consistory and Conversation, and was placed in the Star which is upon the tip of *Calisto*'s Tail, without power to go beyond the bounds of that Parallel under which lies Mount *Caucasus*, where the poor God was consum'd with Cold and Hunger: *Momus*, I say, is call'd home, justify'd, restor'd to his former Condition, and is made Cryer in ordinary, as also upon extraordinary occasions, with a most ample Privilege to reprove Vices, without regard had to the Title or Dignity of any Person whatsoever. He hath forbid *Cupid* to wander any more up and down, in the presence of Men, Heroes, and Gods, without Breeches, as he uses to do; and hath enjoin'd him that he no longer offend the Eyes of the Heavenly Inhabitants, by showing his Buttocks in the *Via Lactea*, and the *Olympic Senate*: but that for the future he be cover'd at least from the Girdle down. And he hath strictly charg'd him not

to

to fhoot an Arrow, unlefs into the natural Mark, under the greateft penalty; and that he make Men love like other Animals, caufing them to fall in love at certain feafons; and as *March* is the ordinary time for Cats, and *May* for Affes, fo let thofe Days be allotted to Men, in which *Petrarcha* fell in love with *Laura*, and *Dante* with *Beatrix*. And this is order'd in form of Interim, till the next general Council, the Sun entring into the tenth Degree of *Libra*, which is in the Head of the River *Eridanus* or *Po*, where *Orion* bends his Knee. Then fhall he reftore that natural Law, by which every Man is allow'd to have as many Wives as he can maintain and impregnate: For 'tis a vain and unjuft thing, and perfectly againft natural Order and Equity, that that Man-making Seed, which might raife up Heroes, and fill the empty Seats of Heaven, fhould be fpilt upon a Woman already impregnated and great with Child, or upon fome other worfe Subjects, as it's often done upon illegitimate Strumpets, who for fear of Shame and Difgrace provoke Abortions.

Saul. Very well provided, in my mind! But what more?

Soph. This fame *Ganymedes*, who, in fpite of *Juno*'s mortal grudge at him, was fo much in favour, and who alone was permitted to accoft *Jupiter*, and reach forth to him the three-furrow'd Thunder-bolts, while the Gods ftood behind him at an awful diftance;

at

at prefent, I believe, if he hath no other thing to recommend him, than what he has loft, 'tis to be fear'd that from *Jupiter*'s Page, he will not ha' fo much intereft as to be made the Squire of *Mars*.

Saul. How came this Change about?

Soph. Both from what I told you of *Jupiter* himfelf and his Change, and alfo from the envious *Saturn*, who fome days ago, under pretence of Merriment and Sport, ftrok'd the young Man's Chin and Vermilion Cheeks with his rude Hand after fuch a manner, that his Face turn'd pale upon the Touch, and by little and little that Grace and Comelinefs diminifh'd, which was fo powerful as to ravifh *Jove* from Heaven, and made him be ravifh'd by *Jove* in his turn to Heaven: And thus the Son of a Man was deify'd, and the Father of the Gods became a Bird.

Saul. Thefe are ftupendous things! Go on.

Soph. He hath enjoin'd all the Gods, that none of their Pages, nor Gentlemen of their Bed-Chambers, fhall be under the Age of Five and Twenty.

Saul. Ah, ah, what does *Apollo* fay now of his dear *Iacinthus*?

Soph. Oh! if you knew how much he is difpleas'd!

Saul. I really believe that his Grief caufes this Gloominefs and Obfcurity in the Heavens, which has lafted above a week. His

Breath

Breath produces thick Clouds, his Groans produce tempestuous Winds, and his Tears produce copious and heavy Rains.

Soph. You have guess'd it.

Saul. But what becomes of the poor Boy?

Soph. Apollo has a mind to send him to study the *Belles Lettres,* in some reform'd University or College, and commit him to the Care of some Pedant.

Saul. O treacherous Fortune! O deceitful Chance! Is this pretty Boy a fit bit for a Pedant? Were it not better to commit him to the Discipline of a Poet? to form him by the hands of an Orator, or to make him Cross-bearer? Were it not more expedient to tie him over to the Rules of——

Soph. No more, no more of that: What must be, shall be; and what was to be, is. But to compleat the History of *Ganymedes;* t'other night hoping to meet with as kind a Reception as he us'd to do, he presented a Bowl of Nectar to *Jupiter,* with his wonted childish Leering : but *Jupiter* fixing his angry Eyes upon him, said, ' Art thou not asham'd,
' O Son of *Tros?* Do'st thou think thou
' wilt always be a Boy? 'Tis strange that
' thou do'st not grow in Discretion and Judg-
' ment, as thou growest in Years. Do'st
' thou not perceive that the time in which
' thou camest to deafen my Ears, as we were
' going out at the utter Court, is now past?
' *Silenus, Faunus,* and he of *Lampsacus,* and
' the rest thought themselves happy, if they
' had

‘ had but the opportunity of rinſing one of
‘ thy little Cups, or even to touch the Hem
‘ of thy Garment. And to preſerve that
‘ Touch, they did not waſh their Hands
‘ when they went to eat, or do whatever elſe
‘ they went about. Now conſider with thy
‘ ſelf, for thou muſt follow ſome other Cal-
‘ ling. I’ll have no more of thy Rogueries
‘ and waggiſh Tricks.’ If you had but ſeen
the Countenance of this poor Boy or Youth,
I know not whether Compaſſion or Jeſt, or
a Strife between both would have affeded
you moſt.

Saul. Upon this occaſion I believe that
riſit Apollo.

Soph. Take notice, for what you have
already heard, is nothing to what you are
to hear.

Saul. Poſſible!

Soph. Yeſterday, which was the Anniver-
ſary for the Victory of the Gods over the
Giants, immediately after Dinner, ſhe who
alone governs univerſal Nature, and to
whom all the Happineſs under Heaven is
owing,

> *Æneadum genetrix, hominum divumque po-*
>   *teſtas,*
> *Alma Venus, cœli ſubter labentia ſigna,*
> *Quæ mare navigerum, quæ terras frugiferenteis*
> *Concelebras : per te quoniam genus omne ani-*
>   *mantum*
> *Concipitur, viſitque exortum lumina ſolis.*
>
> *Te,*

Te, Dea, te fugiunt venti, te nubila cœli,
Adventumque tuum · Tibi fuaves Dædala
tellus
Summittit flores, tibi rident æquora Ponti,
Placatumque nitet diffufo lumine Cælum, &c.

Having order'd a Ball, fhe prefented herfelf
with fuch Grace and Comelinefs, as would
have charm'd and overcome *Charon* himfelf,
and, as it was her bounden Duty, fhe went
firft to pay her Refpects to *Jupiter*, who, inftead of what he us'd to do, did embrace
him with her left Arm, and prefs her Breaft
to his. Then with the two foremoft Fingers
of the right Hand preffing her under Lip,
Mouth touch'd Mouth, Tongue Tongue,
Teeth Teeth (too wanton Careffes of a Fa
ther towards his Daughter) and fo they rofe
to the Ball.

Yefternight he laid his right Hand upon
his Breaft, and ftarted back, (as who would
fay, *Noli me tangere)* with a compaffionate
Look, and a Countenance full of Devotion;
and then fpoke after this manner: ' Ah *Ve-*
' *nus, Venus,* is it poffible that you have not
' confider'd my Cafe, but efpecially your
' own, once in your Life? Can you believe
' that what Men fay of us is true? *viz.* that
' whofoever of us is old, is always old; who-
' foever is young, is always young; who-
' foever is a Child, is always fo; thus eter-
' nally continuing as we were, when we
' were firft taken up into Heaven; and that,
' as

‘ as our Pictures and Images are always the
‘ same upon Earth, so our vital Complexion
‘ is not subject to any Change or Alteration
‘ in Heaven.

‘ This day's Feast brings into my mind
‘ that Disposition which I was in, when I
‘ thunder'd upon and overthrew the fierce
‘ Giants, who were so bold as to set *Ossa*
‘ upon *Pelia*, and *Olympus* upon *Ossa*; when
‘ I was able to throw down to the dark Ca-
‘ verns of devouring Hell the fierce *Briareus*,
‘ to whom his Mother *Terra* gave a hundred
‘ Arms and as many Hands, to enable him
‘ to attack Heaven, and throw a hundred
‘ Rocks against the Gods with great force:
‘ when I banish'd the bold and audacious
‘ *Typheus* to that place where the *Tyrrhenian*
‘ Sea joins it self with that of *Ionia*, thrust-
‘ ing him under the Isle of *Trinacria*, that so
‘ he might have a perpetual Tomb tho he
‘ was alive. From whence the Poet says,

Vasta giganteis ingesta est insula membris
Trinacris, & magnis subjectum molibus urget
Æthereas ausum sperare Typhoea sedes.
Nititur ille quidem, pugnatque resurger sæpe
Dextra sed Ausonio manus est subjecta Peloro
Læva Pachyne, tibi Lilybeo crura premuntur ·
Degravat Ætna caput, sub qua resupinus a-
  renas
Ejectat, flammamque fero vomit ore Typhoeus,
  &c.

‘ I who thunder’d the Iſle of *Prochita* upon
‘ another; I who repreſs’d the Boldneſs of
‘ *Licaon,* and at the time of *Deucalion* melted
‘ the Earth rebellious againſt Heaven; I
‘ who, by ſo many manifeſt and ſignal Per-
‘ formances, have ſhew’d that I am moſt
‘ worthy of my Authority, am not now able
‘ to make head againſt and withſtand certain
‘ puny Men; and I am conſtrain’d to let the
‘ World go as Chance and Fortune would
‘ have it, to my great diſhonour and ſhame:
‘ and he that purſues Fortune, overtakes her;
‘ and he that overcomes her, enjoys her.
‘ Now I am become like *Eſop*’s old Lion,
‘ that the Aſs kick’d without any danger,
‘ the Ape made mouths at, and the Hog
‘ rub’d her dirty ſide againſt, as at an inſen-
‘ ſible Block. Where I formerly had moſt
‘ noble Oracles, Fanes, and Altars; now
‘ they are moſt unworthily demoliſh’d, and
‘ miſerably profan’d, and in their place Al-
‘ tars and Statues are erected to certain Per-
‘ ſons whom I am aſham’d to name, becauſe
‘ they are worſe than our Satyrs, Fauns, and
‘ other Half-Beaſts, viler than even the Cro-
‘ codiles of *Egypt:* For theſe being led only
‘ by Magick and Mechaniſm, ſhew ſome
‘ ſigns of Divinity; but the others are mere
‘ Dung of the Earth. And all this hath
‘ happen’d thro the ill-nature of Fortune,
‘ which is my Enemy, which has not lifted
‘ up and exalted them ſo much to honour
‘ them, as to undervalue, ſlight, and deſpiſe
‘ us.

' us. The Laws, Statutes, Worſhips, Sa-
' crifices and Ceremonies, which I have
' given, ordain'd, commanded and inſtitu-
' ted by my *Mercuries*, are broken and an-
' nul'd; and in their place ſucceed the moſt
' filthy and moſt abominable Villanies that
' ever this blind Jade could encourage and
' favour: that ſo as Men by us became He-
' roes, they may after this become worſe
' than Brutes. The Smoke of roaſted Fleſh
' offer'd upon the Altars in our Service,
' comes no more to our Noſtrils · but if
' ſometimes we have a deſire to taſte, we are
' oblig'd to go thro Kitchins like the *Dii Pa-*
' *tellarii.* And altho ſome Altars ſmoke with
' Incenſe *(quod dat avara manus)* by little
' and little, doubtleſs this Smoke is ſpent,
' that there may not remain any footſtep of
' our holy Inſtitutions. We know very well
' by experience, that this World is juſt like
' a skittiſh Horſe, that knows very well when
' he is rid by one who cannot manage him to
' purpoſe; he bounces, and deſpiſes his Ri-
' der, and ſtrives to throw him out of the
' Saddle; and when he hath thrown him
' down, he turns and kicks him.
' Behold how my Body is dry'd, and my
' Brain moiſten'd; Swellings ariſe, and my
' Teeth fall; my Fleſh turns of a golden,
' and my Hair of a ſilver Colour; my Eye-
' brows enlarge, and my Face contracts,
' my Breath fails, and Coughing grows upon
' me; I ſit firmly, and walk unſteddily, my

' Pulſe

' Pulfe trembles, and my Ribs grow toge-
' ther, my Bones grow fmall, and my Joints
' grow great: and to fhut up all, what tor-
' ments me moft, is, that when my Heels
' grow hard, my Calves grow foft ; and the
' Bags of my Bagpipe grow long, and the
' Pipe it felf is worn fhort. My Wife *Juno*
' is no longer jealous of me ; my Wife *Juno*
' takes no more care of me   Not to fpeak
' of other Gods, I would have you ferioufly
' think of your own Husband *Vulcan.* He
' that us'd to beat the Anvil with fo much
' vigour and force, that his loud and fiery
' Blows pierc'd to the Skies from ignivomous
' *Etna* , and the Eccho of the Concavities of
' the ringing *Vefuvius,* and ftony *Taburnus*
' anfwer'd him ; at prefent what is become
' of the Strength of my Smith, and your
' Husband ? Is it not fpent? Is it not fpent ?
' He has no more force to blow the Bellows
' for kindling his Fire : He has no more
' ftrength to lift the heavy Hammer, to
' ftrike the hot Metal.

' As for you, my dear Sifter, if you will
' not give credit to what others fay of you,
' only ask your Looking-Glafs, and it will
' tell you, that by reafon of the Wrinkles
' which have made bold with your comely
' Face, and the Furrows that the Plough of
' Time has drawn upon your Forehead, the
' Painters find daily more and more difficul-
' ty to draw you to the life, without offend-
' ing you. When you laugh'd or fmil'd, thefe
' two

' two extraordinary genteel Dimples, two
' Centers, and two Points in the midſt of ſo
' charming and lovely Graces, captivated the
' whole World, and added a great many more
' Beauties to your Countenance; ſo that if
' you only dally'd or ſported a little, Love
' pop'd his ſharp and burning Arrows at the
' Hearts of your Admirers. Now if we be-
' gin from the corners of your mouth, and
' end at the foremention'd part, from both
' ſides we begin to diſcover the figure of
' four Parentheſes, which being doubled, it
' looks as if they would ſhut your mouth to
' hinder you from laughing , having alſo
' theſe circumferential Arches which are be-
' tween the Ears and Teeth, to make you
' look like a Crocodile Not to tell you, that
' whether you laugh or no, the internal Geo-
' meter who dries up your vital Moiſture,
' who ſtill makes your Skin come nearer
' your Bones, and devours your Fat, draws
' very deep parallel Lines upon you in great
' numbers, by which he ſhews you the direct
' way that leads you as it were to your
' Grave. What do you cry for, *Venus* ?
' What do you laugh at, *Momus* ? (he ſaid
this, ſeeing *Momus* ſhowing his Teeth, and
Venus ſhedding Tears) ' Likewiſe *Momus*
' knows when one of theſe Jeſters (one of
' which tells more Truths of his Actions in
' the Ear of his Prince, than all the Court
' beſides , and by whom, thoſe who dare
' not ſpeak out, often make Motions and

' Pro-

' Propofals, and caufe others to do the like,
' under the covert of a Jeft) faid that *Efcu-*
' *lapius* had propos'd the Powder of Hartf-
' horn for you, with Conferve of Coral, after
' having dig'd out two great Lumps of proud
' Fleih fo fecretly, that every Boy in Heaven
' knows of it. Look then, dear Sifter, how
' that Traitor Time fubdues and keeps us
' under, and how all of us are fubject to
' Change : And what is moft afflicting of all,
' is, that we have no Certainty, nor fo much
' as Hope, to refume that Being and Form
' which we were fometime poffefs'd of. Let
' us go on, and not tuin back : And as we
' have no remembrance of what we were
' before we were in this ftate of Being, fo
' let us not expect to be able to know what
' we fhall be hereafter. Thus Piety, Reli-
' gion, and the Fear of us, Honour, Refpect,
' and Love vanifh , all which were wont to
' attend our Majefty, Power, Providence,
' Viitue, Dignity and Beauty, as the Sha-
' dow does the Body ; but all thefe are fled
' from us. Truth alone, with abfolute Vir-
' tue, is immutable and immortal : and if fhe
' fometimes droops and hides her head, yet
' no fooner does her Handmaid *Sophia* reach
' forth hei hand to lift her up, but fhe un-
' doubtedly rifes again. Let us take heed
' therefore, that we offend not the Divinity
' of Fate, by injuring this double Deity, fo
' much recommended, and fo much favour'd
' by it. Let us reflect on our approaching
' future

' future State, and not, as if we were in-
' different about the univeisal Deity, be
' wanting to raise our Hearts and Affections
' to this Giver of all Good, and the Distri-
' buter of all Lots and Fortunes. Let us
' supplicate that Divinity, to bestow happy
' Genius's upon us, in our Transfusion, Paf-
' fage, or Metempsychosis, since however
' inexorable he be, we must attend him with
' Wishes, to be either preserv'd in our pre-
' sent state, or to enter into a better, or a
' like, or one but a little worse. Not to
' mention that the being well-affected to-
' ward this Supreme Deity, is as it were a
' sign of a favourable Event: As he who is
' determin'd to be a Man, is ordinarily and
' necessarily led by his Destiny to pass thro
' his Mother's Belly. The Spirit that is pre-
' destinated to be embody'd with a Fish,
' must first be choak'd in Water; after the
' same manner, he that is to be favour'd
' by the Gods, must obtain this by the
' means of good Wishes and good Actions.

The

The Second Part of the First Dialogue.

THE Great Father of the Celeſtial Kingdom having proceeded thus far in his Diſcourſe by gentle ſteps, he groan'd, and having ended his Converſation with *Venus*, the Propoſal of a Ball turn'd to a Reſolution of calling a grand Council of the Gods of the round Table, that is to ſay, all thoſe who are truly and originally Gods, and have a Head for Counſel; excluding all Sheep-Heads, Ox-Horns, Goat-Beards, Aſſes-Ears, Hogs-Eyes, Apes-Noſes, Bucks-Foreheads, Pullets-Gizzards, Horſe-Bellies, Mules-Feet, and Serpents-Tails. For this end Proclamation being made by the mouth of *Miſenus* Son of *Eolus* (for *Mercury* ſcorn'd to do it, tho he had formerly been Trumpeter and Publiſher of Edicts) all the Gods that were diſpers'd thro the Palace, immediately aſſembled together. After they were all met, and ſilence kept, *Jupiter* appear'd with a ſad and ſorrowful Aſpect, in the mean time advancing with a great Preſence, and magiſterial Dignity, but before he mounted his Throne, and appear'd in his Tribunal, *Momus* preſented himſelf before him, who, according to his wonted Liberty of Speech, ſpoke with ſo low a Voice, that every one heard what he ſaid. ' This Council, O Fa-
' ther,

' ther, ought to be delay'd to another day,
' and another occaſion; for this humour of
' holding a Conclave immediately after din-
' ner, I doubt is owing to the liberal Hand
' of your unwary Cup-bearer: For Neſtar
' that is not well-digeſted in the Stomach,
' does not comfort or refreſh, but ſpoils and
' deſtroys the Temper, and diſturbs the Fan-
' cy, makes ſome merry out of meaſure, and
' others extravagantly frolickſom, others ſu-
' perſtitiouſly devout, ſome vainly heroick,
' ſome cholerick, others great Builders of
' Caſtles in the Air: inſomuch that by the
' floating of theſe Vapours which paſs thro
' Heads of a different Make and Complexion,
' every thing miſcarries, and vaniſhes in
' ſmoke. 'Tis evident, *Jupiter*, that Neſtar
' hath put the Species of wanton and frisking
' Thoughts into a terrible commotion in
' your Brain, and made you evil-diſpos'd;
' for every body judges you (tho I am the
' only Perſon that dare tell it) overcome and
' oppreſs'd with Gall. What other Judg-
' ment can be paſs'd upon your going about
' to handle Affairs ſo ſerious and weighty,
' that I don't pretend to underſtand them,
' much leſs to deſcribe them in words, eſpe-
' cially in this juncture, that we are met un-
' prepar'd to give Counſel, on this occaſion,
' that we are aſſembled to feaſt; at this
' time ſo ſoon after Dinner, and with the
' Circumſtances of having eat well and drank
' better?'' Now becauſe it is neither cuſtomary,

mary, nor very lawful for the reft of the
Gods to enter into difpute with *Momus, Jupiter* after he had thrown him a Half-Smile,
and fcornful Leer, without troubling himfelf
to anfwer him, he mounts his high Chair,
fits down, and cafts his eyes about upon
the great Council of State that fat in a Circle to affift him. You may eafily imagine,
that at his Look every Heart begun to beat,
being ftruck with Wonder and Fear, as well
as fill'd with Reverence and Refpect, which
rife in mortal and immortal Breafts, whenever his Majefty prefents it felf. After having lower'd his Eye-brows a little, and
look'd upwards, he empty'd his Breaft of a
fiery Sigh, and broke out in thefe words.

Jupiter's *Speech.*

' DON'T expect, O, ye Gods! that, ac-
' cording to my wonted cuftom, I fhould
' thunder an artful Introduction into your
' ears, and a handfom Thred of Narration,
' together with a pleafant and comprehenfive
' Epilogue to wind up the whole Difcourfe:
' Don't look for an ornate Contexture of
' words, a fine Ranging of Sentences, a rich
' Apparatus of elegant Sayings, a fumptuous
' Pomp of elaborate Expreffions , and, after
' the manner of Orators, Thoughts put thrice
' under the File, e'er they appear once on
' the Tongue.

Non

*Non hoc, non hoc ista sibi tempus spectacula
poscit.*

'Believe me, O ye Gods, for in believing
'me ye shall believe the Truth; the chaste
'*Lucina* hath fill'd her silver Horns twelve
'times, since I resolv'd to call this Assembly
'this day, this hour, and upon such terms
'as you see; and at this present I am more
'concern'd to find out what may hide our
'Disgrace and Misfortune, than I am to
'premeditate and find words suited to the
'Occasion of our meeting.

'I hear you are surpriz'd that I have call'd
'you from your Diversion at this time, and
'summon'd an Assembly of the Gods to
'meet in Council after Dinner. I find you
'grumble that I put you upon serious matters
'on a Day of Rejoicing, and every one of
'you is disturb'd at the Sound of the Trum-
'pet, and the publishing of the Proclama-
'tion. But tho the reason of these Actions
'and Circumstances depends merely upon
'my Pleasure, which has propos'd and insti-
'tuted them, and tho my Will and Decree
'be the very Reason and Ground of Justice;
'yet, before I proceed any farther, I shall
'endeavour to remove all your Amazement
'and Confusion. Resolutions then ought to
'be slow, grave, and well weigh'd; Coun-
'sel mature, secret, and cautious; but Exe-
'cution must be wing'd, swift, and quick.
'Don't

' Don't think therefore, that some strange
' Humour hath seiz'd me at Dinner, and
' holds me captive ever since ; and that my
' Behaviour proceeds not from the Dictates
' of Reason, but from the Force of Nectar's
' Fumes : For just this day twelve-month
' I begun to ruminate within my self, what
' I should execute on this day and hour.
' And I chose to meet you here just after
' Dinner, because bad News are very im-
' proper to be told to an empty Stomach.   I
' thought it best to take you at unawares,
' because I am very sure that you are much
' more forward to come together to a good
' Feast, than to meet in Council, which you
' mortally hate : for some are afraid of it,
' lest they create to themselves Enemies ;
' some because they know not what side
' shall have the better; some lest their Ad-
' vice should be slighted , some because their
' Opinion is often rejected ; some lest they
' should be oblig'd to break thro that Neu-
' trality which they love to observe in doubt-
' ful Cases, some to shun the occasions of
' burdening their Consciences ; in short,
' some for one reason, and some for ano-
' ther.   I put you in mind at this time,
' my Brethren and Sons, that those whom
' Fate has allow'd to taste Ambrosia, and
' drink Nectar, and arrive at the Degree
' and Dignity of Majesty, are under a ne-
' cessity to bear with all the Uneasiness and
' Trouble it brings along with it.   The
' Dia-

‘ Diadem, the Mitre, the Crown, add Dig-
‘ nity only to the Head they burden, the
‘ Royal Robe and Scepter adorn only that
‘ Body which they encumber.

   ‘ Would you know the Reafon why I
‘ have fix’d upon a Feaft-Day for this pur-
‘ pofe, and particularly fuch a Day as this?
‘ Are you really of the mind, are you really
‘ of the mind I fay, that this Day fhould
‘ be fpent in Rejoicing? And are you not
‘ convinc’d that this Day fhould be ac-
‘ counted the moft tragical Day in the whole
‘ Year? Who among you, that has juftly
‘ confider’d, will not judg it a moft dif-
‘ graceful thing to celebrate the Commemo-
‘ ration of our Victory over the Giants, at a
‘ time when we are fet at nought and de-
‘ fiance by the Scum of the Earth? O that
‘ omnipotent and inflexible Fate had pleas’d
‘ then to have driven us from Heaven, when
‘ the Dignity and Prowefs of our Enemies
‘ fhould not have made our Overthrow fo
‘ fhameful! For this day we are in a worfe
‘ Condition, than if we were not in Heaven,
‘ worfe than when we were driven out of
‘ it; fince that Fear of us, which render’d
‘ us fo glorious, is gone; fince the great Re-
‘ putation of our Majefty, Providence and
‘ Juftice, is blafted; and, which is worfe,
‘ we have no Means or Force to repair our
‘ Misfortune, and vindicate our Honour;
‘ becaufe Juftice, with which Fate governs
‘ the Governours of the World, hath quite

‘ taken

' taken away all that Authority and Power
' which was so ill imploy'd by us. Our
' Shame and Nakedness are laid open, and
' made manifest to the Eyes of Mortals; and
' Heaven it self bears witness against our
' Miscarriages, with Evidence as clear and
' certain, as the Stars are bright and shining:
' For the Fruits, Relicks, Reports, Words,
' Writings and Histories of our Adulteries,
' Incests, Whoredoms, Wrath, Indignation,
' Rapine, and other Crimes and Wickednes-
' ses, are openly known upon Earth: And
' for a Reward of our Errors and Crimes
' we have committed greater ones, in ex-
' alting to Heaven the Triumphs of our Vi-
' ces, and Seats of our Debauches, leaving
' Virtue and Justice banish'd, bury'd and
' neglected in Hell.

' And to begin at lesser Matters, as at
' Venial Sins: Why has *Deltaton*, this Tri-
' angle I say alone, obtain'd four Stars near
' *Medusa*'s Head, under *Andromeda*'s Poste-
' riors, and above the *Ram*'s Horn? Why,
' but to shew the Partiality of the Gods.
' What makes the *Dolphin* join'd to *Capri-*
' *corn* on the North, Lord of fifteen Stars?
' 'Tis that he may be able to see and con-
' template the Assumption of him who is
' the good Procurer (not to say Pander) of
' *Neptune* and *Amphytrite*. Why do the seven
' Daughters of *Atlantis* sit upon the Neck of
' the *White Bull*? Because he treasonably
' boasts that he is the Father of us Gods,
' having,

' having, as he pretends, fupported us and
' Heaven that was going to decay ; or to
' fhew the Levity and Inconftancy of our
' Godfhips, for having plac'd them there.
' Why did *Juno* adorn *Cancer* with nine
' Stars, befides the other four which ftand
' round them, and are for no ufe ? only out
' of Caprice, becaufe he pinch'd *Alcides*'s Heel
' when he fought with this huge Giant.

' Who can tell me any other reafon than
' the fimple and irrational Decree of the
' Gods, why *Serpentaurus* (call'd by us
' *Greeks Ophiulcos*) together with his Lady
' poffeffes the Bounds of fix and thirty Stars ?
' What weighty and reafonable Caufe can
' be affign'd why *Sagittarius* ufurps one and
' thirty Stars ? Becaufe he was Son to *Eufche-*
' *mia*, Nurfe or Fofter-Mother to the Mu-
' fes. Why did he not rather own his Mo-
' ther ? becaufe he learn'd to dance, and
' play comical Tricks. Why has *Aquarius*
' four and forty Stars near *Capricorn* ? may
' be becaufe he fav'd the Daughter of *Venus*
' in a Lake. Why not others (to whom we
' Gods are fo much beholden) who have
' their Graves in the Earth, rather than this
' Fellow, whofe Service is not worthy of fuch
' a Recompence as this fpacious Field ? Let
' *Venus* give a reafon why fhe was pleas'd to
' order it fo.

' Altho *Pifces* deferve fome Reward for
' having driven from the River *Euphrates*
' that Egg, which being hatch'd by a Dove,
' brought

' brought forth the Mercy of the Goddefs of
' *Paphus*; yet do you think it reafonable
' they fhould be adorn'd with four and thir-
' ty Stars, befides the other four that ftand
' round them, and dwell out of the Water,
' in the moft noble and pleafant Region of
' Heaven? To what end does *Orion* ftand
' in a warlike Pofture, with his Arms bran-
' difh'd, embroider'd with eight and thirty
' Stars in the Eaftern Latitude of *Taurus*?
' He ftands there upon a mere Caprice of
' *Neptune*, who not fatisfy'd to exercife his
' Power and Prerogatives under Water,
' where his lawful Dominion lies, meddles
' with fuch little Matters out of his own Pa-
' trimony. You know that the Hare, Dog,
' and little Bitch have three and forty Stars
' in the South, only for playing two or three
' little Tricks, fuch as obtain'd Places for
' the *Hydra*, the *Cup*, the *Dragon* and the
' *Raven*, that got one and forty Stars in
' memory of the Gods fending the *Raven*
' one day to bring them fome Water to
' drink; but the Raven by the way met
' with a Fig-Tree which bore Figs. This
' Bird found by the Tafte they were ripe,
' and fo fell to eating. When he had done,
' he remember'd the Water, and fo went to
' fill his Pitcher; but feeing a Dragon there
' he was afraid, and fo return'd to the Gods
' with an empty Barrel. The Gods willing
' to make known how well the *Raven* had
' imploy'd its Wit and Judgment, have de-
' fcrib'd

‘ ſcrib’d in Heaven this Hiſtory of ſo pretty
‘ and uſeful a Servant. You ſee how well
‘ we have ſpent our Time, Ink and Paper.
‘ Who has predeſtinated the Southern Crown,
‘ which lies under the Bow and Feet of *Sa-*
‘ *gittarius,* adorn’d with thirteen ſhining To-
‘ pazes, to be eternally without a Head to
‘ fill it ? Is it not a fine thing to ſee that
‘ Fiſh which is under the feet of *Aquarius*
‘ and *Capricorn,* divided into twelve Eyes,
‘ with ſix other that encompaſs her ? I won’t
‘ ſay any thing of Altars, Cenſers, Lamps,
‘ or Veſtries, becauſe ’twas never ſo neceſſary
‘ to be in Heaven as now, when we have no
‘ Intereſt on earth. At this time the Reli-
‘ gion and Worſhip of the Gods upon earth,
‘ may be conſider’d only as a Relick, or as a
‘ Plank of a Ship that has ſuffer’d Shipwreck.
‘ I ſay nothing of *Capricorn,* becauſe he
appears to me moſt worthy of a heavenly
Poſſeſſion, for doing us the favour to ſhow
us how *Python* was to be overcome : for it
would have been neceſſary elſe for the Gods
to change and transform themſelves into
Beaſts, before they could have the honour
to enter into this War , and he hath in-
ſtructed us in this Doctrine, *viz.* That he
who knows not how to make himſelf a
Brute, cannot maintain his Dignity in a
nobler ſtate.
‘ I don’t ſpeak of the *Virgin,* becauſe her
Virginity is ſafe no where but in Heaven,
having *Leo* on one ſide, and *Scorpius* on the
D ‘ other

' other for a guard. The poor little Girl is
' fled from the Earth, becaufe the exceffive
' Luft and Wantonnefs of the Women, who
' the bigger their Bellies grow, love the
' Sport the better, would violate her Chafti-
' ty, even tho fhe was in her Mother's
' Womb; and therefore fhe enjoys her fix
' and twenty Carbuncles, befides other fix
' which are within her, and lie out of view.
' I dare fay nothing of the fpotlefs Majefty
' of thefe two Affes which fhine in the fpace
' of *Cancer*; becaufe chiefly of thefe, both
' by Juftice and Reafon, is the Kingdom of
' Heaven, as I fhall invincibly demonftrate
' by moft powerful Reafons fome other time,
' for I dare not fpeak now of fuch an im-
' portant matter, fo much as *en paffant*. But
' I am only griev'd and vex'd that thefe two
' divine Animals have been fo fcurvily trea-
' ted, not having fo much as a Houfe of
' their own to dwell in, but are glad to take
' Lodgings of that retrograde aquatick Ani-
' mal Befides, we have beftow'd on them
' only two little pitiful Stars to each one,
' and thefe two only of the fourth Magni-
' tude.

' I fhall determine nothing at prefent a-
' bout the *Altar, Capricorn, Virgo*, or *Afini,*
' altho I am very much difpleas'd that any of
' them fhould not be treated according to
' their Dignity, but inftead of being ho-
' nour'd, are perhaps injur'd and affronted:
' but I turn to other purpofes, which are
                                          ' weigh'd

' weigh'd in the fame Scales with the for-
' mer.

' Is it not reafonable that the other Ri-
' vers on Earth fhould grumble by reafon of
' the wrong they fuffer? For, pray, why
' fhould *Eridanus* have his four and thirty
' Lights, which appear beyond, and on this
' fide of the Tropick of *Capricorn,* rather
' than others as deferving and great, and
' others more deferving and great than he?
' Is it enough to fay that the Sifters of *Phae-*
' *ton* have their Lodgings there? Or perhaps
' you think he fhould be fo celebrated, be-
' caufe at that place fell by my hand the
' thunder-ftruck Son of *Apollo,* for having
' bubbl'd his Father out of his Office, Dig-
' nity and Authority. Why was *Bellerophon*'s
' Horfe mounted up to Heaven to be cloth'd
' with twenty Stars, tho his Rider lies bu-
' ry'd on earth? To what purpofe does that
' Arrow, which fhines with five Stars with
' which 'tis enamel'd, ftand fo near to *Aquila*
' and the *Dolphin?* Surely it is very much
' out of humour, that it is at fuch a diftance
' from *Sagittarius,* who would otherwife
' give him very good Employment, after
' having fhot that which he has bended.
' Now I wou'd fain know what this Harp
' made of Ox-horns, in form of a *Teftudo,*
' does between the Skin of the Lion, and the
' Head of this white fweet Swan. I'd fain
' know if it ftays there in honour of the Tor-
' toife, or of the Horns, or of the Harp;

' or that every one might fee the Art of *Mer-*
' *cury* who made it, or in teftimony of his
' vain and diffolute Boafting.

   ' Behold, O ye Gods, our Bufinefs! This
' is the noble Work of our hands, by which
' we do honour to Heaven. See the fine Fa-
' bricks, not much unlike thofe which Chil-
' dren make of Clay, Mud, Twigs, Boughs,
' and Branches, thus imitating the Work of
' grown Men. Do you think that we muft
' not give account and reafon of thefe things?
' Can you believe we fhall be lefs queftion'd,
' interrogated, judg'd, and condemn'd for
' idle Works, than for idle Words?   The
' Goddeffes Juftice, Temperance, Conftan-
' cy, Liberality, Patience, Truth, Memory,
' Wifdom, and a great many more Goddeffes
' and Gods, are banifh'd not only from Hea-
' ven, but alfo from Earth: and in their
' room, and in the ftately Palaces built by
' the moft high Providence, fucceed Dol-
' phins, Goats, Ravens, Serpents, and other
' Uncleanneffes, Levity, Caprice and Hu-
' mour. If what I fay gives you any uneafi-
' nefs; and if you are touch'd with Remorfes
' of Confcience for the Good you have omit-
' ted and neglected, how much more, think
' ye, ought thofe to be prick'd and pierc'd to
' the heart, for the horrid Crimes and Wic-
' kednefs, which we were fo far from re-
' penting of, that we even celebrated Tri-
' umphs, and erected Trophies for them,
' not only in a decay'd and ruinous Chappel,
' and

' and earthly Temple, but even in Heaven,
' and in the eternal Stars? Miftakes and Mif-
' carriages committed thro Frailty, and un-
' inftructed Levity, may be born with, and
' eafily pardon'd : But what Mercy, what
' Favour can be pleaded for thofe, who being
' placed as the Prefidents of Juftice, never-
' thelefs, as a Reward of moft criminal Mif-
' takes, commit greater ones, by honouring,
' rewarding and exalting to the Heavens the
' Delinquents together with their Crimes?
' For what great and virtuous Action did
' *Perfeus* obtain fix and twenty Stars? For
' having kill'd the *Gorgons* while they were
' afleep, by favour of the Wings, and Shield
' of Cryftal which render'd him invifible, in
the Service of *Minerva*, to whom he prefented *Medufa*'s Head? But this was not
enough, that he fhould ftand there; but
for long and famous Memory, his Wife *Andromeda* muft appear to him with her three
and twenty, as alfo his own Father-in-
law *Cepheus*, with his thirteen Stars, who
expos'd his innocent Daughter to the mouth
of a Whale for a Caprice of *Neptune*, who
was offended at her Mother *Caffiopeia*, who
thought herfelf more beautiful than the
Nereides. And yet his Mother is to be feen
there now fitting in her Chair, adorn'd with
other thirteen Stars, upon the Confines of
the Artick Circle. What does that Father of the Lambs with Wool of Gold,
with his eighteen Stars, befides thefe feven

D 3 ' which

' which encompaſs him ; what does he, I
' ſay, bleating upon the Equinoctial ? 'Tis
' perhaps to proclaim the Simplicity and
' Folly of the King of *Colchos*, the Impu-
' dence of *Meduſa*, the luſtful Temerity of
' *Jaſon*, and the unjuſt Providence of us here
' preſent. Theſe two little Striplings which
' ſucceed the Bull in the Zodiack with their
' eighteen Stars, beſides the ſeven By-
' ſtanders which are without form, pray
' what good or fine thing do they diſcover,
' except the reciprocal Love of two Bur-
' daſhes?

' For what reaſon hath *Scorpius* obtain'd
' the Reward of one and twenty Stars,
' beſides the eight which are in his Fore-
' part, and the nine which are round him,
' and other three without form ? For a
' Reward of the Homicide directed by the
' Levity and Envy of *Diana*, upon her Rival
' Hunter *Orion*. You know, that *Chiron*
' with his Beaſt obtain'd in the Southern
' Latitude of Heaven ſixty ſix Stars, for
' being pedantick Tutor to the Boy who
' ow'd his Original to the Whoredom of *Pe-*
' *leus* and *Thetis*. You muſt know likewiſe,
' that *Ariadne*'s Crown, in which ſhine eight
' Stars, and which is ſituated upon *Boote*'s
' Breaſt and the Serpent's Folds, is placed
' there in perpetual memory of the unlawful
' Love of *Bacchus*, when he embrac'd the
' King of *Crete*'s Daughter, after *Theſeus* who
' had firſt deflower'd her, and then turn'd
                                        ' her

‘ her off. The Lion that carries a Baſilisk in
‘ his Heart, and poſſeſſes the ſpace of five
‘ and thirty Stars ; pray what is he always
‘ a doing in *Cancer?* He is there perhaps in
‘ company with his Fellow-Soldier and Ser-
‘ vant, the Servant of angry *Juno,* whom ſhe
‘ caus’d to deſtroy the *Cleonian* Territories,
‘ that ſo ſhe might have an occaſion to ſet
‘ the mighty *Alcides* at work againſt him.
‘ The invincible and laborious *Hercules,* my
‘ Son, who with his Club and Lion’s Skin
‘ defends himſelf, hath better deſerv’d eight
‘ and twenty Stars, for ſo many heroical
‘ Actions, than any other whatſoever. But
‘ to tell the truth, I don’t think it conve-
‘ nient that he ſhould hold this place, from
‘ whence he puts his Knee before the Eyes of
‘ Juſtice ; the wrong that’s done to the con-
‘ jugal Knot of my *Juno,* by me and the
‘ Whore *Megara* his Mother. The Ship of
‘ *Argus,* in which are fix’d five and forty re-
‘ ſplendent Stars near the Antartick Circle,
‘ is it placed there for any other end, than
‘ to eternize the Memory of the great Miſ-
‘ carriage of the wiſe *Minerva,* who by this
‘ means inſtituted the firſt Pirates, that ſo
‘ the Sea might not be without its buſy Rob-
‘ bers more than the Land ?
‘ But to turn our view to the Girdle of
‘ Heaven : Why does that Bull at the begin-
‘ ning of the Zodiack poſſeſs two and thirty
‘ clear Stars, not to name that which is upon
‘ the point of the Northern Horn, and eleven

D 4 ‘ others

' others which are call'd formless? Because,
' forsooth, *Jupiter* ravish'd the Daughter of
' *Agenor*, the Sister of *Cadmus*! What Ea-
' gle is that in the Firmament, which usurps
' the space of fifteen Stars beyond *Sagittarius*,
' towards the Pole? There *Jupiter* was
' weary when he celebrated the Triumph
' of ravish'd *Ganymedes*, and the victorious
' Flames of Love. This Bear, this Bear, O
' ye Gods! why is she placed in the most
' conspicuous part of the World, as in a
' high Lanthorn, as in the most airy and
' spacious Court, and most famous Spectacle
' in the Universe that can present it self to
' our eyes? Perhaps that every body might
' see the Conflagration which the Father of
' the Gods kindled after the Conflagration
' of the Earth by *Phaeton*'s Chariot, when he
' repair'd the Ruins of the Fire, by calling
' up the frighted Rivers out of the Caverns
' of the Earth; namely, in the *Arcadian*
' Territories. Behold another Fire kindled
' in my Breast, coming from the bright and
' shining Countenance of the Virgin *Nona-*
' *crina*, which enter'd at my Eyes, scalded
' my Heart, burnt my Bones, and penetra-
' ted even to the Marrow. so that neither
' Water, nor any other Remedy, could cool
' or quench my Flame. There was in this
' Fire an Arrow which pierc'd thro my Heart,
' a Band which tied my Soul, and Talons
' which carry'd me away from my self, and
' made me a Prey to her Beauty. I commit-
' ted

' ted facrilegious Whoredom, I violated the
' Society of *Diana,* and was unjuft to my
' moft faithful Confort: I reprefented to my
' felf the Brutality of my Excefs, in the
' form and fhape of a Bear, and was fo far
' from conceiving Horrour at this abomina-
' ble fight, that this fame Monfter appear'd
' fo lovely to me, and pleas'd me to fuch a
' degree, that I was willing the lively Image
' of it fhould be exalted to the higheft and
' moft magnificent Seat of the heavenly Fa-
' brick. This is the Crime, this the Bru-
' tality, this the horrible Blot, which the
' Water of the Ocean difdain'd and abomi-
' nated to wafh, that *Thetis,* for fear of pol-
' luting her Waves, would not fuffer to ap-
' proach her Abode; that *Dictynna* hath for-
' bid entrance into her Defart, for fear of
' profaning her facred College; and the *Ne-*
' *reides* and Nymphs have fhun'd for the
' fame reafon.

' I a poor miferable Sinner tell my Sin, I
' tell my moft grievous Sin, in the prefence
' of abfolute unfpotted Juftice, and before
' you. To this time I have finned moft
' grievoufly, and by my bad Example have
' given you occafion and permiffion to do the
' like. And withal I confefs, that both you
' and I have moft defervedly incurr'd the
' Difpleafure of Fate, which makes us be
' difown'd any longer for Gods; and fo given
' up Heaven to the Abominations of the
' Earth. Fate hath difpens'd with the
' breaking

' breaking down of our Temples, Images
' and Statues upon Earth, that thoſe who
' unjuſtly exalted things of a baſe and low
' nature, may be thrown down from their
' exalted State.——Alas, O ye Gods! what
' ſhall we do? what ſhall we think? what
' can we expect? We have foully prevari-
' cated, we have perſiſted in our Crimes,
' and we ſee Puniſhment is join'd to and
' continu'd with our Crimes.

 ' Let us provide then, let us provide a-
' gainſt what may befal us: For as Fate
' hath not put it out of our power to fall,
' ſo ſhe hath not put it out of our power to
' riſe again. And as we have been forward
' to fall, ſo let us alſo be ready to ſet our
' ſelves upon our Feet again. If we will
' make that Reparation which is in our
' power, we may without difficulty free
' our ſelves from that Puniſhment, which our
' Crimes have made us undergo, and than
' which a worſe could not have befal'n us.
' If we are ty'd by a Chain of Crimes, we
' may be loos'd by the Hand of Juſtice. If
' our Levity hath depreſs'd us, our Gravity
' muſt raiſe us up. Let us return to Juſtice,
' by departing from which, we have de-
' parted from our ſelves ; ſo that we are no
' more Gods, we are no more our ſelves.
' We muſt return to her, if we would return
' to our ſelves. The Order and Manner of
' this Reparation is, firſt to remove from our
' Shoulders the grievous weight of Crimes
     ' which

‘ which burden us ; to remove from before
‘ our Eyes the Veil of Inconfideration which
‘ blinds us ; to empty our Minds of Self-
‘ Love that retards us ; to caft far from us
‘ all thofe vain Thoughts that difturb us ; to
‘ demolifh all the Engines of Errors, and
‘ Edifices of Perverfity, which hinder us in
‘ our way, and ftop our Progrefs. Let us
‘ ruin and annul, as much as poffible, the
‘ Triumphs and Trophies of our ungodly
‘ Deeds, that fo a true Repentance for our
‘ paft Errors may appear at the Tribunal of
‘ Juftice. Up, O ye Gods ! and remove
‘ from Heaven all thefe Spectres, Statues,
‘ Images, Pictures, Figures, Proceffes and
‘ Hiftories of our Avarice, Lufts, Thefts,
‘ Hatred, Contempt and Shame.

‘ Let us leave this dark and gloomy night
‘ of our Errors, and accept of the Invita-
‘ tion from the charming Morning of a
‘ new day of Juftice : And let us place our
‘ felves in fuch a manner, that the Rifing
‘ Sun may not fee our Uncleanneffes. We
‘ muft not only make our felves clean and
‘ beautiful, but we muft alfo fcour and po-
‘ lifh our Abodes and Houfes. We muft pu-
‘ rify our felves both without and within.
‘ We muft firft, I fay, place our felves in the
‘ intellectual Heaven which is within us, and
‘ afterwards in that fenfible corporeal Hea-
‘ ven which prefents it felf to our Eyes.
‘ Let us remove from the Heaven of our
‘ Minds the Bear of Deformity, the Arrow
‘ of

' of Detraction, the Horfe of Levity, the
' Dog of Murmuring, the little Bitch of
' Flattery. Let us banifh the *Hercules* of
' Violence, the *Harp* of Confpiracy, the
' *Triangle* of Impiety, the *Bootes* of Incon-
' ftancy, the *Cepheus* of Cruelty, the *Dragon*
' of Envy, the *Swan* of Imprudence, the
' *Caffiopeia* of Vanity, the *Andromeda* of La-
' zinefs, the *Perfeus* of vain Anxiety. Let
' us chafe away the *Ophiulcus* of Evil-fpeak-
' ing, the *Eagle* of Arrogance, the *Dolphin* of
' Luft, the *Horfe* of Impatience, the *Hydra*
' of Concupifcence, the *Whale* of Gluttony,
' the *Orion* of Rage, the *River* of Superfluity,
' the *Gorgon* of Ignorance, the *Hare* of vain
' Fear. Let us no longer carry in our Breaft
' the *Argo* of Avarice, the *Bowl* of Infobrie-
' ty, the *Balance* of Iniquity, the *Cancer* of
' Slownefs, the *Capricorn* of Deceit. Let us
' not come near the *Scorpion* of Guile, the
' *Centaur* of animal Affection, the *Altar* of
' Superftition, the *Crown* of Pride, the *Fifh*
' of fhameful Silence. May the *Twins* inde-
' cent Familiarity, the *Bull* of Concern for
' mean things, the *Ram* of Inconfideratenefs,
' the *Lion* of Tyranny, the *Aquarius* of Dif-
' folutenefs, the *Virgin* of fruitlefs Conver-
' fation, and the *Sagittarius* of Detraction
' fall with them. If we thus purge our Ha-
' bitations, O ye Gods ' if we thus renew
' our Heaven, the Conftellations and In-
' fluxes fhall be new, the Impreffions and
' Fortunes fhall be new ; for all things de-
' pend

pend upon this upper World, and contrary
Effects depend on contrary Caufes. O happy! O truly fortunate we! if we could
make a good Colony of our Minds and
Thoughts. If any among you is not pleas'd
with his prefent Condition, yet I hope he
is pleas'd with the prefent Counfel. If we
would change our State, we muft change
our Manners. If we would have that
good and better, thefe muft not be as they
are now, or worfe. Let us purify our inward Affections, fince by informing this
internal World, it will not be hard to make
' Advances towards reforming the fenfible
' and external World. I fee you have done
' the firft, O ye Gods! I fee your Determi-
' nation; it is made, it is fuddenly made,
' becaufe it is not fubject to the Counterpoife
' of Time.

' Now let us go on to the fecond, that is,
' to the external, corporeal, fenfible and lo-
' cal World. But we muft proceed upon
' certain Reafon, with Succeffion and Order;
' we muft view and compare one thing with
' another, one Reafon with another, before
' we determine. For as fome time is fpent
' in the difpofing of corporeal things, fo the
' execution of them cannot be made in an
' inftant. I allow then that you have three
' days to decide and determine among your
' felves, whether this Reformation fhould
' be made or no. For by the Ordinance of
' Fate, I no fooner propos'd this, but you
' judg'd

' judg'd it moſt convenient and neceſſary.
' 'Tis not by external Signs, Figures and Sha-
' dows, but really and in truth, that I per-
' ceive your Diſpoſitions, as you reciprocal-
' ly ſee mine ; and I no ſooner touch'd your
' Ears with my Propoſals, but you touch'd
' my Eyes with the Splendour of your Con-
' ſent.

' It remains then that you think and con-
' fer with one another, about the manner
' how we muſt provide for thoſe things that
' are to be diſpatch'd from Heaven, for
' which we muſt prepare and order other
' Countries and Habitations ; and how theſe
' Seats may be fill'd, ſo that Heaven may
' not remain a Deſart, but be better adorn'd
' and inhabited.   When the three days are
' over, you muſt come into my Preſence
' with mature Thoughts and Reflections up-
' on all theſe things ; ſo that when we meet
' the fourth day, we may be able to deter-
' mine and pronounce what ſhall be the Form
' of this Colony. *Dixi.*'

Thus, O *Saulinus !* Father *Jupiter* touch'd
the Ears, kindled the Spirits, and mov'd the
Hearts of the celeſtial Senate and People,
when he openly diſcover'd in their Counte-
nances and Geſtures (while he diſcours'd)
that what he propos'd to them was concluded and determin'd in their Minds.
They all with one Voice and Tone ſaid, We
very willingly conſent, O *Jupiter*, to effect
what

what you have propos'd to us, and what
Fate hath certainly predeftinated. Here
fucceeded the approving Hum of the Multitude, there appear'd Signs of a glad Refolution; here appear'd Tokens of a voluntary
Obedience, there of Thought; here Ap-
plaufe, there wagging the Head, here one
fort of Look, there another, till the time of
Supper drew near, and then one went to
one place, another to another place.

Saul. Thefe are no fmall Matters, *Sophia.*

The Third Part of the Firft Dialogue.

Sophia. THE fourth Day being come,
and it being about the Hour of
Twelve, they all met in the General Council,
where not only all the principal Gods were allow'd to come, but likewife all the reft who
have a Place in Heaven by the Law of Nature. The Senate and the whole Tribe of
Gods being fet, and *Jupiter,* according to
Cuftom, being mounted upon his Throne of
Saphire, with that kind of Diadem and Robe
which he ufes to appear with only in the moft
folemn Councils: All things being fettled,
and the Company in a Pofture of Attention,
and profound Silence commanded, in fuch
fort, that the whole Affembly feem'd to be
fo many Statues or Pictures, the God *Mercury* prefented himfelf with his Orders, En-
figns

figns and Inftructions; and placing himfelf
before *Jupiter*, he declar'd, interpreted and
explain'd what none of the Council was ignorant of: which however was fit to be pronounc'd, to obferve the Form and Decorum
of the Statutes; that is, that the Gods were
ready and prepar'd, without Deceit or Guile,
and with a free and fpontaneous Will, to receive and put in execution whatfoever fhould
be concluded, appointed and order'd by the
prefent Synod. When he had faid this, he
look'd round upon the Gods that ftood about
him, and requir'd them to declare and ratify what he had fet forth in their name in
the prefence of the Almighty Thunderer,
by lifting up their hands, and fo it was done.
Then the great *Protoparent* open'd his Mouth,
and broke out into thefe words: ' If our
' Victory, O ye Gods! over the Giants, was
' glorious, over the Giants, I fay, who all of
' a fudden rofe up againft us, who were fo-
' reign and open Enemies, who attack'd us
' only from *Olympus*, and who endeavour'd,
' but could not throw us down from Hea-
' ven; how much more glorious and honou-
' rable will a Victory over our felves be, who
' were victorious over them? How much
' more honourable and glorious, I fay, will
' a Victory over our Affections be, which
' have fo long triumph'd, which are our in-
' ward and domeftick Enemies, which ty-
' rannize over us on every quarter, and
' which have tofs'd and driven us from our
' felves?   ' If

' If then that Day on which we obtain'd a
Victory, the Fruits whereof difappear'd in
a moment, was thought worthy to be a
Day of Feafting and Rejoicing, how much
more ought this Day to be celebrated with
Joy and Gladnefs, the fruitful Glory of
which will laft to all future Generations?
Let us change the Day of Rejoicing for our
Victory over the Giants, to a Day of Rejoicing for our Victory over our felves.
Let the Day in which we purg'd Heaven,
be more folemn and joyful to us, than
ever the Departure of the leprous People
' could be to the *Egyptians*, or the Freedom
' from the *Babylonifh* Captivity to the *He-*
brews. This day Sicknefs, Peftilence, Le-
profy, are banifh'd from Heaven to the Defarts, this day is broken that Chain of
Crimes, and thofe Fetters of Errors which
bound us over to eternal Chaftifement.
Now then, you being all in a good Difpofition to go on in this Reformation, and
having (as I underftand) premeditated
upon the manner of perfecting it; I fhall
go on, in order to fpeak to every Particular,
' according to my beft Judgment. And
' when any thing I propofe feems worthy of
' Approbation, tell me fo, if any thing feems
' inconvenient, let me know it; if you think
' you can do better, declare fo; if any thing
' ought to be abolifh'd, tell me your Opi-
' nion, if any thing ought to be added, let
' me hear it: for every one has full liberty

E   ' to

' to give his Vote ; and whoever is filent, is
' fuppos'd to acquiefce.' At this all the Gods
rofe up, and by that fign ratify'd what was
propos'd.

' To begin then at the Head, (faid *Jupiter)*
' let us confider in the firft place the Affairs
' of the North, and make provifions about
' them ; and then, by regular Steps, let us
' proceed in order till we arrive at the end.
' Tell me freely what your Judgment and
' Thoughts are concerning that Bear there?'
The Gods who firft heard thefe words, laid
it upon *Momus* to anfwer ; who faid, ' 'Tis
' a great Scandal, O *Jupiter*, and greater
' perhaps than you are aware of, that in the
' moft celebrated part of Heaven, in that
' part which *Pythagoras* (who underftood that
' the World had Arms and Legs, a Body
' and a Head) faid was the upper part of
' that, to which is oppofite the other Ex-
' treme which he call'd the lower Region :
' according to what a Poet of that Sect fings.

Hic vertex nobis femper fublimis, & illum
Sub pedibus Styx atra videt, manefque pro
   fundi.

' There where the Mariners confult in the
' uncertain and untrodden Paths of the Sea,
' towards which all the Paffengers who fuf-
' fer Storms and Tempefts lift up their hands;
' which the Giants afpire at , there where
' the fierce Generation of *Belus* rais'd the
                                  ' Tower

‘ Tower of *Babel*; where the Magicians of
‘ the Steel Looking-Glaſs ſought for the Ora-
‘ cles of *Floron*, one of the great Princes of
‘ the artick Spirits; where the Cabaliſts ſay
‘ *Samael* would have rais'd a Throne, that
‘ he might be like the mighty Thunderer;
‘ there have you placed this ugly huge Mon-
‘ ſter of a Brute, not with ſupernumerary
‘ Eyes, or Beard, or Hands, or Feet, or any
‘ other leſs noble part of the Body, but with
‘ a Tail, (which againſt the nature of the
‘ Bear-kind, *Juno* tack'd on behind) which
‘ ſerves as a worthy Index to the magnificent
‘ Pole and Support of the World, to all Con-
‘ templators in Heaven, in the Sea, and
‘ Earth. And as you did very ill in fixing
‘ her there, ſo you will do well to remove
‘ her from thence · And ſee you tell us where
‘ you will ſend her, and what you would
‘ have to come in her room.’ ‘ Let her go
‘ (ſaid *Jupiter*) where you Gods think beſt,
‘ either to the Bear-Garden of *England*, or
‘ the *Orſini* or *Ceſarini* of *Rome*, if you would
‘ have her go into a City of great renown.’
I would have her impriſon'd in the Dens of
Bern, ſaid *Juno*. ‘ Don't be ſo ill-natur'd,
‘ my dear Wife, (ſaid *Jupiter*) ſhe may go
‘ where ſhe will, provided ſhe is free. And
‘ becauſe this is the moſt eminent place,
‘ when ſhe leaves it, I will have Truth to
‘ ſucceed her. For there the Nails of De-
‘ traction do not come; the Poiſon of Envy
‘ does not kill; the Darkneſs of Error does

E 2 ‘ not

' not penetrate. There she shall stand firm
' and stable; there she shall not be agitated
' by Waves and Tempests; there she will
' be a sure Guide to those that wander thro
' this Sea of Errors and Mistakes; from
' thence will be seen the clear and pure Mir-
' ror of Contemplation.'

   Old Father *Saturn* said, ' What shall we do
' with this *Ursa Major?*' *Momus* answer'd,
' Let her go (for she is old) and be Waiting-
' Maid to the young *Ursa Minor*; but take
' care that she don't become her Bawd:
' which if she do, we will condemn her to
' serve some Beggar, who may get his Living
' by her, by making a Show of her, and
' causing little Children and the like to ride
' upon her, to cure the Quartan Ague, and
' other lesser Diseases.'

   Mars demanded of *Jupiter*, What they
should do with their huge Dragon? Says
Momus, ' Our Father hath given an answer
' to that; and it is this: It is an useless
' Beast, and better dead than alive; how-
' ever, if you please, we will send it to *Ire-*
' *land*, or to some of the *Orkney* Isles to feed
' but have a care that it don't throw down
' some of the Stars into the Sea with its
' Tail.' ' Never fear that, answer'd *Apollo*,
' for I will order some *Circe* or *Medea* to lull
' it asleep, with the Verses by which I made
' it fall asleep when it guarded the golden
' Apples, that so it may be softly transported
' to the Earth: but let it go wherever there
                                                     ' is

is barbarous Beauty ; for the golden Apples ſhall be Beauty, the Dragon ſhall be Fierceneſs, *Jaſon* ſhall be the Lover, and the Enchantment which makes the Dragon fall aſleep, ſhall be propoſing Love, waiting and embracing Opportunities, crying, and ſometimes bribing, for there is no Heart ſo hard which may not be melted, no Deſire ſo cold which may not be warm'd by theſe means. What would you have to ſucceed in the Dragon's place, O Father? Prudence, (anſwer'd *Jupiter*) which ought to be near Truth ; becauſe this ought not to deſign, move or do any thing without that ; and becauſe it is not poſſible that one of theſe without the other can do any thing uſeful or honourable.' A good Reſolution, ſaid the Gods.

Mars ſubjoin'd, ' This *Cepheus*, when he was King, manag'd his Arms in a very troubleſom manner, to aggrandize his Kingdom, which Fortune beſtow'd on him : Now I don't think it convenient, that he ſhould have ſuch a large Court in Heaven, thus ſpreading his Arms, and enlarging his Strides.' ' Well then (ſaid *Jupiter*) he muſt drink a Draught of *Lethe*, that ſo he may forget his Poſſeſſions both in Heaven and Earth, and riſe up an Animal that has neither Legs nor Arms.' It muſt be ſo, added the Gods. ' But *Sophia* muſt ſucceed to his place, becauſe the poor Creature muſt partake of the Fortune and Misfortune of

E 3 ' Truth

' Truth her inseparable Companion, with
' whom she has always partaken in all Straits,
' Afflictions, Injuries and Labours : besides,
' if she is not taken into the Administration
' with Truth, I don't know how this last
' can ever be respected and honour'd.' ' I
' consent to it with all my heart, said *Jupi-*
' *ter*, because 'tis both agreeable to Order
' and Reason; and because I should think I
' had ill placed the one in this place without
' the other : and Truth could not be easy at
' a distance from her so much lov'd Sister,
' and desir'd Companion.

   ' *Aritophylax* who is so well enamel'd with
' Stars, (said *Diana*) and manages the Cha-
' riot , what do you think, *Momus*, shall be
' done with him ?' ' Because he is that *Ar-*
' *cadian*, said *Momus*, the Fruit of that sacri-
' legious Womb, that generous Birth which
' witness'd the horrid Thefts of our great
' Father ; he must go from hence, and do
' you provide a Habitation for him.' *Apollo*
said, ' Since he is the Son of *Califto*, let him
' follow his Mother.' *Diana* subjoin'd, ' And
' since he was a Bear-Hunter, 'tis fit he
' should follow his Mother , with this pro-
' viso, That he don't fix his Javelin in her
' Tail at any time.' *Mercury* added, ' Be-
' cause you see that he can take no other
' way, let him go to guard his Mother in
' her Return to the *Erymantian* Woods.'
' That will be best, said *Jupiter*; and be-
' cause the unhappy Woman was ravish'd by
                       ' force,

'force, I will repair her Loſs, when I ſend
'her from this place (if *Juno* pleaſes) and
'reſtore her to her former beautiful Form.'
'I am contented (ſaid *Juno*) when you have
'firſt put her in the ſtate of Virginity, and
'conſequently in favour with *Diana.*' 'We'll
'ſay no more of this at preſent, ſaid *Ju-*
'*piter*; but let us ſee what muſt ſucceed
'him in this place.' After a great many Re-
ſolves and Diſcuſſions, *Juno* ſaid, 'Let the
'Law ſucceed him; becauſe that is a very
'neceſſary Inhabitant of Heaven, ſince ſhe
'is the Daughter of the divine and celeſtial
'*Sophia*, as this is the Daughter of the infe-
'riour *Sophia* into which this Goddeſs ſends
'her Influxes, and irradiates the Splendour of
'her own Light, while ſhe goes thro the
'deſart and ſolitary places of the Earth.'
'Well order'd, *Jupiter*, ſaid *Pallas :* For
'there is no good and true Law which has
'not *Sophia* for its Mother, and the rational
'Intellect for its Father, and therefore this
'Daughter ought not to be far from her
'Mother. And that Men may contemplate
'how things ought to be order'd among them
'below, let *Jupiter* agree to this Reſolution
'here if he pleaſes.

'Next follows the Seat of the Northern
'Crown, made of Sapphire, enrich'd with
'ſo many ſhining Diamonds, and makes that
'fine Proſpect, with four and four, which
'are eight burning Carbuncles. And be-
'cauſe this came from below, and was tranſ-

E 4   'ported

' ported thence, I think it very proper it
' fhould be prefented to fome heroick Prince,
' who is worthy of it . therefore let *Jupiter*
' look who among us is moft worthy to pre-
' fent it.' ' Let it remain in Heaven (an-
' fwer'd *Jupiter*) till the time when it fhould
' be given to that invincible Arm, which is
' to bring back the fo much defir'd Peace to
' miferable *Europe*, by crufhing the many
' Heads of that worfe than *Lermean* Mon-
' fter, which fpreads the fatal Poifon of mul-
' tiform Herefy, which creeps thro her Veins
' into all parts with incredible Velocity.'
Momus added, ' 'Twill be a noble Work to
' put an end to this daftardly Sect of Pe-
' dants, who without doing good according
' to the natural and divine Law, efteem
' themfelves, and would be efteem'd by o-
' thers to be religious Perfons, and accepta-
' ble to God , and fay that doing good is
' good, and doing evil is evil, but that do-
' ing good, or abftaining from evil, does not
' render them acceptable to God ; but only
' hoping and believing according to their
' Catechifm. I leave you to judg, O ye
' Gods! if there was ever fuch Ribaldry and
' Roguery as this in the world , which every
' one who is not ftone-blind muft fee at firft
' glance.' ' Indeed (faid *Mercury*) he who
' is ignorant of Trick and Chicane, is igno-
' rant of that which is the Mother of all.
' If *Jupiter* himfelf, and all of us together,
' fhould propofe fuch a Bargain and Cove-

' nant

' nant to Men, we fhould deferve to be abo-
' minated more than Death; as if we were
' follicitous only about our own Vain-Glory,
' to the great prejudice of human Happinefs.'
' The worft of it is (faid *Momus)* that they
' defame us, by faying this is the Inftitu-
' tion of the Gods; withal they reproach
' Effects and Events, by giving them the
' title of Defects and Vices: In the mean
' time they labour for no-body, and all Men
' labour for them; they do nothing elfe but
' fpeak evil of Works, and yet they live upon
' the Works of thofe who work'd for others
' befides them, and who inftituted Temples,
' Chappels, Hofpitals, Colleges and Univer-
' fities for others: wherefore they are open
' Robbers and Poffeffors of the hereditary
' Goods of others, who if they are not fo
' good and perfect as they ought, yet they
' are not, like them, perverfe and pernicious
' to the World, but rather neceffary to the
' Commonwealth, fkill'd in the fpeculative
' Sciences, Lovers of Morality, follicitous
' for enlarging the Zeal and Care of helping
' each other, and maintaining Society (for
' which all Laws are ordain'd) by propofing
' certain Rewards to fuch as do well, and
' threatning certain Punifhments to Crimi-
' nals. Befides, they tell us all their Care is
' taken up about invifible things, which nei-
' ther they, nor any others for them, ever
' underftood. They fay that immutable
' Deftiny produces all things, by means of
' certain

' certain inward Affections and Fancies,
' which the Gods infinitely entertain them-
' selves with. And therefore, said *Mercury*,
' if some believe Works to be necessary,
' this ought not to offend them, or excite
' their Zeal ; because their Destiny, as well
' as that of those who believe the contrary,
' is prefix'd, and does not change according
' as they believe or disbelieve, but remains
' always unchangeable. And for the same
' reason they ought not to molest those who
' do not believe them, but esteem them very
' wicked ; because they cannot believe them
' good Men, not being able to change De-
' stiny, it not being in their Choice to alter
' their Faith But those that believe the
' contrary, may not only justly vex them ac-
' cording to their Conscience, but also esteem
' it a great Sacrifice to the Gods, and Bene-
' fit to the World, to persecute, kill, and
' drive them off the face of the Earth ; be-
' cause they are worse than Caterpillars and
' barren Locusts, and those Harpies which
' do no good, but trample under foot, and
' foul all those they cannot devour, and are a
' hindrance to those that would exercise them-
' selves in doing Good.'

' All those who are capable to judg (said
' *Apollo)* will agree that the Laws are good,
' inasmuch as they have Practice for their
' Scope ; and those are always the best, that
' give the best Encouragement to the best
' Actions. For all Laws have been given
                              ' either

' either by us, or invented by Men chiefly
' for the Convenience of human Life : And
' becaufe fome do not fee the Fruit of
' their Merits in this Life, Good and Evil,
' Rewards and Punifhments in another
' Life, are promis'd and laid before their
' Eyes, accoiding to their Deeds. All thofe
' then that think otherwife, faid *Apollo*, de-
' ferve to be perfecuted by Heaven and
' Earth, and exterminated from the World
' as Pefts, and deferve no more Mercy than
' Wolves, Bears and Serpents, the driving
' of which out of the World is an honoura-
' ble and meritorious Work: And he that
' fhall remove them, will incomparably me-
' rit fo much the more, by how much they
' are greater Pefts than thefe. And there-
' fore *Momus* hit very right, when he propos'd
' that the Southern Crown fhould be given
' to him, who is difpos'd by Fate to take a-
' way this ftinking Naftinefs from the
' World.'

' Well (faid *Jupiter*) I am willing and de-
' termin'd that this Crown be beftow'd, as
' *Mercury*, *Momus*, and *Apollo* have propos'd,
' and the reft of you have confented. This
' Peftilence being fo violent, and contrary
' to all Law and Nature, certainly it cannot
' laft long, as you may eafily underftand.
' And Fate and Deftiny are their mortal
' Enemies, for fuch fort of People never
' grow numerous, but to fuffer the greater
' Ruin.' ' The Crown (faid *Saturn*) is a
' very

‘ very worthy Reward for him that fhall fend
‘ them out of the way ; but to be driven
‘ from human Converfation, is too fmall and
‘ difproportion’d a Punifhment for the per-
‘ verfe Wretches, and therefore I think it
‘ will be juft, that when they leave this Bo-
‘ dy, they fhould pafs from one Body into
‘ another thro many Ages and Generations,
‘ till at laft they take up their Habitation
‘ in Swine, which are the vileft Animals in
‘ the World, or Oyfters, which are fix’d to the
‘ Rocks.’

‘ Juftice (faid *Mercury*) judges otherwife :
‘ It appears juft to me that Idlenefs fhould
‘ be punifh’d with Labour and Fatigue, and
‘ therefore ’tis better they fhould go into
‘ Afles, and retain their Ignorance, and be
‘ rid of their Idlenefs. In this condition let
‘ them have a little Hay or Straw in return
‘ for their continual Labour, and many
‘ Blows for Reward.’ This Propofal was
approv’d by all the Gods together. Then
Jupiter pronounc’d, that the Crown fhould
be his for ever who fhould give them the
laft Tofs, and that they fhould ftill go from
Afs to Afs for the fpace of thirty thoufand
years. He pronounc’d Sentence farther, that
in place of this particular Crown fhould fucceed an Ideal one, that is communicable *in
infinitum*, from which might proceed infinite
Crowns as from a Lamp without Diminution,
and without lofing any of its Virtue or Effi-
cacy, by kindling an infinite number of o-
theis

thers at it. And to this Crown he propos'd
to join the Ideal Sword, which has likewise
much more reality than any particular one
that subsists within the Limits of natural
Operations. By which Sword and Crown
Jupiter understands the universal Judgment,
by which every one in the World shall be rewarded or punish'd, according to the measure of his Merits or Sins. All the Gods very much approv'd this Provision, because 'tis
fit that Judgment should have a Place near
the Law; because Judgment must govern for
the Sword, and the Sword execute for Judgment; Judgment must dictate, and the
Sword execute. In the one consists all the
Theory of Justice, in the other all the Practice.

After many Reasonings and Digressions
had been made upon this Subject, *Momus*
presented *Hercules* to *Jupiter*, and said, ' What
' shall we do now with this Bastard of
' yours?' ' You have heard (said *Jupiter*)
' the Cause why my *Hercules* must go hence
' with all the rest; but I will not have his
' going away to be like that of the rest,
' because the Cause, Manner and Reason of
' his Assumption was very unlike theirs: For
' he merited Heaven only for the singular
' Virtues and Merits of his heroick Actions,
' and tho he is spurious, yet he hath shewn
' himself worthy to be the legitimate Son
' of *Jupiter*; and you clearly see that the on-
' ly Reason of his being deny'd a Place in
                                          ' Heaven,

' Heaven, is, becaufe he is an adventitious
' God, and not one by Nature. And 'tis
' my Fault, not his (as has been faid) that
' he is a Baftard. And I believe your Con-
' fciences tell you, that *Hercules* fhould be
' the only Perfon excepted out of that gene-
' ral Rule and Determination. However,
' if we remove him from hence, and fend
' him to the Earth, let us take care that he
' be not without his Honour and Reputa-
' tion, which ought not to be lefs there, than
' that was which he had in Heaven.' Many
(I mean the greateft part) of the Gods rofe
up, and faid, *Let it be Greater*, if greater
be poffible.' ' Let us appoint then (added
' *Jupiter*) that fo ftrong and laborious a Per-
' fon have a Commiffion and Charge, by
' which he may make himfelf fo great a
' Terreftrial God, that all may efteem him
' greater than when he was a Celeftial De-
' mi-God.' They all anfwer'd, *So be it*
And becaufe fome of them did not rife at
the firft, and fpeak immediately, *Jupiter*
turn'd towards them, and faid, he would
make them underftand the Matter alfo.
Wherefore fome of them faid, *PROBA-
MUS*, others faid, *ADMITTIMUS*,
and *Juno* faid, *NON REFRAGAMUR*.
Then *Jupiter* rofe up, and pronounc'd the
Decree in this Form: *Becaufe at this very time,
in fome parts of the Earth, there have appear'd
Monfters, who if they are not of the fame Nature with thofe in the Times of the ancient Inha-*
bitants

bitants of it, yet, I am sure, are much worse;
I Jupiter, *Father and Proveditor-General,* appoint, *That* Hercules *go as my Lieutenant, and
the Minister of my potent Arm on Earth; not
with the like or greater Bulk of Body, but furnish'd and enrich'd with greater Vigilance, Vigour of Mind, and Power of Spirit And as he
seem'd great, First, when he was born, and brought
forth in it, for having overcome so many fierce
Monsters; and, Secondly, when he return'd to it
victorious from Hell, appearing to the Comfort of
his despairing Friends, and to the Surprize and
Destruction of outrageous Tyrants: So at present may this new, this so necessary and desir'd
Proveditor appear the third time to the Joy of his
Mother. See if any* Nemean *Lion dares to ravage in the* Arcadian *Cities, if the* Cleonean
Lion dare appear a-new in Thessaly. *See if that*
Hydra, *that Pest of* Lerna *dare rise up again
with her many growing Heads. Look if that*
Diomedes, *who fed Horses in* Hebron *with the
Blood of Strangers, dare appear again in* Thrace.
Lift up your Eyes to Lybia, *to see if that* Anteus, *who so often regain'd Strength, has again
reassum'd his Body. Consider if there be any
three-body'd* Gerion *in the* Iberian *Kingdom.
Raise your Heads, and see if the most pernicious*
Stymphalides *dare fly thro the Air at this time;
those Harpies, I say, that us'd sometimes to
darken the Air, and hinder the View of the luminous Stars. Spy if any bristly Wild-Boar
walk thro the* Erymanthian *Deserts If any Bull
like that which struck so many People with a pa-*
nick

nick Fear is to be met with : If *it be neceſſary to make ſome three-headed* Cerberus *go into the open Air, in order to vomit up the mortal* Aconitum : *If any butcherly* Buſiris *takes his Walks about his bloody Altars · If any* Hart *that adorns her Head with gilded Horns appears in thoſe Deſarts, like her that with her brazen Hoofs run as ſwift as the Wind : If any new* Amazonian *Queen has gather'd her rebellious Forces   If any perfidious and vain* Archelous, *with inconſtant, manifold and various Aſpect, tyrannizes any where : If any* Heſperides *have committed the Golden Apples to the Guardianſhip of a Dragon : If the unmarry'd bold Queen of the People of* Thermodon *appears · If any plundering* Lancinius, *or robbing* Cacus *over-run* Italy, *and defend themſelves with Smoke and Flame. If theſe, or the like, or any new unheard of Monſters ſhall meet him upon the ſpacious Back of* Terra *as he goes along to ſpeculate, let him toſs, tumble, reform, chaſe, purſue, bind, daunt, ſpoil, ſcatter, break, ſplit, bruiſe, throw down, overwhelm, burn, kill and annihilate them.   In reward for ſuch Deeds, and ſo many glorious Actions, I ordain that in the Places where he ſhall perform his heroick Exploits, there may be Trophies, Statues, Coloſſus's rais'd, beſides Chappels and Temples, if Fate don't thwart me.*

‘ In truth *Jupiter* (ſaid *Momus*) now by
‘ degrees you ſeem to me to be a good God,
‘ becauſe I ſee you are not tranſported by pa-
‘ ternal Affection beyond the Bounds of a
‘ juſt

just Retribution to the Merits of your *Alcides*; who if he is not worthy of so much, yet perhaps deserves something else, even in the Opinion of *Juno*, who, I see by her smiling, agrees with me in what I say.'

But here comes my *Mercury*, whom I expected with so much eagerness, *Saulinus*; for whose sake this our Conference must be defer'd to another occasion. and therefore be pleas'd to be gone, and leave us to discourse together by our selves,

Saul. Very well, we shall see one another to morrow. Behold him to whom I directed my Wishes yesternight, and who, after too long a stay, now presents himself to me! Yesternight my Wishes must have come to him, the same night have been heard by him, and this morning answer'd. If he did not appear immediately upon my Call, 'twas because he was taken up with some important matter, for I am confident I am no less belov'd by him than by my self. Behold he comes forth out of a bright shining Cloud, which from the Spirit of the South runs towards the Center of our Horizon; and yielding to the bright Rays of the Sun, opens it self in a Circle to crown my noble Planet. O Holy Father and High Majesty! I return you my hearty Thanks, because I see my wing'd Deity peep out of this *Medium*, and with expanded Wings beating the Air, glad to divide the Heavens in my Sight with his Rod, swifter than the Bird of *Jove*, more charm-

F ing

ing than that of *Juno*, rarer than the *Arabian* Phenix : He approaches me quickly, he prefents himfelf to me courteoufly, and appears as if all his Affections were wholly center'd on me alone.

Mercury. Behold me obfequious and favourable to thy Wifhes, O my *Sophia*; becaufe thou haft invok'd me, and thy Prayer came not to me like Aromatic Smoke, as ufual, but as a penetrating and well-feather'd Arrow of refplendent Rays.

Soph. But, my Deity, what was the reafon of your fo long Delay?

Mer. I'll tell you the Truth, *Sophia*, thy Prayer found me juft at my return from Hell, where I had been committing into the hands of *Minos*, *Eacus* and *Rhadamanthus*, two hundred forty fix Thoufand five hundred and twenty two Souls, which had compleated the Courfe of the Animation of the prefent Bodies, by divers Battles, Punifhments and Offices. There was prefent with me the Celeftial *Sophia*, commonly call'd *Minerva*, and *Pallas*, who immediately knew by the Habit and Gate that the Embaffy was from you.

Soph. She might well know it; for fhe ufes to converfe with me as often as with you.

Mer. And fhe faid to me, Lift up your Eyes, *Mercury*, for this Embaffy comes to you from our Sifter and Earthly Daughter, that lives by my Spirit, and proceeds from

the

the Light of my Father ; and therefore I
would recommend her to you. 'Tis needlefs
(reply'd I) to recommend to me, O Daughter
of *Jupiter*'s Brain, our moft beloved and
common Sifter and Daughter. I approach'd
your Meffage then, I embrac'd it, I kifs'd it,
I unbutton'd my Coat, and put it betwixt
my Shirt and my Skin, fo that my Heart
beat again and again upon it. *Jupiter* (who
was in the Room, but ftept a little afide to
talk with *Eolus* and *Oceanus* in private, who
were impatient to return quickly to their Bufinefs here below) faw what I was a-doing ;
he broke off his Difcourfe, and was inquifi-
tive to know what that Memorial was I put
in my Bofom : and I anfwering him, that it
came from you ; Oh my poor *Sophia*, faid
he, how does fhe do ? Alas, poor Creature!
I underftood immediately by that Piece of
coarfe Paper, not very nicely folded, that it
came from her ; and 'tis a long time fince
we have had any News from her : But, pray,
what does fhe ask ? What does fhe want ?
What does fhe propofe to you ?

Nothing (faid I) but that I would hear
her for one Hour. 'Tis well (faid *Jupiter*)
and fo return'd to finifh his Difcourfe with
thefe two Gods ; and when he had done, he
call'd me to him in all hafte, faying, Come,
come, let us quickly put our Affairs in order, e'er you go to fee what that poor Drudg
would have, and I to vifit my uneafy Wife,
that really burdens me more than the whole

weight

weight of the Univerfe. He was pleas'd to order (for 'tis lately decreed thus in Heaven) that every thing that is to happen in the World this day, fhould be regifter'd by my Hand.

Soph. Let me hear fome News, if you pleafe, after you have unbofom'd your felf to me about your Charge.

Mer. I'll tell you . He has ordei'd that this day at twelve a clock, two Melons, from a-mong a great many moie in the Melon-Plot of *Franzino*, fhould be perfectly ripe ; but that they be not gather'd till three days af-ter, when they fhall be good for nothing. At the fame time he will have thirty Jubebs gather'd in the Jubeb-Plot of *John Boromeo*, at the foot of the Mountain of *Cicada*, thirty of which are to be gather'd ripe, and feventeen to fall wither'd upon the Ground, and fouiteen worm-eaten. That *Vefta*, the Wife of *Albentio*, buin feven and fifty Hairs, by mak-ing the Iron too hot, when fhe curls the Hair of her Temples and Forehead , but that fhe don't fhake her Head ; even tho fhe fhould fmell a ftinking Smell, fhe muft bear it pa-tiently. That two hundred and fifty Beetle-flies grow out of the Dung of her Bull, thiiteen of which are to be trampled and kill'd by *Albentio*'s Foot ; that twenty fix die, by being turn'd topfy-turvy ; that twenty two live in a Cavern ; that eighty go in Pilgri mage thro the Court-yard , that foity twc lead a retir'd Life, under that Block near the

Gate

Gate ; that sixteen tofs Balls where they find it most convenient ; and that others go and seek their Fortune : That when *Laurenza* combs her Hair, thirteen may fall, seventeen break ; that ten of thefe grow again in three days, but the other seven never any more. That *Antonio Saulino*'s Bitch conceive five Puppies; that two of them die in their Mother's Belly, and three of them come to their time, that the first be like the Father, the second like both Father and Mother, the third like neither, but fomething like *Poldoro*'s Whelp. At that time the Cuckoo muft be heard from his Houfe, and muft cuckoo neither more nor lefs than twelve times, and then depart, and go to the Ruins of the Caftle. Let her cuckoo there seven minutes, and afterwards fly to *Scarvatta*, and what is to become of her next, we fhall provide afterwards. That the Gown that Mr. *Daneſe* cuts on his Table be fpoil'd, that twelve Bugs leave the Boards of *Conftantine*'s Bed, and march to his Pillow, four of them very little, and seven of them huge great ones, and one of a middle Size, and what becómes of them at Candle-light we fhall fee : That at the fifteenth Minute of the fame Hour, *Furtulo*'s old Wife fhall lofe the third Tooth of her Right Jaw, without any Blood or Pain (by moving her Tongue four times in her Mouth) becaufe that Tooth had been in a State of Trepidation for the fpace of almoft feventeen annual Revolutions of the

F 3   Moon :

Moon: That *Ambruoggio* do bufinefs with his Wife, after a hundred and twelve fruitlefs Attempts, and yet not get her with Child after all, but the next time he impregnate her with the Seed of that roafted Onion, which he eats now with Sauce and Millet-Bread: That the Hair of Puberty begin to fprout upon *Martinello*'s Son's Privities, and that withal he begin to have a manly Voice: That *Paulinus*, while he ftoops to heave up a great fhovel-full of Earth, break the red String that ties his Breeches; and if he fhall fwear or blafpheme, I'll lay him under this Punifhment, *viz.* his Pottage fhall be too falt, and tafte of Smoke: That he fall, and break a Bottle full of Wine, for which if he fwears, we fhall confider afterwards what fort of Punifhment to inflict on him: That of feven Moles, which began their Journy from under Ground four days ago, taking different Roads towards the Air, two may arrive at the Surface of the Earth the fame Hour, the one juft at twelve a clock, the other fifteen Minutes and nineteen Seconds after, at three Paces diftance from one another, and one Foot half an Inch over, in the Garden of *Anton'o tarvano.* The Time and Place of the reft will be provided for at more leifure.

Soph. You would have a very large Task, *Mercury*, if you fhould recount to me all the Acts of Father *Jupiter*'s Providence, and in relating to me all his particular Decrees one by one, you would, in my opinion, be like

him

him that had a mind to take an account of all the Particles whereof the Earth is compos'd. And if you have taken up so much time in recounting a few Trifles from among an infinite number that have fallen out at the same time, in a little Spot of Ground, where there are only four or five Seats, and these not very great ones neither; what Work would you have, if you were to give a full account, in order, of all things that happen at this Hour, thro this Village, that stands at the Foot of the Mountain *Cicada?* In short, a whole year would not suffice to set forth every thing prrticularly, as you have begun. But what work do you think you would have, if you were to relate every thing that happen'd about the City of *Roan* in the Kingdom of *France*, in *Italy*, in *Europe*, in the whole Terrestrial Globe, in all the Globes of the Universe *in infinitum*; as indeed the Worlds under the Providence of *Jupiter* are infinite? And really it would be necessary for you to have a hundred Mouths, and as many Tongues of Iron (agreeable to the Fiction of the Poets) to relate only what has happen'd in one instant, in the Compass of one only of those Orbs or Worlds; nay a thousand Millions would not be sufficient to execute the thousandth part of it. To tell you freely, *Mercury*, I don't know what that Relation of yours means, which some of my Worshipers, call'd Philosophers, believe gives a great deal of Trouble, Business and

F 4   Incum-

Encumbrance to this poor Father *Jupiter* the Magnificent: And they believe his Fortune to be fo bad, that the meaneft Mortal has no reafon to envy him ; not to fay, that the time he fpent in difpofing and appointing thefe Events, muft make him lofe infinite Occafions of providing for other things. And it would require an infinite number of Ages for you to difcourfe over to me all thefe things.

Mer. You know, *Sophia,* (if you be *Sophia)* that *Jupiter* does every thing without Carefulnefs, Labour, or Encumbrance: For he provides for innumerable Species and infinite Individuals, giving order, not in a certain fucceffive Duration, but all at once, for all thefe things : And he does not perform things after the manner of individual Efficients, one by one, by many Actions; and by infinite Actions come to infinite Acts; but he does all things paft, prefent, and to come, by one fimple and fingular Act.

Soph. I know this very well, *Mercury,* viz. That you do not relate and execute all thefe things at once , and that they are not in one fimple and fingular Subject : and therefore the Efficient of thefe things muft be proportionated, or at leaft muft proportion it felf to them.

Mer. What you fay is neceffarily true, and cannot be otherwife in a particular, proximate, and natural Efficient , becaufe the Meafure and Reafon of a particular Act about

bout a particular Subject, is according to the
Reason and Measure of a particular effective
Virtue : but it is not so in the universal Efficient ; for that is proportion'd (if I may
say so) to the whole infinite Effect which
depends upon it, according to the reason of
all Places, Times, Modes and Subjects, and
not definitely to certain Places, Subjects,
Times and Modes.

Soph. I know, *Mercury,* that universal Knowledg is distinct from particular, as infinite
is from finite.

Mer. As Unity is from an infinite Number,
would have been better said.   And you must
know moreover, *Sophia,* that Unity is in infinite Number, and infinite Number in Unity ; besides that Unity is an implicit Infinite,
and Infinite is an explicit Unity.   Moreover,
where there is not Unity, there is neither
finite nor infinite Number : and wheresoever
there is either finite or infinite Number,
there is necessarily Unity.   Unity therefore
is the Support and Substance of Infinity , and
therefore he that knows Unity, not acciden-
tally as certain particular Intellects, but ef-
sentially as the universal Intelligence, knows
One and Number, Finite and Infinite,
the End and Term of Comprehension, and
Surplusage of all things : And this can do
every thing, not only in general, but also in
every Particular , for as there is no Particular but what is comprehended in what is universal, so there is no Number in which Uni-

ty

ty is not more truly than Number it self.
Thus then, without any difficulty or encumbrance, *Jupiter* takes care of all Things,
in all Places and Times , as Being and Unity
are necessarily found in all Numbers, in all
Places, and in all Times, and in every Atom
of Times, Places, and Numbers: and the
only Principle of Being is in infinite Individ-
duals, that ever were, are, or shall be. But
this Dispute is not the End for which I am
come hither, and for which I presume I was
call'd upon by you.

Soph. 'Tis true, I am very sensible that
these are matters worthy to be decided by
my Philosophers, and fully understood, not
by me (who can hardly understand them
without Comparisons and Similitudes) but
by the Celestial *Sophia* and you; and so I
was mov'd by your Accounts to engage in
this Debate, before I came to discourse about
my own particular Interests and Designs.
And really I was convinc'd, that so judicious a Deity did not enter into this Discourse
of so small and mean things, without some
Design.

Mer. I did it not out of Vanity, *Sophia,*
but by great Providence , because I judg'd
this Advertisement necessary for you; knowing that you are so vexed with many Afflictions, that your Affections may be transported so as not to think too well of *Jupiter's*
Government, and that of the rest of the
Gods ,

Gods; which is moft juft and holy *ad finem
finalem*, altho things may appeai in a very
confus'd and diforderly State to you. I was
willing therefore to provoke you to fuch a
Contemplation, before I treated of any other
matter, to free you from all Doubts which
you might entertain, and perhaps have often
fhewn; becaufe you being earthly and dif-
cuifive, cannot clearly underftand the Importance of *Jupiter*'s Providence, and the
Bufinefs of us his Collaterals.

Soph. But pray, *Mercury*, what is the reafon of your uncommon Zeal at this time?

Mer. I'll tell you (what I have delay'd to
tell you till now) why your Wifh, your
Prayers, your Embaffy, tho coming to us
very fwiftly and fpeedily, were frozen even
in the middle of Summer, cold and trembling, as rather thrown out by Chance, than
addiefs'd and committed to Providence; as
if they had been in doubt, whether they
could reach the eais of fuch as are efteem'd
bufy about things of more importance. But
you aie miftaken, *Sophia*, if you think that
the minuteft things, as well as the greateft,
aie not under the Care and Providence of the
Gods; fince the greateft and chiefeft things
confift of the fmalleft and moft abject. All
the meaneft things, then, are under a Providence infinitely great, nay, all the pooreft
Trifles whatfoever, are moft important in
the Order of univerfal Nature · for the great
are compos'd of little things, and the little
of

of the leaft, and thefe laft of fingle and pri_mary Particles. I conceive of great Sub-ftances, as of great Powers, and great Ef-fects.

Soph. 'Tis very true, for the greateft, moft magnificent, and moft beautiful Fa-brick, is made up of things which are leaft, bafeft, and appear and are judg'd without any Beauty.

Mer. The Act of the Divine Knowledg is the Subftance of the Being of all things; and therefore all things, whether their Eſſence be finite or infinite, are known, order'd, and govern'd. The Divine Knowledg is not like ours, which follows things, but is before things, and is in every thing: fo that if it were not in all things, there would be no proximate and fecondary Caufes.

Soph. Therefore, *Mercury*, you would not have me be furpriz'd at any thing, great or fmall, that befalls me, not only as principal and direct, but even as indirect and accef-fary, and that *Jupiter* is in All, compleats All, and watches over All.

Mer. 'Tis fo: and therefore, for the future I would have you remember, to warm your Embaffy better, and not fend it in a negli-gent fafhion, ill-cloth'd and cold, in the pre-fence of *Jupiter*; and both he and your *Pal-las* chaig'd me, e're I fpoke to you of any thing elfe, I fhould lay this before you with fome addrefs.

Soph. I am oblig'd to you all for this.

Mer.

Mer. Tell me now the reaſon, why you call'd me hither.

Soph. Becauſe of the Change of *Jupiter*'s Manners, which I underſtand by what I have learnt from you by other Conferences. I have taken the Aſſurance to ask, and make inſtances to him for what I durſt not have mention'd formerly ; when I was afraid, left ſome *Venus, Cupid,* or *Ganymedes,* ſhould have rejected my Embaſſy, as ſoon as it preſented it ſelf at the door of *Jupiter*'s Anti-Chamber. Now that all things are reform'd, and other Porters, Maſters of Ceremonies, and Aſſiſtants are appointed, and that he is well-diſpos'd towards Juſtice, I wiſh you would pleaſe to preſent my Requeſt to him, which relates to great Wrongs that have been done me by divers ſorts of Men upon earth; and to pray him to be favourable and propitious to me, according as his Conſcience ſhall dictate to him.

Mer. Becauſe this your Requeſt is long, and of no ſmall importance, and likewiſe becauſe 'tis lately decreed in Heaven, that all Expeditions civil as well as criminal be regiſter'd in the Chamber, with all their Occaſions, Means, and Circumſtances ; therefore 'tis neceſſary that you give it me in writing, and ſo it ſhall be preſented to *Jove* and the Heavenly Senate.

Soph. What was the reaſon of giving that new Order ?

Mer. That by this means all the Gods might be tied to the strict Observance of Justice : For they are afraid that their Infamy may thus become eternal by Registry (which eternizes the Memory of Deeds) and that they may incur perpetual Blame and Condemnation from absolute Justice, which reigns over Governours, and presides over all the Gods.

Soph. I shall do so then : But I must have time to think and write. Wherefore I beseech you, come to me to-morrow, or the day after.

Mer. I shall not fail. In the mean while mind your Business.

The End of the First Dialogue.

THE

THE

Second DIALOGUE.

Saulinus. I Intreat you, *Sophia*, before we
go any farther, give me an ac-
count of the Reasons of this Or-
der and Disposition of the Gods, which *Jupiter* has form'd in the Stars. And let me
know, in the first place, why he was pleas'd
to place the Goddess Truth in the most eminent place, as 'tis commonly esteem'd ?

Soph. I shall satisfy you about this with
the greatest ease. Truth is plac'd, *Saulinus*,
above all other things; because she is the Unity which presides over all, and the Goodness
which shines above all: For *Ens est unum,
verum, bonum; idem est verum, Ens, bonum.*
Truth is that Entity which is not posteriour to
any thing whatsoever; for if you would suppose any thing before Truth, you must reckon it something different from Truth, and
if you suppose it different from Truth, you
must necessarily suppose it to have nothing
of Truth in it; without Truth, not true,

and

and confequently falfe, Nothing, a Non-Entity. Moreover, nothing can be before Truth, if the fame be not alfo before and above Truth, and fuch a Being cannot be a true Being, but by the Truth: Hence it can be no other but Truth, and the very fame with Truth, becaufe if it is not a true Being by Truth, 'tis a Non-Entity, falfe, and nothing. In like manner, there can be nothing after Truth; becaufe if 'tis after, 'tis without it; if 'tis without it, 'tis not true, becaufe it has not Truth in it felf; therefore 'twill be falfe, therefore 'twill be nothing. Therefore Truth is before all things, with all things, after all things, above all things: It has the Reafon of Beginning, Middle, and End. It is before things, by way of Caufe and Principle; fince upon it things have their Dependance. It is in things, and is it felf the Subftance of things; fince by it they have their Subfiftence. It is after things, fince by it they are conceiv'd without Falfity. It is Ideal, Natural, and Notional It is Metaphyfical, Phyfical, and Logical. Truth then is above all things, and what is above all things, tho conceivable in another manner, and otherwife named, yet in fubftance 'tis neceffarily Truth it felf. For this reafon then, *Jupiter* has been pleas'd to fet Truth in the moft eminent place in Heaven. But indeed that which you fee after a fenfible manner, and can found by the Depth of your Underftanding, is not the chief and

fiift,

firſt; but only a certain Figure, a certain Image, a certain Splendour of that which is ſuperiour to this *Jupiter* whom we often ſpeak of, and who is the Subject of our Metaphors.

Saul. Worthily ſaid, *Sophia* · for Truth, of all things, is the moſt pure and the moſt divine; or rather, Truth is the Divinity, Purity, Goodneſs, and Beauty of all things; which is neither deſtroy'd by Violence, nor corrupted by Antiquity, nor diminiſh'd by Secrecy, nor loſt by Communication : For Senſe does not confound it, Time does not crumble it, Place does not hide it, Night does not interrupt it, Darkneſs does not veil it ; but the more it is oppos'd, the more it riſes and grows: It defends it ſelf without a Patron or Protector, and therefore loves the Company of the few Wiſe, hates the Multitude, and ſhews it ſelf to thoſe only who ſearch for it by it ſelf, and is willing to declare it ſelf only to thoſe who lay themſelves open to it with Humility, and not to thoſe who ſearch after it with Fraud ; and is therefore placed very high, where all may admire it, and few reach it. But pray, *Sophia*, why is Prudence placed next it ? Is it becauſe thoſe who would contemplate and preach Truth, ought to be govern'd by Prudence ?

Soph. That is not the reaſon. That Goddeſs who is join'd and dwells next to Truth, comes under two denominations, *viz.* Providence

G and

and Prudence : and is call'd Providence, as she influences and is present with the superiour Principles, and Prudence, by the Effects she produces in us : as we call that the Sun, which diffuses its Warmth and Light thro the World ; and that Light and Splendour, which appears in Glasses and other Subjects. Providence then is properly said to be in things which are above ; it is the Companion of Truth, and never without it, and is Necessity as well as Liberty. So that Truth, Providence, Liberty, and Necessity, Unity, Verity, Essence, and Entity, are all one absolute Being, as I shall explain to you more at large another time.

But the better to direct the present Contemplation, you must know, that Providence instils Prudence into us, which consists in a certain temporal Reasoning, and is the principal Reason that is conversant about Universal and Particular ; and has Logick for her Waiting-Maid, and acquir'd Sapience or Wisdom, commonly call'd Metaphysicks, for her Guide, which considers the universal Principles of all things that fall under human Cognizance : and these two reduce all their Considerations to the use of this. She then has likewise three treacherous vicious Enemies ; on the right hand, Subtilty, Craftiness and Malice ; on the left, Stupidity, Sloth and Imprudence : and is conversant about consultative Virtue, as Fortitude is about the Impetuosity of Wrath, Temperance about
the

the Confent of Concupifcence, and Juftice about all Operations, as well external as internal.

Saul. You mean then that Providence infpires into us Prudence, and that in the Archetypal World anfwers to this in the Phyfical World : This, that holds out a Shield to Mortals, by which with the affiftance of Reafon they fortify themfelves againft the Shocks of Fortune ; by which we are taught to take the readieft and moft perfect Caution, where the greateft Difadvantages are threaten'd and fear'd , by which inferiour Agents accommodate themfelves to Things, Times, and Occafions ; and the Will and Inclination is not chang'd, but adapted to Circumftances : by which nothing happens, to the Welldifpos'd, unexpectedly and by furprize ; on the contrary, they fufpect nothing, but guard againft Accidents ; remembring what is paft, making their advantage of what is prefent, and forefeeing what is to come. Tell me now, if you pleafe, why *Sophia* fucceeds, and is next to Prudence and Truth.

Soph. Sophia, or Wifdom, (like Truth and Providence) is of two kinds , the one is fuperiour, fupra-celeftial, and ultra-mundane, if I may fo fpeak, and is Providence it felf ; it is it felf both Light and Eye ; Eye that is Light it felf, and Light that is Eye it felf : The other is confecutive, mundane and inferiour , and is not Wifdom it felf, but the true Receptacle and Partaker of

Wifdom :

Wiſdom : She is not the Sun, but the Moon, Earth, and Star which ſhines by that Sun. Thus ſhe is not Wiſdom by Eſſence, but by Participation, and an Eye which receives Light, and is illuminated by external and foreign Light ; and is not an Eye from her-ſelf, but from another ; and has not Being by her-ſelf, but by another : becauſe ſhe is not the *Unum, Verum, Bonum*, but from *Unum, Verum, Bonum*; to *Unum, Verum, Bonum* ; by *Unum, Verum, Bonum*; and in *Unum, Verum, Bonum*. The firſt is inviſible, ineffigiable, incomprehenſible, above all, in all, and thro all : The ſecond is figur'd in Heaven, illuſtrated by Knowledg, communicated by Words, digeſted by Arts, poliſh'd by Diſcuſſions, delineated by Writings ; by which he who ſays he knows what he knows not, is a raſh Sophiſt; he who denies he knows what he knows, is ungrateful to the active Intellect, injurious to Truth, and outrageous to me. And ſuch are all thoſe who do not ſeek me by my ſelf, or by the ſupreme Virtue, and Love of the Divinity, which is above all *Jupiters* and all Heavens; but ſell me for Riches, for Honour, or any other ſort of Gain: who are not ſo careful to be wiſe, as to be thought ſo ; or who love to detract from, and oppoſe the Felicity of others, or are troubleſom Cenſors and rigid Obſervers of their Neighbours. The firſt of theſe are miſerable, the ſecond vain, the third malicious, and of a baſe Temper. But thoſe who ſeek

me

me to inftruct themfelves, are prudent Thofe
who pay me their Refpects to inftruct others,
are humane.   Thofe who feek me abfolutely
and without conditions, are curious : And
thofe who enquire after me, out of love for
the fupreme and firft Truth, are wife, and
confequently happy.

Saul. From whence comes it, *Sophia*, that
all thofe who thus poffefs you, don't become
thus difpos'd ; but fometimes he that poffeffes
you moft, is leaft edify'd and inftructed ?

Soph. From whence comes it, *Saulinus*,
that the Sun does not warm all thofe on
whom it fhines ; and that fometimes it falls
out, that thofe on whom it fhines moft, are
leaft warm'd by it ?

Saul. I underftand you, *Sophia* ; and know
that 'tis you who in various ways contemplate, comprehend, and explain this Truth,
and the Effects of that heavenly Influence of
your Being ; which many afpire, endeavour,
ftudy, and earneftly contend to arrive at, by
divers fteps and degrees ; which prefents it
felf the very End and Scope of the different
Studies of Mankind, and actuates the diverfe
Subjects of intellectual Virtues according to
different Meafures , and is her felf that one
fimple Truth which directs all Men, And
as there is none who has not fome Notices of
Truth, fo there is none here below, who is
able perfectly to comprehend it , becaufe it is
not comprehended and truly conceiv'd by
any thing, but that in which it dwells effen-

tially,

tially; and that is no other than her felf:
And therefore fhe is not feen externally, but
in a Shadow, a Similitude, a Glafs, and fu-
perficially ; to which none in this World can
approach by an Act of Providence, and Effect
of Prudence, except your felf, *Sophia.* How
ever, fhe brings you many Sects, fome of
which admire her, others approve, others
enquire, others fuppofe, others judge and determine : fome by the Sufficiency of natural
Magick, others by fuperftitious Divination,
others by way of Negation, others by way
of Affirmation, others by way of Compo-
fition, others by way of Divifion, others by
way of Definition, others by way of Demon-
ftration, others by acquir'd Principles, others
by divine Principles, afpire at her. In the
mean time, fhe who is prefent in no place,
nor abfent from any, cries aloud to them,
and prefents before the Eyes of their Underftanding all things by Writings and natural
Effects , and thunders into the Ears of the
inward Mind, by the conceiv'd Species of
things vifible and invifible.

To Wifdom fucceeds Law her Daughter.
By this Princes reign, and Kingdoms and
Commonwealths are maintain'd ; and by
adapting her felf to the Complexions and
Manners of People and Nations, fhe fuppref-
fes Audacioufnefs by Fear, and makes Goodnefs fafe even among the Wicked ; and always caufes in the Guilty a Remorfe of
Confcience, with a Fear of Juftice, and Expectation

peftation of fuch Punifhment as humbles
proud Daringnefs, and introduces humble
Submiffion, by virtue of her eight Servants,
which are *Lex Taltonis*, Prifons, Scourging,
Exile, Ignominy, Servitude, Poverty, and
Death. *Jupiter* has placed her in Heaven,
and exalted her, on this condition, That fhe
fuffer not the Potentates of the Earth to be
fecure, becaufe of their Dignity and Power,
but that they refer all to a higher Providence
and fuperiour Law (by which the Civil is
regulated, as by a Divine and Natural Law)
and declare, that Nets, Cords, Chains, and
Fetters are appointed for fuch who break
thro Spiders Webs. For it is ratify'd by order of the eternal Law, that the moft potent
fhould be moft powerfully held and bound,
if not in the fame Prifons, and with the fame
Bonds, yet with worfe than what are prepar'd
for other Men. Then fhe was order'd and
enjoin'd to fhew the utmoft Rigour about
thofe things, which from the beginning were
thought moft important and neceffary, that
is, about thofe things which relate to the
mutual Duties of Men in human Societies,
that fo the Powerful may be fupported by
the Impotent, that the Weak be not opprefs'd
by the Stronger, that Tyrants be depos'd,
and juft Governours and Kings be eftablifh'd
and firmly fettled, that Commonwealths be
cherifh'd, that Reafon be not inculcated by
Violence and Force, that Ignorance defpife
not Knowledg, that the Poor be affifted by
the

the Rich; that Virtues and Studies neceſſary and uſeful to the Community be promoted, advanc'd, and maintain'd; that thoſe who advance and make progreſs in them, be honour'd and rewarded; that the Negligent, Avaritious, and Miſer, be deſpis'd and ſet at nought; that none be put into a Place of Power, unleſs recommended by his Merits, either thro a prevailing and ſuperiour Virtue and Genius, which may make him riſe of himſelf, which is rare and next to impoſſible; or by the Recommendation and Counſel of others, which is the due, ordinary, and neceſſary Method. *Jupiter* has confer'd on her the Power of binding, which conſiſts chiefly in this, That ſhe do nothing which may make her incur Contempt and Indignity; which ſhe cannot eſcape, if ſhe walks in either of theſe two Roads, one of which is that of Iniquity, which recommends and propoſes things that are unjuſt, the other is that of Difficulty, which propoſes and recommends things that are impoſſible, and therefore unjuſt: and for that reaſon the two Hands by which all Laws are made effectual, are Juſtice and Poſſibility; one of which is moderated and temper'd by the other: for tho many things are poſſible, which are unjuſt; yet nothing can be juſt, which is impoſſible.

Saul. You have very good reaſon, *Sophia,* to ſay, that no Law which is not uſeful to human Society ought to be receiv'd. *Jupiter*

has

has difpos'd and order'd the matter very well: for that Inftitution or Law, which brings not along with it Convenience and Utility, and Fitnefs to lead us to our beft End, whether it defcend fiom Heaven, or arife out of the Earth, ought to be rejected and condemn'd. Now a greater and nobler End cannot be conceiv'd, than that which direfts the Mind, and regulates the Inclinations, and correfts our Miftakes in fuch a manner, that they may bring forth fruits ufeful and neceffary to human Society ; which muft certainly be a Divine Thing, the Art of Arts, and Difcipline of Difciplines ; that by which Men muft be govern'd and kept under, who of all Animals have the moft different Complexions and Tempers, the moft various Cuftoms, the moft divided and feparate Inclinations, the moft difagreeing Wills, and the moft inconftant Impulfes But alas! *Sophia*, that we are come to fuch a pafs (and who would ever have thought this was poffible?) that that muft be chiefly efteem'd Religion, which defpifes, neglefts and condemns Good-works as criminal, fome not fticking to fay that the Gods care not for thofe things, and that however great they may be, yet Men are not juftify'd by Good-works.

Soph. Really, *Saulinus*, I think you dream ; I believe that what you fay is not true, but only a Fantafm or Apparition of a troubled Brain : 'Tis neverthelefs certain that there are fome fuch who piopofe and

offer

offer fuch things to the Belief of wretched People, but be affur'd, the World will ea fily difcern that this can never be digefted, 'twill perceive this as eafily, as that it cannot fubfift without Law and Religion. We have now feen in fome meafure how well the Law has been made and fettled; you muft next hear on what Condition Judgment is join'd to it. *Jupiter* has put the Sword and the Crown into the hands of Execution, with this he rewards thofe who do Good, and abftain from Evil; with that he chaftifes thofe who are forward in finning, and are unprofitable and unfruitful Plants. He hath enjoin'd on Execution, the Defence and Care of the true Law, and the Deftruction of the wicked and falfe, that is dictated by per-verfe Minds, and Enemies to the peaceable and happy State of Mankind. He hath commanded Execution, that being join'd to the Law, it extinguifh not, but (as much as poffible) kindle the Appetite of Glory in human Breafts, becaufe that is the fole and moft efficacious Spur that ufes to pufh Men on, and warm them to thofe Deeds which inlarge, maintain and fortify Commonwealths.

Saul. Our Profeffors of a falfe Religion cry, That this Glory is all vain, and fay, we ought to glory in I don't know what Caba-liftical Tragedy.

Soph. In earneft, 'tis not much matter what one fancies or thinks, provided his

Words

Words and Actions don't corrupt the peaceable State of Things: And Duty confifts chiefly in correcting and keeping up ufeful Practices, not in judging of the Tree by its beautiful Leaves, but by its good Fruits; and that thofe which bring not forth good Fruit be remov'd, and others put in their place that do. Who can believe that the Gods find themfelves interefted any way in thofe things in which no Man is interefted? For the Gods are concern'd about thofe things only wherein Men are concern'd, but are not difpleas'd or exafperated on their own account, for any thing done, or faid, or thought, that has not fome Tendency to make Men lofe that Refpect, by which Commonwealths are preferv'd. For the Gods would ceafe to be Gods, if they were either pleas'd or difpleas'd, forry or glad for any thing which Men do or think: And they would be more neceffitous than Men; or at leaft as Men receive Benefits and Advantages from them, fo they might come to want the fame from Men The Gods therefore being exempted from all Paffion, they can only have active Anger or Liking, but not paffive: For which reafon we do not threaten Punifhments, and promife Rewards, for any Evil or Good that can refult to our felves; but only for the Good and Tranquillity of Communities and Civil Societies, which we have taken care to affift by our Divine Laws, when human Laws were infufficient.

cient. 'Tis therefore foolish, unworthy, profane and injurious, to imagine that the Gods seek Reverence, Fear, Love, Worship and Respect from Men, for any other Good, Advantage or End, than that of Men themselves; for being most glorious in themselves, and not capable of receiving any Glory from without, they have made and constituted Laws, not so much (or at all for themselves or their own Glory) as to communicate Glory to Men. And therefore Laws and Judgments want so much of the Goodness and Truth of Laws and Judgments, as they come short in ordering and approving, in a special manner, the moral Actions of Men, with regard to other Men.

Saul. This Appointment and Decree of *Jupiter,* *Sophia,* most effectually demonstrates, that the Trees, which are in the Gardens of the Law, are planted there for their Fruits, but especially for those Fruits, by which Men are fed, nourish'd and preserv'd; and the Smell of these only is grateful and pleasing to the Gods.

Soph. Hear me out: 'Tis the Pleasure of *Jupiter,* that Execution make the Gods to be lov'd and fear'd, only in so far as they favour human Society, and discourage those Vices which are dangerous to it: And therefore inward Sins ought only to be judg'd Sins, inasmuch as they produce, or may produce outward Effects. And inward Righteousness is never Righteousness without outward

ward Performances, as Plants are ufelefs and unprofitable without Fruit actually in being, or in expectation. And 'tis his Pleafure that thofe fhould be efteem'd the greateft Crimes that are prejudicial to the Commonwealth; that thofe which are prejudicial to a particular innocent Perfon fhould be efteem'd leffer; fuch as are committed between two Perfons by Agreement, leaft of all; and that fuch as don't give bad Example, or produce not bad Effects, and arife from an accidental Impetus in the Complexion and Temper of a particular Perfon, be judg'd no Crime at all. And thefe are Errors and Mifcarriages which the exalted Gods are moft, lefs, leaft, and not at all offended at; and by Works contrary to thefe, they judg themfelves moft, lefs, leaft, and not at all ferv'd. He hath moreover commanded Execution, by all means, to approve Repentance for the future, but never to put it on an equal foot with Innocence, to approve Faith and Opinion, but never to put them on an equal foot with Deeds and Works. He means the fame with refpect to Confeffion and Profeffion, as they regard Amendment and abftaining from Evil. He commends Thoughts, in fo far as they fhine in outward Signs, and poffible Effects. He will not allow him that vainly mortifies his Body, to fit in as honourable a Seat as he who curbs his Temper; nor equal that folitary unprofitable Drone, with one of a profitable Converfation. He will not diftinguifh

Cuftoms

Cuftoms and Religions fo much by the Diftinction of Gowns, and Difference of Habits,
as by the good and more ufeful Habits of Virtue and Difcipline. He is not fo much pleas'd
with him that has bridled the Fervour of his
Luft, and who perhaps is cold and impotent,
as with another that is really fearlefs, and
foftens the Impetus of Anger by Patience.
He does not fo much applaud one who has
oblig'd himfelf to no purpofe to abftain from
Luft, as one who is determin'd to be no more
a Back-biter, or Evil-doer. He does not
pronounce the proud Defire of Glory, which
has often been the occafion of Good to the
Commonwealth, to be a greater Fault than
the fordid Thrift of Riches. He does not
make fo much account of one that has cur'd a
vile and unprofitable Cripple, who perhaps
is little or nothing better found than infirm,
as of one who has deliver'd his Country from
Slavery, and reform'd a diforderly Mind.
He does not efteem it a more heroick Deed,
to have, fome way or other, been able to extinguifh the Fire of a burning Furnace without Water, as to have extinguifh'd the Sedi-
tions of an inflam'd People without Blood.
He does not allow Statues to be erected to
Poltroons, Enemies to the State of the Commonwealth, who corrupt the Manners of
Men by Words and Whims; but to thofe
who raife Temples to the Gods, who inlarge the Worfhip and Zeal of that Law and
Religion, that kindles the Magnanimity and

Ardour

Ardour of Glory, which purfues the Service of the Republick, and the Advantage of Mankind : From whence it appears, that Univerfities were inftituted for the Difcipline of Manners, Letters and Arms. And he is very far from promifing Love, Honour, and the Reward of eternal Life and Immortality, to fuch as are approv'd by Pedants, and Tellers of Parables ; but to thofe who pleafe the Gods, by adorning and perfecting their own and others Underftandings, in the Service of the Community, in the exprefs Obfervance of all the Acts of Magnanimity, Juftice and Mercy. 'Twas for this reafon the Gods rais'd the *Roman* People fo far above other Nations : for they underftood how to imitate and conform themfelves to the Gods, by their magnificent Actions, more than other Nations; which confifted in pardoning the fubmiffive, humbling the proud, forgiving Injuries, not obliging to make Returns for Benefits, fuccouring the Needy, defending the Afflicted, relieving the Opprefs'd, bridling the Violent, promoting the Deferving, abafing the Tranfgreffors, putting thefe in Terror, and punifhing them with utter Deftruction by Whips and Axes, while it honours thofe with Statues and Coloffus's. From whence it neceffarily follow'd, that this People was more bridled and aw'd from the Vices of Incivility and Barbarity, and more exquifite and ready at generous Enterprizes, than any other People whatever. And fince
their

their Law and Religion were such, their Manners and Actions, their State, Honour and Felicity must have been agreeable to them.

Saul. I wish he had order'd something exprefly against the Temerity of those Pedants of our time, who plague all *Europe.*

Soph. *Jupiter* has not been wanting, *Saulinus*, to enjoin, command, and give Orders to Execution concerning these Cattel, who at this time swarm all over *Europe.*

Soph. *Jupiter* has given very good Orders to Execution concerning them. He has order'd Execution to see if 'tis true, that they induce the People to despise, or at least to disregard Legillators and Laws, by teaching them, that they propose things impossible to be done, and command them as it were in jest; that is, to make Men believe, that the Gods command that which can never be put in practice: to see whether they affirm, that those who come to reform corrupted Laws and Religions, do really intend to spoil all that is just and good, and to confirm and exalt to the skies all their perverse and vain Fictions: to see if they bring forth any other Fruits than to destroy Societies, diffipate Concord, diffolve Union, make Sons rebel against their Fathers, Servants against their Masters, Inferiours against Superiours, put Schisms between People and People, Nation and Nation, Companion and Companion, Brother and Brother; to diforder Families, Cities, Republicks, and Kingdoms: And in

con-

conclufion, if while they give the Salutation
of Peace, they carry the Dagger of Divifion,
and the Fire of Difperfion wherever they
enter, taking away the Son from the Father,
Neighbour from Neighbour, the Inhabitant
from his Country, and making other horrible
Separations, againft Nature and Law : to fee
if while they call themfelves the Minifters of
one who rais'd the Dead, and heal'd the Sick,
they do not maim and hurt thofe who are
whole, worfe than all others on the face of
the earth, killing not fo much with Fire
and Sword, but which is worfe, with their
pernicious Tongues.

He has order'd Execution to fee what kind
of Peace and Concord they propofe to miferable People; if they are willing and defirous
that the whole World agree and confent to
their malicious and moft prefumptuous Ignorance, and approve their wicked Confcience;
while they themfelves will not agree and
confent to any Law, Juftice, or Doctrine,
and fo much Difcord and Difagreement appears not in the whole World, and in all the
Ages of it, as amongft them : for among ten
thoufand of fuch Teachers, there is not to
be found one, who has not form'd to himfelf a Catechifm, ready to be publifh'd to the
World, if not publifh'd already ; approving
no other Inftitution but his own, finding in
all others fomething to be condemn'd, dif-
approv'd, or doubted of : befides that the
greater part of them difagree with them-
H felves,

felves, blotting out to day what they had wrote yefterday. He has order'd Execution to fee what Succefs they have, and what Manners they form in others, as to the Acts of Juftice and Mercy, and the Confervation and Enlargement of Publick Good: If by their Doctrine and Authority, Academies, Univerfities, Temples, Hofpitals, Colleges, Schools, and Places of Arts and Difcipline are rais'd, or if where thefe are to be found, they are not the very fame, and endow'd with the very fame Powers and Privileges, as they were before thefe Men appear'd in the World. Next, if thefe are enlarg'd by their Care, or rather, are not diminifh'd, ruin'd, and diffolv'd by their Negligence: Moreover, if they are Poffeffors of other Peoples Goods, or Beftowers of their own: Finally, if thofe who take their part, augment and eftablifh the publick Good, as their Predeceffors did, or if they diffipate, fquander, and devour it, and withal difcourage good Works, and extinguifh all Zeal to perform new, and prefeve old Benefits. If it is fo, and if fuch be apprehended and convicted, and if after admonition they fhew themfelves incorrigible, and perfift in their Obftinacy; *Jupiter* commands Execution under pain of his Difpleafure, and of lofing its Degree and Pre-eminence in Heaven, to diffipate, deftroy, and annihilate them, and to ufe any manner of Force, Power and Induftry, to the deftruction of the very Memory of fo noxious a Seed. And

And to this he adds, that it make known to all Generations of the World, under pain of their Ruin, that they arm themselves in favour of Execution it self, till the Decree of *Jupiter* against this Plot of the World, be fully put in execution.

Saul. I presume, *Sophia*, that *Jupiter* will not thus rigidly execute this Punishment upon this miserable Set of Men, and compleat their final Ruin, till he has first try'd to reform them, and make them sensible of their Wickedness and Error, and so provok'd them to Repentance.

Soph. 'Tis so: and therefore *Jupiter* has order'd Execution to proceed in the manner I tell you. He will have all those Goods taken from them, which they who preach'd up, prais'd, and taught Good Works, had acquir'd, and which were left and appointed by those who did, and trusted in Good Works, and were confirm'd by them, who believ'd they should render themselves acceptable to the Gods by such Works, Benefits, and Testaments. And so let them curse those Trees which brought forth these Fruits from a Seed so much hated by them. And let them be maintain'd, preserv'd, defended and nourish'd only by those Fruits, those Revenues, those Grants, which those who believe in them, and approve and defend this Opinion, furnish them with. And it is his Pleasure, that they be no longer allow'd to acquire by Rapine and violent Usurpation

that

that which others have acquir'd and fown
with a free and grateful Mind, for the common Good. And thus let them depart from
thofe profane Houfes, and not eat of that ex-
communicated Bread, but go to dwell in
thofe pure and undefiled Houfes, and feed on
that Meat, which by means of their newly
reform'd Law, is appointed for them, and
brought forth by thofe pious Perfonages, who
have fo little efteem for *Opus Operatum*; and
merely from a vile, impertinent, and foolifh
Fancy, reckon themfelves Kings of Heaven,
and Sons of the Gods; and believe and attribute more to a vain, fheepifh, and ftupid
Faith, than to a ufeful, real, and magnificent
Action.

Saul. We fhall quickly fee, *Sophia,* how
thofe who are fo liberal and profufe in be-
ftowing Kingdoms of Heavens, fhall be driven to their fhifts to get a Hand-breadth here
on earth : and they fhall know of their Em-
perors in the Empyreal Heaven, how libe-
rally their *Mercuries* live upon their own
Subftance, who perhaps (for want of Faith
in Works of Charity) will reduce thofe their
Ambaffadors to the Neceffity of manuring
the Ground, or following fome other mecha-
nick Trade ; and would fain perfuade Men,
that I know not what Righteoufnefs of another, is made theirs, without their being at any
pains or trouble about it, but that all fuch as
have been guilty of Affaffinations, Rapine,
Violence and Homicide, and who made light
of

of Alms-deeds, the Acts of Liberality, Mercy, and Justice, will be excluded from the Benefit of this Righteousness of another.

Soph. How is it possible, *Saulinus,* that Consciences of this make can ever have a true Love for Good Works, and true Penitence, and Fear of committing any kind of Villany, if they are so secure, notwithstanding all the Crimes they commit, and so diffident of Works of Justice?

Saul. You see the Effects of this Persuasion, *Sophia ·* for it is as true and certain as any thing can be, that if any come from any other Profession and Faith to this; from Liberal, as he was before, he becomes Covetous; from Meek he becomes Insolent, from Humble you see him Proud, from a Benefactor, a Robber and Usurper of what belongs to others, from Good and Sincere, a Hypocrite; from Kind, Ill-natur'd; from Simple, Malicious; from Grateful, most Arrogant; from able in all Goodness and Learning, forward in all sort of Ignorance and Knavery: and in fine, if he was Bad before, he becomes perfectly Wicked then, so as that he cannot be worse.

H 3

The Second Part of the Second Dialogue.

Sophia. LET us now purſue our Subject,
which was interrupted by *Mer-*
cury's Arrival yeſterday.

Saul. 'Tis high time, after having given
an account of the Reaſons of placing good
Deities inſtead of thoſe Beaſts that have been
driven from thence.   Let us ſee what Deities
are appointed to ſucceed the remaining Beaſts,
and if it be not troubleſom, let me underſtand the Cauſe and Reaſon of theſe Changes.
We were yeſterday on the Hiſtory of *Jupiter's*
diſpatching *Hercules,* and brought that Narration to a period : and conſequently the firſt
thing we are to conſider, is, what has ſucceeded in his place.

Soph. I underſtand, that thing has in reality happen'd in Heaven, *Saulinus,* which
Crantore ſaw in a Fancy, or in a Dream, and
in the Shadow or Spirit of Prophecy, about
the Debate between Riches and Pleaſure,
Health and Strength.   For no ſooner had *Ju-*
piter ſent *Hercules* from thence, but immediately *Riches* preſented her ſelf before him,
and ſaid, ' This Place belongs to me, O Fa-
' ther.'   To which *Jupiter* anſwer'd, ' For
' what reaſon ?'   ' I wonder, ſaid ſhe, that
' you have delay'd ſo long to give me that
' Place : and you have not only placed other
' Gods

‘ Gods and Goddeſſes, much inferiour to me,
‘ before ever you thought of me, but you
‘ have likewiſe given out, that the greateſt
‘ favour you could do me, was to hear what
‘ I could ſay upon ſo ſtrange a Paradox, as
‘ my pretending to any Place at all.’ *Jupi-*
ter anſwer’d *Riches*, ‘ Tell me your Claim :
‘ for I am ſo far from thinking I have done
‘ you any wrong in not giving you any of
‘ the Manſions already fill’d, that I think my
‘ ſelf oblig’d to refuſe you thoſe which are
‘ ſtill empty : and perhaps ſomething worſe
‘ may fall to your ſhare than you are aware
‘ of.’ ‘ And what worſe can or ought to be-
‘ fal me by your Judgment, than what has
‘ befaln me already, ſaid *Riches* ? Tell me
‘ with what reaſon you have placed Truth,
‘ Prudence, Wiſdom, Law and Judgment
‘ before me ? If I am ſhe for whom Truth
‘ is eſteem’d, Prudence practis’d, Wiſdom
‘ priz’d, by which Law reigns, and Judg-
‘ ment is executed : and if without me Truth
‘ is cheap, Prudence is Folly, Wiſdom neg-
‘ lected, Law mute, and Judgment lame :
‘ Why then have you not given me the firſt
‘ place ? for to the firſt I give Scope, to the
‘ ſecond Strength, Light to the third, Au-
‘ thority to the fourth, and Execution to the
‘ fifth , to them all together, Pleaſure, Beau-
‘ ty and Ornament , and I free them from
‘ Trouble and Miſery.’ ‘ O *Riches* ! an-
‘ ſwer’d *Momus*, what thou ſayeſt is neither
‘ falſe nor true: For thou art ſhe likewiſe

H 4 ‘ that

‘ that makes Judgment halt, the Law ſtand
‘ mute, Wiſdom be trampled upon, Pru-
‘ dence impriſon’d, and Truth cruſh’d; when
‘ you make your ſelf a Companion of
‘ Rogues and Fools, when you protect Folly
‘ by the force of Chance , when you in-
‘ flame and captivate the Mind with Plea-
‘ ſures; when you adminiſter Aims to Vio-
‘ lence, and bare-facedly reſiſt Juſtice.   And
‘ after all, you bring no leſs Pain than Plea-
‘ ſure, no leſs Deformity than Beauty, no
‘ leſs Rudeneſs than Ornament to ſuch as
‘ poſſeſs you. and you are not the Hand to
‘ put an end to Miſeries and Troubles, but
‘ only change their Names and Forms.   So
‘ that in Opinion you are good, in Truth you
‘ are bad ; in Appearance you are valuable,
‘ but in Reality you are baſe, in Fancy you
‘ are uſeful, but in effect you are moſt per-
‘ nicious : For when once you appear in your
‘ own Authority and Shape, however per-
‘ verſe (as I ordinarily ſee you in the Houſes
‘ of the Wicked, and rarely in the Company
‘ of good Men) you baniſh Truth out of all
‘ Cities there below, to the Deſarts , you
‘ break the Legs of Prudence, you make
‘ Wiſdom bluſh , you ſhut the mouth of the
‘ Law, you take away Courage from Judg-
‘ ment, and render all things moſt contemp-
‘ tible.’   ‘ In theſe very things, anſwer’d
‘ *Riches,* O *Momus,* you may diſcern my
‘ Power and Excellence; that by opening or
‘ ſhutting the Hand, and imparting my ſelf
‘ to

' to this or t'other, I give to thefe Deities
' Strength, Power, and Action ; or can have
' them defpis'd, banifh'd, and refifted ; and
' to tell you plainly, I can banifh them out
' of Heaven, and thruft them into Hell, as I
' pleafe.'

Here *Jupiter* interpos'd : ' We will have
' none but good Deities in Heaven, and in
' thefe Seats. We remove from hence all
' that are more bad than good, as well as
' thofe that are indifferently good and bad,
' of which fort I take you to be ; *viz.* That
' you are good with the Good, and evil with
' the Evil.'

' You know, O *Jupiter*, faid *Riches*, That
' of my felf I am good, and am not indiffe-
' rent, or neutral, or fometimes one thing
' fometimes another, as you fay, but in as
' much as fome make a good, others make a
' bad ufe of me.' Here *Momus* anfwer'd ;
' You, *Riches*, are a manageable, ferviceable,
' tractable Goddefs ; you do not govern
' your felf, and don't truly govern and dif-
' pofe of others ; but others difpofe of you,
' and you are govern'd by others : wherefore
' you are good when others manage you well,
' evil when you are ill-govern'd. You are
' good, I fay, in the hands of Juftice, Wif-
' dom, Prudence, Religion, Law, Liberali-
' ty, and other Deities . You are bad, if
' Deities of contrary qualities manage you ,
' fuch as Violence, Avarice, Ignorance, and
' others. As therefore of your felf you are
' neither

' neither good nor bad, fo I believe it will
' be convenient (if *Jupiter* confent to it)
' that we be neither the Caufe of Honour or
' Difgrace to any body ; and confequently,
' that you be not worthy to have a proper
' permanent Station, either on high among
' the Gods and heavenly Deities, or below
' among the infernal Deities, but that you
' wander eternally from place to place, and
' from region to region upon earth.'

All the Gods agreed to the Sentence of
Momus , and *Jupiter* pronounc'd accordingly,
in thefe words : ' When you belong to Juf-
' tice, *Riches*, you fhall dwell in the Houfe
' of Juftice ; when you belong to Truth,
' you fhall be where the Excellency of Truth
' is , when you belong to *Sophia* or Wifdom,
' you fhall fit in her Throne; when you be-
' long to voluptuary Pleafures, you may go
' where they are to be found , when you be-
' long to Gold and Silver, you may hide your
' felf in Purfes and Coffers , when you belong
' to Wine, Oil, and Corn, you may ftow
' your felf in Cellars and Magazines , when
' you belong to Sheep, Goats, and Oxen, go
' feed with them, and keep company with
' Flocks and Herds.'

In like manner, *Jupiter* gave her Direc-
tions how to behave her felf, when fhe fhould
be in the company of Fools, and how to
manage her felf in the company of Wife
Men, and in what manner fhe fhould perfevere for the future to do as fhe had done

for the time paft (becaufe perhaps it could not
be otherwife) to make her felf be eafily found
in one certain manner, and with difficulty in
another manner. But thofe Ways and Manners he has not communicated to many; fo
that *Momus* rais'd his Voice, and declar'd
another Manner, if indeed it can be faid to
be different from the former, and that is,
' That none may be able to find thee, with-
' out having firft renounc'd a good Mind
' and a found Brain.' I believe he meant,
that it was neceffary firft to lofe the Confideration of Judgment and Prudence, never
thinking of the Uncertainty and Unfaithful-
nefs of the Times; having no regard to the
doubtful and unftable Promife of the Sea;
not believing Heaven, nor regarding Juftice
or Injuftice, Honour or Difgrace, Calm or
Tempeft; but committing all to Fortune.
' And, adds he, beware ever to make thy felf
' too familiar with thofe, who feek thee with
' too much Judgment: And take care that
' thofe who purfue thee with the Snares, Gins
' and Nets of Providence, be fartheft from
' catching thee; but go for the moft part
' where the moft fenflefs, ftupid, carelefs and
' foolifh are to be found. In fine, when thou
' art upon Earth, keep thy felf from the
' Wife, as thou wouldft from Fire: And
' thus always come near and make thy felf
' familiar with People that are half Beafts,
' and always obferve the fame Rule which
' Fortune does.'

Sau'.

Saul. It is ordinary, *Sophia*, that the wifeſt are not the richeſt; either becauſe they are contented with a little, and that little they eſteem enough, if it can make them live; or for other Reaſons, as that while they are intent upon more worthy Enterprizes, they don't wander too much here and there to make their Court to theſe Deities, I mean Riches and Fortune. But purſue your Diſcourſe.

Soph. No ſooner did *Poverty* ſee her Enemy *Riches* ſhut out, but ſhe preſented herſelf in a moſt miſerable plight, and ſaid, ' That for the ſame Reaſon that *Riches* was ' judg'd unworthy of that Place, ſhe that ' was her Antagoniſt ought to be eſteem'd ' moſt worthy and deſerving of it.' To which *Momus* anſwer'd, ' O *Poverty, Poverty,* you were not *Poverty,* if you were not ' poor in Arguments, Syllogiſms, and good ' Conſequences. It does not follow, unhap- ' py Goddeſs, that you ſhould be inveſted ' with what ſhe is deſpoil'd of, and that you ' ought to be all that which ſhe is not, be- ' cauſe you are contrary to her. as *Verbi gratia* (ſince 'tis neceſſary to illuſtrate the ' thing to you by an Example) that you ' ſhould be *Jupiter* and *Momus,* becauſe ſhe is ' neither *Jupiter* nor *Momus,* and in fine, ' that what is deny'd of her, ſhould be af- ' firm'd of you. For thoſe who are better ' ſtock'd with Logick than you are, know ' that Contraries are not the ſame with *Po-*
' ſitiva

' *sitiva & Privativa, Contradictoria, Varia, Dif-*
' *ferentia, Altera, Divisa, Distincta & Diversa.*

' They know likewise, that by reason of
' Contrariety it follows, that you cannot both
' be in the same Place at the same time; but
' not, that where she is not, nor cannot be,
' therefore you are, or may be.' Here all the
Gods smil'd, seeing *Momus* ready to teach *Po-*
verty Logick : And this has remain'd a Proverb in Heaven, *Momus is* Poverty's *Master,*
or Momus *teaches* Poverty *Logick.* And this
the Gods say, when they would ridicule any
thing done aukwardly. ' What do you
' think then should be done with me, *Momus ?*
' said *Poverty ·* resolve me quickly, for I am
' not so rich in Words and Conception, as to
' be able to dispute with *Momus,* nor of so
' happy a Genius, as to be able to learn much
' from him.'

Then *Momus* ask'd *Jupiter* permission to
make a Decree for once. To whom *Jupiter*
said, ' Do you yet mock me *Momus,* you
' who have so much Licence, that you are
' more licentious than all the other Gods ta-
' ken together, insomuch that we might take
' you for a Licentiate ? Nay, give Sentence
' as you please ; and if 'tis good, we will ap-
' prove it.' Then *Momus* said, ' It appears
' to me convenient, that she go and walk
' thro those publick Places, in which Riches
' is seen to stalk about, that she pass and re-
' pass, go and come thro the same Fields.
' Now (according to the Rules of Reason-
' ing,

' ing, with regard to such Contraries) *Po-*
' *verty* must not enter into any Place, but
' what *Riches* has forsaken; nor succeed, till
' she has departed: and on the other hand,
' let *Riches* succeed and enter, where *Poverty*
' is gone. Let the one always be at the o-
' ther's Heels; the one must always give the
' other a Push, but never Face to Face: but
' where one has her Breast, the other must
' have her Back, as if they were playing (as
' we sometimes do) at Leap-Frog.'

Saul. What did *Jupiter* and the rest say
of this?

Soph. They all ratify'd and confirm'd the
Sentence.

Saul. What said *Poverty?*

Soph. She said, ' It does not seem just, O
' ye Gods! (if my Opinion may have place,
' and if I am not altogether bereft of Judg-
' ment) that my Condition should be exact-
' ly like that of *Riches.'* To whom *Momus*
answer'd, ' From your appearing on the same
' Theatre, and acting the same Tragedy or
' Comedy, you ought not to draw this Con-
' sequence, *viz.* that you are in the same
' Condition; *Quia contraria versantur circa*
' *idem.'* ' I see, *Momus,* said *Poverty,* that
' all mock me; and you among the rest, who
' make Profession to tell the Truth, and speak
' ingenuously, despise me; which appears
' not to me to be your Duty, because *Poverty*
' is frequently more worthy of Defence than
' *Riches.'* ' What would you have one to
       ' do,

' do, anfwer'd *Momus*, if you are altogether,
' and in every refpect poor? Poverty is not
' worth defending, if fhe is poor in Judg-
' ment, Reafon, Merits and Syllogifms, as
' you are, who have forc'd me to fpeak to you
' very poorly by the Rules of Analyticks, of
' the *priora* and *pofteriora* of *Ariftotle.*'

Saul. What do you tell me, *Sophia?* The
Gods then fometimes took *Ariftotle* in their
hands? They ftudy the Philofophers?

Soph. I'll fay no more of *Pippa*, *Nanna*, *An-
tonia*, *Burchiella*, *Ancroia*, and fuch like; and
of another Book, whofe Author is not known,
but is afcrib'd to *Ovid* or *Virgil*, I don't remember the Title of it.

Saul. And do they indeed meddle with
things fo grave and ferious?

Soph. Do you think thefe are not grave and
ferious Matters, *Saulinus?* If you were more
a Philofopher, and more difcerning, you
would believe there was no Subject, no Book
but what was examin'd by the Gods; and
that it never fails of being perus'd by them;
if 'tis not altogether without Spirit and Life,
if 'tis not all over fimple and impertinent,
'tis approv'd and chain'd in the Publick Li-
brary: For they take pleafure in the manifold Reprefentations of Things, and in the
manifold Fruits of all manner of Talents and
Endowments: For they have as much pleafure in all things that are, and in all the Reprefentations that are made, as they have in
taking care that they be, and giving Order
and

and Permiſſion that they be made. And do you think that the Judgment of the Gods is any other than what is common to us with them; and that every thing that is Sin to us, is no Sin to them? Theſe Books, any more than Theological Books, ſhould not be allow'd to be read by ignorant Men, who would thereby become wicked, and receive evil Inſtruction from them. This is a way of reaſoning, which is as ridiculous as it is common.

Saul. What do you ſay then of Books compos'd by Men of bad Fame, diſhoneſt and diſſolute, and which are written perhaps to a bad End?

Soph It cannot be deny'd but ſuch Books are written, but then it is of ſome uſe to know who was the Author of them, the Manner he obſerves in handling his Subject, the Reaſon why he writes; how ſuch a one was cheated, and how he cheated others, how one declines from, and inclines to a virtuous and vicious Affection; how Laughter, Uneaſineſs, Pleaſure, Squeamiſhneſs are raiſ'd: In every thing there is Wiſdom and Providence, and in all things there is every thing; but eſpecially a thing is where its contrary is, and the knowledg of one flows very neceſſarily from another.

Saul. Let us now return to the purpoſe, from which the Name of *Ariſtotle*, and the Fame of *Pippa* diverted us. How was Po-

 verly

verty difmifs'd by *Jupiter*, after fhe was fo
fcurvily us'd by *Momus* ?

Soph. I will not relate to you all the ridiculous Particulars that pafs'd between him
and her, who no lefs mock'd *Momus*, than
Momus mock'd her. *Jupiter* declar'd that fhe
had a right to Privileges and Prerogatives,
which *Riches* had not in things here below.

Saul. Pray tell me what they are.

Soph. ' 'Tis my Pleafure, faid *Jupiter*, that
' in the firft place thou, *Poverty*, be quick-
' fighted, and know how to return quickly
' to the place you left, and that you chafe
' *Riches* away, with greater force than thou
' art chas'd by her, whom I decree to be
' eternally blind. Next, 'tis my Pleafure,
' *Poverty*, that thou be very nimble, and
' that thou have on thee the Wings of an Ea-
' gle or a Vultur; but that thy Feet be like
' thofe of an old Ox, which tugs the Plough
' when it cuts deepeft into the earth. I will
' on the contrary, that *Riches* fhall have flow
' and heavy Wings, like thofe of a Goofe or
' Swan, but her Feet like thofe of the fwifteft
' Courfer or Hart, to the end that when fhe
' flies from any place by employing her Feet,
' thou may'ft come there with thy Wings:
' and wherefoever thou diflodgeft by the
' means of thy Wings, fhe may fucceed by
' ufing her Feet : fo that thou may'ft purfue
' and chafe her away with the very fame
' Swiftnefs with which fhe purfues and chafes
' thee away.'

I   *Saul.*

Saul. Why does he not give them both either good Wings or good Heels? For they could, nevertheless, pursue and chase one another away either slowly or speedily.

Soph. Because *Riches* going always with a Load, her Wings come to be encumber'd thereby, and *Poverty* going always bare-foot, her Feet are easily pain'd by going thro rugged Ways and therefore this would have swift Feet, and that swift Wings in vain.

Saul. I am satisfy'd with your Resolution Now go on.

Soph. Moreover, he orders *Poverty* to follow *Riches*, and she to be banish'd by her when she comes into those Houses or Palaces where Fortune has her Empire: But when she holds to those things which are high, and out of the reach of Time's and blind Fortune's Rage, he orders her not to have so much Impudence and Power, as to attempt to make her fly, and take her place. For he will not have *Riches* easily depart from those places, which requir'd so much Difficulty and Honour to arrive at. ' And thus have thou
' as much Steddiness and Resolution in things
' of an inferiour, as she can have in things
' of a superiour nature. But (added *Jupiter)* I order you to have a certain Concord,
' in a certain way with one another, and
' that not of a slight importance, to the end
' thou may'st not think that by being banish'd from Heaven, thou should'st be sent
' to Hell, but that on the contrary, by being
' taken

taken up from Hell, thou fhould'ft be fent
to Heaven. So that the Condition of
Riches, as I have faid, comes to be incomparably better than thine. However, I
will, that you be fo far from always ba-
nifhing one another from your places, that
the one fhall rather maintain and cherifh
the other, fo that there be a moft ftrict
Friendfhip and Familiarity bttween you.'

Saul. Pray explain this to me as foon as
ou can.

Soph. *Jupiter* faid, ' Thou *Poverty*, when
thou art converfant about inferiour things,
thou mayft be join'd by the ftricteft Ties to
Riches in fuperiour things. For no-body
who is wife, or is willing to be wife, will
ever endeavour to join himfelf with her
in great things . fince *Riches* are a hindrance to Philofophy, and Poverty makes
the way plain and eafy. For Contemplation cannot be, where a Throng of many
Servants crowd, where an importuning
Multitude of Debtors and Creditors is;
where Merchants Accounts, and the Rec-
konings of Stewards appear, where fo
many ill-manner'd Bellies are to be fed ;
where the Snares of fo many Robbers, the
Eyes of greedy Tyrants, and the Exac-
tions of unfaithful Minifters perplex and
trouble us: So that no-body can tafte the
Sweetnefs of Tranquillity, if he is not
poor, or very like a poor Man.

I 2   ' Now

' Now 'tis my Pleasure, that he who is
' rich in Poverty, be great, becaufe he is
' contented , and that he who is poor in
' Riches, be a mean Slave, becaufe he is
' not fatisfy'd. Thou fhalt be fecure and
' calm ; fhe troubled, follicitous, fufpicious,
' and reftlefs. By defpifing her, thou fhalt
' be more magnificent and great than ever
' fhe can be by valuing and efteeming her felf.
' I will make meer Opinion fufficient to fa
' tisfy thee to the full : but for her, fhe fhall
' not be full with the Poffeffion of all things.
' I will make thee greater with taking away
' Defires from thee, than fhe can be by the
' addition of Poffeffions : I will make thee
' open Friends, and her hidden Enemies. I
' will make thee rich with the Law of Na-
' ture, her extremely poor, in fpight of all
' her Care and Induftry. For 'tis not he
' who hath little, but he who defireth much,
' who is truly poor. To thee (if thou wilt
' curb Defire) what is neceffary fhall be e
' nough, and a little fhall be fufficient. But
' to her nothing is enough, altho fhe grafps
' at all things with extended Arms. Thou
' by confining thy Defires, may'ft contend
' for Felicity with *Jove* ; fhe, by enlarging
' the Borders of Concupifcence, more and
' more plunges her felf in the Gulf of Mi-
' feries.' When *Jupiter* had difpatch'd her,
fhe very contentedly ask'd leave to go
her way : And *Riches* made a fign, that
fhe defir'd to come near, and follicit the
Council

Council once more upon fome new Propofal: But fhe was not allow'd to make more words.

'Away, away, faid *Momus* to her · Do'ft not hear how many call thee, cry for thee, pray to thee, facrifice to thee, and complain to thee, with fo great noife and din, that we are almoft deafen'd here? And do'ft thou divert thy felf fo much, and frisk about in thefe parts? Go quickly in an ill Hour, if you are not pleas'd to go in a good one.' 'Don't trouble your felf about this, *Momus*, faid Father *Jupiter* · Let her depart, and go when and whither fhe pleafes.' 'In truth, faid *Momus*, it feems to me a matter worthy of Compaffion, and a kind of Injuftice (which you, who can, do not provide againft) that fhe fhould leaft regard thofe who cry and cry over again for her, and always keep at the greateft diftance from thofe who deferve her beft.' 'My Will, faid *Jupiter*, concurs with the Will of Fate.'

Saul. Do otherwife if you can, *Momus* fhould have faid.

Soph. 'I will, that with refpect to things below, fhe be deaf, and that fhe never anfwer or come when call'd, but led by Chance and Fortune, fhe go blindfold, and groping in the dark, to him fhe meets firft among the Multitude.' 'From whence it will fall out, faid *Saturn*, that fhe will fooner communicate her felf to Knaves and Scoun-

'drels

' drels (the number of which is as the Sand)
' than to any body that is but tolerably good,
' and fooner to thefe ordinary fort of Peo-
' ple, who are numerous enough, than to
' one of the principal, who are perhaps very
' few ; and perhaps never, nay moſt certain-
' ly never, to him who is more deferving
' than others, and fingle by himfelf.'

   Saul. What faid *Jupiter* to that?

   Soph. ' It muſt be fo : Fate has laid this
' Condition on *Poverty*, that fhe fhould be
' rarely call'd upon in earneſt, and by very
' few, but that fhe communicate and pre-
' fent her felf to more than call upon her,
' which are much the greateſt number:
' *Riches* on the contrary is that which is
' call'd upon, defir'd, invok'd, ador'd, and
' expected by almoſt every body, fhe com-
' municates her felf to very few, and leaſt
' of all to thofe who worſhip and reverence
' her moſt. Fate hath decreed that *Poverty*
' fhall be quite deaf; that fhe be not frighted
' away by the greateſt and moſt thundring
' noife; and that fhe fhall be deaf to and
' proof againſt all the huffing of thofe who
' hate her, and be at the heels of him who
' has not only not call'd for her, but with
' great diligence would hide himfelf from
' her.' While *Riches* and *Poverty* gave up
their places, ' Holà ! faid *Momus*, what Sha-
' dow is this which is the Familiar of thefe
' two Oppofites, and which is both with
' *Riches* and *Poverty*? I ufe to fee divers
                   ' Shadows

' Shadows of the fame Body, but I have ne-
' ver obferv'd divers Bodies have the fame
' Shadow, till now.' To which *Apollo* anfwer'd, ' Where there is no Light, there all
' is Shadow, altho there be divers Shadows,
' if they are without Light, they are con-
' founded and become one: as when there
' are many Lights without the intervention
' of thick and opake Bodies, they all concur
' to make one Splendour.' ' I don't think
' this holds here, faid *Momus* ; for where
' there is *Riches,* and *Poverty* is quite exclu-
' ded ; and where there is *Poverty* abfolutely
' diftinct from *Riches,* not like two Lights
' concurring in one illuminable Subject, we
' fee this Shadow to belong to the one and
' the other.' ' Look well to it, *Momus,* faid
' *Mercury*; and you will fee that it is not a
' Shadow.' ' I did not fay that it was a
' Shadow, faid *Momus* ; but that 'tis join'd
' to thefe two Deities, as one and the fame
' Shadow to two Bodies. O now I confider,
' *Avarice* appears there to me, which is a
' Shadow ; and is the Darknefs of *Riches,* and
' the Darknefs of *Poverty.'* ' 'Tis fo, faid
' *Mercury*; fhe is the Daughter and Compa-
' nion of *Poverty,* a mortal Enemy to her
' Mother, and flies from her as much as fhe
' can : enamour'd and charm'd with *Riches,*
' to which fhe fometimes joins her felf, fhe
' is always fenfible of the Rigour of her Mo-
' ther who torments her ; and tho fhe is near
' her, yet fhe is far from her, and tho fhe is

I 4   ' far

' far from her, yet fhe is near her: for if
' fhe is feparate from her in truth and rea-
' lity, yet in common Eftimation fhe is moft
' intimate with her, and united to her.   And
' don't you perceive, that being join'd in
' company with *Riches*, fhe makes *Riches* not
' to be *Riches*; and being far diftant from
' *Poverty*, fhe makes *Poverty* not to be *Po-*
' *verty?* This Darknefs, this Shadow, this
' Obfcurity, is that which makes *Poverty*
' not to be evil, and *Riches* not to be good,
' and is never prefent without throwing a
' blot upon one of the two, or on both to-
' gether; very rarely on neither the one nor
' the other : and that is only when they are
' encompafs'd on all fides with the Light of
' Reafon and Knowledg.'   Here *Momus* defir'd *Mercury* to explain to him, how *Avarice*
made *Riches* not to be *Riches*.   *Mercury* anfwer'd, ' The rich covetous Perfon is ex-
' tremely poor ; becaufe *Avarice* can never be
' where *Riches* are, if there is not *Poverty* in
' that Perfon's Mind, which is not lefs truly
' prefent *virtute affectus*, than it may be faid
' to be *virtute effectus*.   So that this Shadow,
' in fpight of its teeth, can never depart from
' its Mother, more than from it felf.'

   While thefe things were difcours'd, *Momus*
who has a very good Eye (tho 'tis none of
the fharpeft) when he looks very attentively,
faid, ' O *Mercury*, that which I told you was
' like a Shadow, I now difcover to be fo
' many Beafts all confufedly jumbled toge-
                                    ' ther;

' ther ; for I fee it to be canine, porcine,
' arietine, apifh, urfine, aquiline, corvine,
' falconian, leonine, afinine, and fo many
' other *ines, ians,* and *ifbes,* as the like was
' never feen : and fo many Beafts, and yet
' but one Body ! There really appears to me
' a Pantamorphofis of all brute Animals !'
' To fpeak more truly, anfwer'd *Mercury,*
' 'tis one multiform Beaft : it appears one,
' and it is one, but 'tis not uniform : as it is
' the Property of Vices to have many forms,
' becaufe they are without form, and have
' not a proper Face. This is quite contrary
' to what we fee in the Virtues. Thus you
' fee Liberality, the great Enemy of Ava-
' rice, is fimple and one; Juftice is one and
' fimple; once more you fee Health is one,
' and Difeafes are innumerable.'

While *Mercury* was faying this, *Momus* interrupted him, and faid, ' I fee it has three
' Heads, and be hang'd to it. I thought,
' *Mercury,* my Eyes deceiv'd me when I dif-
' cover'd one, and one, and a third Head
' upon the Body of this Beaft. But after
' turning my Eyes every where, and feeing
' no other thing like it, I conclude, that 'tis
' no otherwife than as I fee it.' ' You fee
' very well, faid *Mercury,* of thefe three
' Heads one is Illiberality, another bruitifh
' Gain, and a third Tenacity.' *Momus* ask'd
whether they fpoke. *Mercury* anfwer'd,
' Yes; and that the firft fays, 'Tis better to
' be rich, than to be efteem'd liberal and
' grateful.

‘ grateful. The fecond, Don’t die of Hunger,
‘ becaufe you are a Gentleman. The third
‘ fays, If it does not bring me Honour, it
‘ brings me Utility.’ ‘ And have they only
‘ two Arms, faid *Momus?* ’ ‘ Two Hands
‘ are enough, faid *Mercury*, of which the
‘ right is open, and large, to take, the other
‘ is clofe, clofe, narrow, narrow, to hold,
‘ and whenever it lets out, it looks like Dif-
‘ tillation, without regard to Time, or Place,
‘ or Meafure.’ ‘ Come a little nearer me,
‘ you *Riches* and *Poverty*, faid *Momus*, that
‘ I may be the better able to difcover the
‘ Charms of this your fair Waiting-Maid.’
Which being done, *Momus* faid, ‘ ’Tis one
‘ Face, many Faces; ’tis one Head, and ma-
‘ ny Heads; a Woman, a Woman, a Wo-
‘ man; fhe has a very little Head, tho her
‘ Face be more than moderately large, fhe
‘ is old, ugly, and nafty, fhe has a drooping
‘ Countenance; fhe is of a black Com-
‘ plexion; I fee her full of Wrinkles; her
‘ Hair is ftrait and black; her Eyes little,
‘ her Mouth open and gaping; her Nofe
‘ and Nails crooked. Strange! that fo little
‘ an Animal fhould have fo capacious and
‘ devouring a Belly; that fo weak, merce-
‘ nary and fervile an Animal, fhould direct
‘ her Looks to the Stars! She ftoops, digs,
‘ and enditches her felf; and if fhe expects
‘ to find any thing, fhe will dig down to
‘ the Centre of the Earth, and with her
‘ Back to the Light, and her Face to Dark-
‘ nefs,

' nefs, fhe never knows the Diftinction of
' Day and Night; uneafy to the perverfe
' Hopes of thofe who have never much, e-
' nough, or fufficient, how much foever
' they receive, and whofe Defires inlarge
' with their years, as the Flame devours ac-
' cording to its Greatnefs.   Difpatch, dif-
' patch, banifh, banifh, both *Poverty* and
' *Riches* quickly from thefe Tenements, O *Ju-*
' *piter* , and do not fuffer them to approach
' the Habitations of the Gods, if they don't
' come without this vile, abominable and
' favage Beaft.'   *Jupiter* anfwer'd, They will
' come or go according to the Reception they
' find with you.   At prefent let them go a-
' way, according to the Refolution already
' made ; and let us come quickly to our Bu-
' finefs, to determine what Deity fhall be
' Poffeffor of this Place.'

And behold as the Father of the Gods
was looking round, *Fortune*, without being
call'd, impudently, and with her ufual Arrogance, prefented her felf, and faid, ' It is
' not good, O ye Confular Gods ' and thou
' great Judge *Jupiter*, that *Poverty* and *Riches*
' fhould be allow'd to fpeak fo much, and be
' heard fo long; and I be thought unworthy
' to be heard, and fhew my felf, and declare
' my Refentment, as I have too much reafon
' to do: I who am fo honourable and power-
' ful, that I advance *Riches*, guide and pufh
' her on where and how I pleafe, who chafe
' her from, or lead her to what Places I will,
' who

' who effect her Succeffion, and the Viciffitude
' between her and *Poverty*: And every one
' knows that Felicity in external Goods is not
' more owing to *Riches*, as her Principle,
' than to me. Juft as the Beauty of Mufick,
', and Excellency of Harmony, ought not to
' be more afcrib'd to the Inftruments, than
' to the Art, and Artificer who handles them.
' I am that Divine and Excellent Goddefs, fo
' much defir'd, fo much fought after, fo
' much lov'd, for whom *Jupiter* is moft
' frequently thank'd, from whofe open hand
' flows Riches, and for whofe clofe Fift the
' World fo much laments, and Cities, King-
' doms and Empires are turn'd topfy-turvy.
' Tell me, who ever offer'd up Devotions to
' *Riches* or *Poverty?* Who ever return'd them
' Thanks? Every one that defires to have
' them, calls upon me, facrifices to me.
' Whofoever is contented with thefe, thanks
' me, owns his Obligation to *Fortune*, burns
' Incenfe to *Fortune*, the Altars fmoke for
' *Fortune*. And I am a Caufe that am vene-
' rable and formidable in propoition to my
' Uncertainty; and I am the more defirable,
' the lefs I make my felf known and familiar ·
' For ordinary things leaft difcover'd, moft
' hid and fecret, are efteem'd to have the
' greater Dignity and Majefty. I with
' my Splendour darken Virtue, blacken
' Truth, and fubdue and undervalue the
' greater and better of thefe Gods and God-
' deffes, whom I fee prepar'd and fet in or-
' der

' der to take their Places in Heaven: And I
' also, in the presence of so great a Se-
' nate, put all in Terror. For tho I have
' no Eyes to serve me, yet I have Ears, by
' which I understand that a great part of
' them quake and tremble at my formidable
' Presence. And yet notwithstanding all
' this, they have had the Boldness and Pre-
' sumption to present themselves, to be
' nam'd to Places, without consulting and
' advising with my Dignity; who often,
' and more than often, have Empire and Do-
' minion over Truth, Reason, Wisdom, Jus-
' tice, and other Deities, who (if they will
' not deny what is most evident to all the
' World) can tell whether they are able to
' reckon up the number of Times that I have
' already turn'd them out of their Chairs,
' Seats and Tribunals; and have bound,
' suppress'd, shut up and imprison'd at my
' Pleasure. At other times I have out
' of my Mercy let them escape, set them-
' selves at liberty, restore and confirm them-
' selves again, but never without apprehen-
' sions of my Displeasure.'

  Then *Momus* said, ' Ordinarily, blind Ma-
' tron, all the other Gods expect the Retribu-
' tion of these Seats for the good Works they
' have done, do, or are to do; and the Se-
' nate has resolv'd to reward such: And do
' you pretend to put in your Claim, which
' don't lessen the List and Crowd of your
' Sins, for which you deserve not only to be
                                    ' banish'd

' banifh'd from Heaven, but likewife from
' the Earth ?" *Fortune* anfwer'd, ' That fhe
' was no lefs good than other good Deities ;
' and if fo, then fhe was not evil ; for all is
' good that Fate orders : and tho her Na-
' ture was like that of a Viper, which is na-
' turally venemous ; yet this could not be
' her fault, but either the fault of Nature,
' or of any other that had fo fram'd her.
' Befides that, nothing is abfolutely Evil ; for
' the Viper is not mortal and poifonous to the
' Viper, nor the Dragon to the Dragon, the
' Lion to the Lion, the Bear to the Bear, *&c.*
' but every thing is evil with refpect to a-
' nother, as you virtuous Gods are evil with
' refpect to the vicious, thofe of the Day
' and of the Light, are evil to thofe of
' Night and Darknefs ; you among your
' felves are good, and they among themfelves
' are good. It happens after the fame man-
' ner among different Sects in the World,
' where thofe of all Sects call themfelves juft,
' and the Sons of God ; whereas the chiefeft
' and moft dignify'd of other Sects are rec-
' kon'd the moft reprobate and wicked. And
' therefore I *Fortune*, however much I may
' be condemn'd by fome, by others I am
' efteem'd divinely good. And 'tis a Sen-
' tence pafs'd by the greateft part of the
' World, That the Fortune of Men depends
' on Heaven, from whence there is not a
' Star in the Firmament, great or fmall, but
' what I am thought to have the difpofal of.'

Here

Here `Mercury` anfwer'd, ' That her Name
' was taken too equivocally; for fometimes
' by Fortune is underftood nothing elfe but
' an uncertain Event of Things, which is
' no Uncertainty to the Eye of Providence,
' tho it may be very much fo to the Eyes of
' Mortals.'

Fortune did not hear this, but proceeded;
and to what fhe had faid, fhe added, ' That
' the moft celebrated and excellent Philofo-
' phers in the World, fuch as *Empedocles* and
' *Epicurus*, attributed more to her than to
' *Jupiter* himfelf, nay than to the whole
' Council of the Gods together. In like man-
' ner all the reft, faid fhe, underftood me
' to be a Goddefs, and underftood me to be
' a heavenly Goddefs; as I believe this Verfe
' is no Stranger to your Ears, there being no
' School-boy but can repeat it:

' *Te facimus, Fortuna, Deam, cæloq; locamus.*

' And I would have you underftand, O ye
' Gods, with what Truth fome call me filly,
' foolifh, inconfiderate; while they them-
' felves are fo filly, foolifh and inconfiderate,
' that they can give no account of my Be-
' ing; and whence others, who are efteem'd
' more learned than their Neighbours, in
' effect demonftrate and conclude the con-
' trary: And this Truth foices from them.
' They likewife call me irrational, and with-
' out Judgment; and yet they don't for all
' this

' this think me bruitish and stupid : For by
' this Negation they are not for detracting
' any thing from me, but for attributing
' more to me ; as I my self sometimes deny
' small things, that I may give the greater.
' I am not therefore conceiv'd by them as
' one that works by the Rules of Reason, but
' above all Reason, above all Discourse, and
' above all Knowledg. Not to mention that
' in effect they agree and confess, that I ob-
' tain and exercise Government and Domi-
' nion, especially over the rational, intelli-
' gent and divine Beings. And none that is
' wise will say, that I extend my Power over
' Things void of Reason and Understand-
' ing, such as Stones, Beasts, Children, Mad-
' men, and others, that have no notion of fi-
' nal Causes, and cannot act for an End.'

' I'll tell you, *Fortune*, said *Minerva*, why
' they say you are without Reason and Judg-
' ment : Whoever wants any Sense, wants
' also some Science ; particularly that Science
' which depends on that Sense. Now consi-
' der with your self, that you are without
' the Light of the Eyes, which are the grea-
' test Help to Science.' *Fortune* answer'd,
' That *Minerva* either impos'd upon herself,
' or had a mind to impose upon *Fortune* ; and
' she hop'd to satisfy her why she saw her
' blind. But however I be depriv'd of
' Sight, said she, yet I am not without good
' Ears and Understanding.'

Saul.

Saul. And do you believe she spoke true, *Sophia?*

Soph. Hark, and you shall find how she is able to distinguish, and how familiar *Philo-sophy* is to her, in so much that she is no stranger to *Aristotle's* Metaphysicks: ' I know, ' said she, there are some who maintain, ' that Sight is the most necessary Sense in or- ' der to become wise and learned ; but I ne- ' ver knew any so foolish as to affirm, that ' Sight was the chief Cause of Knowledg : ' And when any one says Sight is chiefly de- ' sirable, he does not thereby mean, that 'tis ' most necessary in any other sense, than for ' the knowledg of certain Things , such as ' Colours, Figures, bodily Symmetries, Beau- ' ties and Charms, and other visible things, ' which use rather to disturb the Fancy, and ' distract the Intellect, than to inform them ; ' but not that 'tis absolutely necessary for all ' or the best kinds of Knowledg. For 'tis ' very well known, that many have pull'd ' out their Eyes, in order to become wise ; ' and of those who have been blind either by ' Chance or Nature, some have become the ' most admirable Men in the World, as *De- ' mocritus, Tiresius, Homer,* and many more, as ' the blind Poet of *Adria,* &c. Now I believe ' you can distinguish, if you are *Minerva,* ' that when a certain *Stagirite* Philosopher ' said, The Sight is most to be desir'd for ' Knowledg, he did not compare Sight with ' other kinds or means of Knowledg, as

K   ' with

'with Hearing, Cogitation, Intellect, &c.
'but he was making a Comparison betwixt
'that end of Sight, which is Knowledg,
'and another End, which might be propos'd
'by the same. Therefore if you don't
'grudge going as far as the *Elyſian* Fields to
'reaſon the matter with him (if he is not
'gone from thence thro another Life, and
'drunk of the Water of *Lethe*) you'll ſee he
'will make this Concluſion, *We deſire Sight*
'*chiefly for the end of knowing*; and not that
'other Concluſion, *We deſire Sight for Know-*
'*ledg more than all the other Senſes.*'

Saul. 'Tis wonderful, *Sophia*, that *Fortune*
ſhould be able to reaſon better, and underſtand Texts better than *Minerva*, who is the
Superintendant of theſe Intelligences.

Soph. Don't wonder, for if you ſhall pro-
foundly conſider, and practiſe, and rummage
over and over, you will find that the Gods,
who are graduated in the Sciences, and Eloquence, and Judgment, are not more judicious, more wiſe, nor more eloquent than
the reſt. But to follow the Thread of *For-*
tune's Cauſe in the Senate, ſhe addreſs'd to
them all in theſe words : 'My Blindneſs, O
'ye Gods, takes nothing, nothing from me,
'nothing that's worth having, nothing which
'makes for the Perfection of my Being : For
'if I were not blind, I ſhould not be *For-*
'*tune* ; and this Blindneſs is ſo far from giv-
'ing you a Right to diminiſh and leſſen the
'Glory of my Merits, that from that very

'　Blindneſs

' Blindnefs I draw Arguments for the Great-
' nefs and Excellency of them. For from
' hence 'tis evident, that I am lefs diverted
' from the Acts of Confideration, and can-
' not be unjuft in Diftributions.' *Mercury*
and *Minerva* faid, ' You'll do a confiderable
' thing, if you make this out.' *Fortune* reply'd, ' 'Tis agreeable to my Juftice to be
' fuch : It does not agree, it does not qua-
' drate with true Juftice to fee. The Eyes
' are made to diftinguifh and know Diffe-
' rences (I will not at prefent fhew how of-
' ten thofe who judge by Sight are deceiv'd.)
' I am a kind of Juftice that cannot diftinguifh,
' or make Differences ; but as all Things
' are principally, really and finally one Being,
' and one Thing (for *Ens verum & bonum* are
' the fame) fo I may put all things upon a
' certain Equality, value every thing alike,
' reckon all things but one, and not be more
' ready to regard or notice one thing than a-
' nother ; and not more difpos'd to give to
' one than to another, and be more inclin'd
' to a Neighbour than to a Stranger. I don't
' fee Mitres, Crowns, Gowns, Arts, Scien-
' ces ; I don't difcover Merits and Demerits,
' becaufe wherever they are found, they are
' always naturally the fame in like Subjects ;
' but they are moft certainly found in this
' or that Perfon, according to Circumftan-
' ces, Occafions and Accidents : And there-
' fore when I give them, I don't fee to
' whom I give them ; when I take them a-

' way,

'way, I do not fee from whom I take them,
'that by this means I may treat them all e
'qually, and without any manner of Diftinc-
'tion. And thus I intend and do all things
'with Equality and Juftice; and I difpenfe
'juftly and equally to all. I put all things
'into an Urn, in whofe moft capacious Bo-
'fom I fhake, mix and fhuffle them: And
'.then have who lift; well for him who gets
'Good, bad for him who gets Evil. In this
'manner, in *Fortune's* Urn, there is no dif
'ference of Great and Small, but there all
'things are equally great, and equally little
'Whatever Difference there may be in them
'before they come into, or after they go out
'of the Urn, they have no Diftinctions from
'me. While they are within, they all come
'from the fame Hand, in the fame Veffel,
'tumbled over and tofs'd with the fame
'fhake: And therefore when the Lots come
'to be drawn, 'tis unreafonable for him who
'has bad Luck, to complain either of him
'who owns the Urn, or of the Urn, or of
'the Shake, or of him who puts his Hand in
'the Urn; but he ought, with the beft and
'greateft Patience he can, to bear with that
'which Fate has order'd, or with Fate it
'felf which is under Orders; fince as to
'what remains, he was equally written, his
'Ticket was equal to that of any others,
'was number'd alike, put in and fhak'd. I
'therefore, who treat every thing alike, and
'reckon all as one Mafs, no part of which I
'efteem

‘ efteem more or lefs worthy than another,
‘ either for being a Veffel of Honour or Dif-
‘ honour: I who throw all into the fame Vef-
‘ fel of Mutation and Motion, am equal to
‘ all, behold all equally, or behold not one
‘ particular thing more than another. I, I
‘ fay, by all this, cannot but be moft juft,
‘ tho the contrary appears to you. Now
‘ that a great Number of bad Lots, and ve-
‘ ry few good ones, occur to him who puts his
‘ Hand in the Urn, and draws the Lots
‘ which are there, this proceeds from the
‘ Inequality, Iniquity and Injuftice of you
‘ others, who do not make all Lots equal,
‘ and who have the Eyes of Comparifons,
‘ Diftinctions, Imparities and Orders, by
‘ which you make Differences, and teach o-
‘ thers to do fo: From you, from you, I
‘ fay, comes all Inequality, all Iniquity, for
‘ the Goddefs *Goodnefs* does not beftow her
‘ felf on all equally. Wifdom does not com-
‘ municate her felf to all with the fame mea-
‘ fure; Temperance is found but in few,
‘ and Truth fcarce in any. Thus you good
‘ Gods are very niggardly, very partial,
‘ making the wideft Differences, the moft
‘ unmeafurable Inequalities, and the moft
‘ confus’d Difproportions in particular things.
‘ I, I am not unjuft, who regard all without
‘ difference, and to whom all are as it were
‘ of one Colour, one Merit, and one Sort.
‘ ’Tis thro your Fault, that when my Hand
‘ draws the Lots, there occur frequently

‘ bad,

‘ bad, seldom good ones, frequently unfor-
‘ tunate, seldom fortunate ones ; oftner the
‘ Wicked than the Good, oftner the Foolish
‘ than the Wife, oftner the False than the
‘ True. Why this ? Why ? Because not a-
‘ bove two or three are thrown in with Pru-
‘ dence, not above four or five are thrown
‘ into the Urn with Wisdom. You throw
‘ in but one with Truth, and less, if less can
‘ be. And then of Hundreds of Thousands
‘ of Lots, which are in the Urn, would you
‘ have one of these eight or nine come to the
‘ Hand that shakes the Lots, sooner than
‘ one of the eight or nine Hundred Thou-
‘ sands ? Now do the quite contrary ; thou
‘ Virtue, I say, make the Virtuous to be
‘ more numerous than the Vicious ; thou
‘ Wisdom, make the number of the Wife
‘ greater than that of Fools ; and thou
‘ Truth, do thou come open and manifest to
‘ the greatest part : And then most certainly
‘ more of your sort of People, than of their
‘ Opposites, shall meet with ordinary Prizes
‘ and good Chances. Make all to be just,
‘ true, wife and good ; and then most cer-
‘ tainly I will never bestow Degree or Digni-
‘ ty on Hypocrites, Knaves and Fools. I
‘ am not therefore more unjust than you ; I
‘ who treat all equally, and you who do not
‘ make all things equal : So that when a das-
‘ tardly Fellow, or a Bully becomes a Prince
‘ or rich, ’tis not my Fault, but yours, who
‘ are so saving of your Light, that you will
‘ not

‘ not beftow any of it on fuch Rafcals, and
‘ fo prevent Chairs and Thrones being fill’d
‘ with Rogues. ’Tis no Crime to make a
‘ Prince, but ’tis a Crime to make a Scoun-
‘ drel a Prince. Now thefe being two things
‘ very diftinct, the Fault confifts not in my
‘ giving Principality, but in your leaving
‘ Rafcality to be join’d and continue with
‘ it. Becaufe I move the Urn, and hide the
‘ Lots, I don’t look to him more than ano-
‘ ther; and therefore I did not determine
‘ him to be a Prince or rich (tho ’tis determi-
‘ nately neceffary that one fhould come to
‘ the Hand among fo many others) but you
‘ who make Diftinctions by looking on, and
‘ communicating your felves to one more, to
‘ another lefs, to this too much, to that no-
‘ thing: You become guilty of leaving this
‘ determinately a Rafcal and Poltroon. If
‘ then Injuftice confifts not in making a
‘ Prince, or enriching one, but in determin-
‘ ing a Subject of Rafcality and Poltroonery;
‘ I fhall not be found unjuft, but you. Be-
‘ hold then how Fate has made me moft equi-
‘ table and juft, and could not have made
‘ me unjuft; for fhe has made me without
‘ Eyes, to the end that I might promote all
‘ equally.’

Here *Momus* fubjoin’d, and faid, ‘ We
‘ don’t call you unjuft for your Eyes, but for
‘ your Hand.’ To which fhe anfwer’d,
‘ Not for my Hand neither, *Momus*; for my
‘ taking things in my Hand does not make

K 4 ‘ them

‘ them evil; but they were evil before they
‘ came into my hand. I am not the Caufe of
‘ Evil, if I only take them as they come to
‘ me; but thofe who offer them to me fuch
‘ as they are, and others who do not make
‘ them otherwife, are the caufe of all the
‘ Evil that happens. I am not perverfe, I
‘ who blindfold ftretch out my Hand indiffe-
‘ rently to whatever prefents it felf, be it
‘ clear or obfcure; but thofe who make them
‘ fo, thofe who leave them fo, and fend them
‘ fo to me.’

Momus fubjoin’d : ‘ But tho they were all
‘ indifferent, equal, and alike, yet you
‘ would not even then ceafe to be wicked
‘ and unjuft: becaufe they being all equally
‘ worthy of Rule, you don’t make them all
‘ Princes, but only one from among them.’
Fortune anfwer’d fmiling: ‘ We are fpeaking,
‘ *Momus*, of what is actually unjuft, and not
‘ of what would be unjuft: and indeed by
‘ your way of reprefenting and anfwering,
‘ you feem to me to ftand fufficiently con-
‘ victed; fince from what is in fact, you
‘ proceed to what might be: and becaufe
‘ you cannot fay that I am unjuft, you fay I
‘ may be unjuft. It remains then, accor-
‘ ding to your own confeffion, that I am
‘ juft, but would be unjuft; and that you are
‘ unjuft, but would be juft. But to what
‘ is faid, I add, that I am not only juft, but
‘ would be lefs juft, if you fhould offer me
‘ all things equal: for what is impoffible,
‘ has

' has neither refpect to Juftice nor to Inju-
' ftice. Now 'tis not poffible that Rule
' fhould be given to all ; 'tis not poffible that
' all fhould have one Lot : but 'tis poffible
' it fhould be offer'd to all. Fiom this Pof-
' fibility follows a Neceffity, that is, that of
' all, one muft neceffarily fucceed ; and In-
' juftice and Evil confift not herein, becaufe
' 'tis impoffible there fhould be more than
' one. But the Crime confifts in what fol-
' lows, and that is, that this one is bafe,
' this one is rafcally, this one is not viituous ;
' and *Fortune* that gave Rule and Riches to
' this one, is not the Caufe of Evil ; but the
' Goddefs *Virtue*, that did not make him
' virtuous.'

' *Fortune* has moft excellently difplay'd her
' Arguments, faid Father *Jupiter*, and fhe
' feems to me by all means moft woithy of
' a Seat in Heaven ; but it does not feem
' convenient fhe fhould have one by her felf,
' being fhe has no fewer than the Stars : for
' *Fortune* is in all of them, no lefs than on
' Earth ; and they do not want their Inhabi-
' tants more than the Earth does hers. Be-
' fides, according to the general Eftimation
' of Mankind, all things depend on *Fortune* ;
' and undoubtedly, if they were a little bet-
' ter furnifh'd with Intellectuals, they would
' fay and think fomewhat more. And there-
' fore, let *Momus* fay what he will, thy Ar-
' guments, O Goddefs, appearing to me to
' be too ftrong, I conclude, that if they bring
' not

' not other Allegations againſt your Claims,
' better than any they have yet brought; I
' will not be ſo bold as to mark out a Seat
' for you, as if I had a mind to ſtraiten or
' tie you to it: but I give, nay rather I
' leave you that Power which you juſtly
' claim in all Heaven; ſince of your ſelf
' you have ſo much Authority, that you can
' open thoſe places which are ſhut to *Jove*
' himſelf, and to all the reſt of the Gods
' with him. And I will not ſay any more to
' you about it, becauſe we are altogether in-
' finitely oblig'd to you. You by unlocking
' all Doors, opening all Paſſages, and diſpo-
' ſing of all Manſions, make all things that
' belong to others your own; and therefore
' the Seats which belong to the reſt of the
' Gods, cannot fail to be yours likewiſe: for
' whatſoever is under the Fate of Mutation,
' comes all thro the Urn, thro the Hand,
' and thro the Revolution of your Excel-
' lency.'

The Third Part of the Second Dialogue.

AFTER this manner then, *Jupiter* re-
fus'd *Fortune* the Seat of *Hercules*; but
left that and all others in the Univerſe to
her Diſpoſal. From which Sentence (ſuch
as it was) none of the Gods diſagreed. And
the blind Goddeſs perceiving the Determination

tion made, but without any hurt or injury
to her, took leave of the Senate in these
words:

'I then go both open and hid to all the
'Univerfe; I run thro Cottages and Palaces;
'and I know, as well as Death, how to ex-
'alt bafe things, and deprefs high things:
'And in fine, by the force of Viciffitude, I
'make all things equal, and by uncertain
'Succeffion, and unreafonable Reafon, which
'I am Miftrefs of (that is, above and be-
'yond particular Reafons) and by undeter-
'min'd Meafure, I turn the Wheel, and fhake
'the Urn; to the end that my Intention
'may not be blam'd by any one Individual.
'Thou, *Riches*, come to my right hand, and
'thou, *Poverty*, to my left; and bring your
'Train along with you: Thou, *Riches*, bring
'thy Servants that are fo acceptable; and
'thou, *Poverty*, thine that are fo unwelcome
'to the Multitude: and firft, I fay, bring
'Sorrow and Joy, Happinefs and Unhappi-
'nefs, Sadnefs and Mirth, Gladnefs and Me-
'lancholy, Wearinefs and Reft, Idlenefs and
'Bufinefs, Plainnefs and Ornament. then,
'Aufterity and Loofenefs, Luxury and So-
'briety, Luft and Abftinence, Drunkennefs
'and Thirft, Surfeit and Hunger, Appetite
'and Satiety, Longing and Loathing, Ful-
'nefs and Emptinefs; moreover, Giving
'and Taking, Profufion and Parfimony,
'Clothing and Nakednefs, Gain and Lofs,
'Going out and Coming in, Profit and Squan-
'dering,

' dering, Avarice and Liberality, with Num-
' ber, Meaſure, Exceſs and Defect, Equality
' and Inequality, Debt and Credit: after-
' wards, Security and Suſpicion, Zeal and
' Flattery, Honour and Diſreſpect, Reve-
' rence and Rudeneſs, Obſequiouſneſs and
' Neglect, Favour and Diſgrace, Succour
' and Helpleſneſs, Affliction and Conſolation,
' Envy and Congratulation, Emulation and
' Compaſſion, Confidence and Diſtruſt, Do-
' minion and Servitude, Liberty and Capti-
' vity, Company and Solitude.

' Thou, *Occaſion*, go before me, precede
' my Steps, open a thouſand and a thouſand
' Ways to me, go uncertain, unknown and
' hid; for I will not have my Coming too
' well known before-hand. Give a blow to
' all Prophets, Diviners, Fortune-Tellers,
' and Prognoſticators; and all ſuch as tra-
' verſe and run about to ſpoil my progreſs.
' Remove all poſſible Stumbling-blocks from
' before my feet. Lay flat and pluck up all
' Buſhes of Deſigns, which may be trouble-
' ſome to a blind Deity. And thus by thy
' guidance I may conveniently mount up, or
' come down; turn to the right, or left
' hand; move or ſtand ſtill; advance for-
' ward, or go backward: I go and come,
' fix and move, riſe and ſit in one moment,
' and all at once, while I ſtretch forth my
' hands to diverſe and infinite things, by di-
' verſe means of *Occaſion*. Let us roam then
' from every thing, thro every thing, *in eve-*
' ry

' ry thing, to every thing : here with Gods,
' there with Heroes ; here with Men, there
' with Beafts.'

Now this Procefs being ended, and *For-*
tune difpatch'd ; *Jupiter* turn'd to the Gods,
and faid, ' 'Tis my opinion that *Fortitude*
' fhould fucceed in *Hercules*'s room ; becaufe
' where Truth, Law, and Judgment are,
' *Fortitude* fhould not be far off, for that
' Will which adminifters Juftice with Pru-
' dence, by Law, and according to Truth,
' ought to be conftant and ftrong. For as
' Truth and Law form the Underftanding,
' Prudence, Judgment and Juftice regulate
' the Will ; fo Conftancy and Fortitude bring
' to effect. From whence a wife Man pro-
' nounc'd ; Take not upon you to be a Judge,
' unlefs you are able to break the Fetters of
' Iniquity by Virtue and Power.' All the
Gods anfwer'd, ' You have order'd very well,
' *Jupiter*, that till now *Hercules* fhould be a
' Type of that Power which ought to fhine
' in the Stars. Succeed, thou *Fortitude*, with
' the Lanthorn of Reafon before you ; for
' otherwife thou fhouldft not be Power, but
' Stupidity, Boldnefs, and Fury : nor wouldft
' thou be efteem'd *Fortitude*, but any thing
' rather than that. And if thro Folly, Er-
' ror, or Alienation of Mind, thou fhouldft
' not fear Evil and Death ; this Light will hin-
' der thee from venturing where there is caufe
' of Fear. And as the Fool and Madman
' fear not, where a wife and prudent Man
' would

' would find caufe to tremble; fo this Light
' will make thee unmov'd and intrepid,
' where Honour, publick Utility, and the
' Dignity and Perfection of thy own Being,
' together alfo with the Care of the divine
' and natural Laws, are at ftake. Be ready
' and expedite, where others are torpid and
' flow: bear that with eafe, which others
' fuffer with uneafinefs; and what others
' efteem a great deal and enough, reckon
' thou little or nothing. Moderate your bad
' Companions: both that which comes on
' the right hand, with her Servants, Rafh-
' nefs, Boldnefs, Prefumption, Infolence, Fu-
' ry, Affurance; and that which comes on
' the left, with Poornefs of Spirit, Dejection,
' Fear, Bafenefs, Pufillanimity, Defpair. Con-
' duct and bring along thy virtuous Daugh-
' ters, Sedulity, Zeal, Toleration, Magna-
' nimity, Longanimity, Brisknefs, Alacrity,
' Induftry. Carry thy Book with thee, which
' contains a Catalogue of things that are to
' be govern'd with Caution, or with Perfe-
' verance, or with Flight, or with Suffe-
' rance, and in which are mark'd thofe
' things that the Strong ought not to fear,
' that is, fuch things as do not make them
' worfe; as Hunger, Nakednefs, Thirft,
' Pain, Poverty, Solitude, Perfecution, Death:
' and other things which ought to be avoided,
' becaufe they make one worfe, as profound
' Ignorance, Injuftice, Infidelity or Unfaith-
' fulnefs, Falfhood, Avarice, and the like.
' And

'And if thou shalt thus behave and manage
'thy self, not turning to the right or left
'hand, not forsaking thy Daughters, reading
'and observing thy Catalogue, not extin-
'guishing thy Light; thou shalt be the sole
'Defence of Virtue, the only Guard of Jus-
'tice, and the single Fortress of Truth, im-
'pregnable against Vice, invincible by Toils,
'fearless in Dangers, rigid against Pleasures,
'a Despiser of Riches, a Conqueror of For-
'tune, and a Triumpher over all.

'Thou shalt not enterprize precipitately,
'thou shalt not fear groundlessly, thou shalt
'not affect Pleasure, nor shun Pain; thou
'shalt not have pleasure in false Praise, nor
'be discourag'd by Reproach, thou shalt
'not be lifted up with Prosperity, nor cast
'down with Adversity; thou shalt not sink
'under the Weight of Uneasiness, nor mount
'up on the Wind of Levity, Riches shall not
'puff thee up, nor Poverty confound thee;
'thou shalt reject Superfluity, and desire
'only a little that is necessary; thou shalt
'turn away from mean things, and be always
'intent on noble Enterprizes.'

'I desire to know what Orders you will
'make about my Harp, said *Mercury.*' *Mo-*
mus answer'd, 'You may pass the time with
'it, in a Boat, or in an Inn: and if you
'have a mind to make a Present of it to the
'most deserving, you need not go far to seek
'such a one; only go to *Naples,* or the Mar-
'ket-place of *Olmo,* or *Venice,* in the Mar-
'ket-

' ket-place of St. *Mark,* in an Evening ; for
' in either of thefe places you fhall find
' the very Flower of fuch as mount the
' Stage, and there you may meet with one
' who deferves it *jure meriti.*' *Mercury* ask'd,
why he fhould give it to the beft of that, rather than any other fort. *Momus* reply'd,
' Becaufe in thefe times the Harp is become
' the chief Inftrument of Mountebanks, by
' which they conciliate and entertain their
' Audience, and fell their Pills and Gally-
' pots to the beft advantage : as the Rebeck
' or Kit is become the great Inftrument of
' blind Beggars.' *Mercury* faid, ' It is in my
' power to do with it what I pleafe.' ' 'Tis
' true, faid *Jupiter* But it muft not be left
' in Heaven for all that. And I order (if it
' feem good alfo to you of the Council) that
' in place of this Harp with nine Strings, the
' great Mother *Mnemofyne* with her Daugh-
' ters the nine Mufes fucceed.'

Here all the Gods nodded their Heads, in
token of their Approbation. And the Goddefs that was prefer'd, with her nine Daughters, return'd thanks. *Arithmetick,* which is
the eldeft, faid, fhe gave them more Thanks
than all the Individuals and Species of Numbers fhe conceiv'd ; and moreover, more
thoufands of thoufands of times, than the
Underftanding could make up by Addition.
Geometry, more than all the Forms and Figures that could be made, and more than
all the Atoms that could come out of the
fan

fantaſtick Reſolutions of *Continuums. Muſick,* more than ever Fancy can combine Forms of Symphony and Harmony. *Logick,* more than the Abſurdities of her Grammarians, than the falſe Perſuaſions of her Rhetoricians, or Sophiſms and falſe Demonſtrations of her Logicians. *Poetry,* more than the Feet her Poets have made to make their Fables run, and more than there are Verſe-makers and Singers. *Aſtrology,* more than the Stars in the immenſe Space of the etherial Region, if more can be. *Phyſick* render'd as many Thanks as there can be proximate and firſt Principles and Elements in the Womb of Nature. *Metaphyſicks,* more than there are kinds of Ideas, and ſorts of Ends and Efficients above natural Effects, as well according to the Reality that is in things, as according to the repreſenting Conception. *Ethicks,* as many as there can be Cuſtoms, Uſages, Laws, Judgments, and Faults in this, and other Worlds of the Univerſe. Mother *Mnemoſyne* ſaid, ' I return you as many ' Thanks, O ye Gods, as there can be parti- ' cular Subjects for Memory and Forgetful- ' neſs, for Knowledg and Ignorance.'

In the mean time, *Jupiter* order'd his eldeſt Daughter *Minerva* to reach him that Box which lay under the Bolſter of his Bed. In that were hid three little Boxes, which contain'd nine Collyriums that were appointed for purifying the human Mind, both as to its Knowledg and Affections. And firſt of

L   all

all he gave three of them to the three firſt of the Muſes, ſaying, ' This here is the beſt ' Ointment for purifying and clearing the ' ſenſitive Power, with reſpect to the Num- ' ber, Greatneſs, and harmonical Proportions ' of ſenſible things.' He gave one of them to the fourth, and ſaid, ' This will ſerve to ' regulate the inventive and judicative Fa- ' culties.' ' Take this, ſaid he to the fifth, ' which by raiſing a certain melancholy Im- ' pulſe, is a powerful Incentive to delightful ' Fury and Prophecy.' He gave the ſixth her Box, ſhowing her the way how to uſe it for opening the Eyes of Mortals to the Contemplation of archetypal and heavenly things. The ſeventh receiv'd that by which the rational Faculty is beſt inform'd in the Contemplation of Nature. He gave the eighth, one no leſs excellent for aſſiſting the Intellect in the apprehenſion of ſuper- natural things, inaſmuch as they influence Nature, and are in a certain manner ab ſtracted from her. He gave the laſt, which is the greateſt, the moſt precious, and moſt excellent, to his youngeſt Daughter, who as much as ſhe is poſterior to all the reſt, ſo much is ſhe more worthy than they all. ' Look, ſaid he, O *Morality*, here's an Oint- ' ment for you, by which you will be able ' to inſtitute Religions, appoint Worſhip, ' eſtabliſh Laws, and execute Judgments, ' with Prudence, Sagacity, Circumſpection, ' and generous Philanthropy , and approve, ' confirm,

' confirm, preferve and defend every thing
' that is well-inftituted, order'd, fettled, and
' executed, accommodating as much as pof-
' fible the Affections to the Worfhip of the
' Gods, and the Society of Men.'

' What muft we do with the Swan, de-
' manded *Juno?*" *Momus* anfwer'd, ' Let us
' fend it, in the Devil's name, to fwim with
' the reft, either in the Lake of *Pergufa*, or
' in the River *Caiftra*, where it fhall have ma-
' ny Companions.' ' I will not have it fo
' (faid *Jupiter*) but I order that it be mark'd
' on the Bill with my Seal, and put in the
' *Thames*; becaufe there it will be more fafe
' than in any other part. And thus none
' will dare to rob me of it, for fear of capi-
' tal Punifhment.' The Gods anfwer'd,
' You have wifely ordain'd, O great Father,
' and we expect that you will determine a-
' bout its Succeffor.' Whereupon the firft
Prefident purfu'd his Decree, and faid, ' It
' feems to me very proper that *Penitence*
' fhould be plac'd there, which is among the
' Virtues, like the Swan among the Birds:
' becaufe fhe dares not nor cannot fly high,
' by reafon of the Weight of Shame, and
' humble Recognition of her felf, which
' keeps her under: and fo raifing her felf
' from the hated Earth, and yet not daring
' to fly up to Heaven, fhe loves the Rivers,
' and plunges her felf in the Waters, which
' are the Tears of Compunction, in which
' fhe feeks to wafh, purify, and cleanfe her

' felf.

' felf · after that fhe has defil'd her felf on
' the flimy fhoie of Error, fhe is difpleas'd,
' and mov'd by a Senfe of this Difpleafure,
' fhe refolves upon amending, and as much
' as poffible becoming like white Innocence.
' By this Virtue Souls afcend, that are caft
' down from Heaven, and funk to the dar-
' keft Hell ; that have pafs'd the *Cocytus* of
' fenfual Pleafures ; that have been inflam'd
' by the *Periphlegon* of burning Love, and
' Appetite of Generation ; the firft of which
' overwhelms the Mind with Sadnefs, the fe-
' cond renders the Mind fretful and uneafy,
' as it were by remembrance of its high In-
' heritance, returning into it felf, it is dif-
' pleas'd with it felf for its prefent Condi-
' tion : it forrows becaufe it is delighted,
' and would not have its Pleafure from it
' felf. And thus it comes by little and little
' to defpoil it felf of its prefent State, by at-
' tenuating its carnal Matter, and the Weight
' of its grofs Subftance. It becomes all over
' Feathers, it warms and kindles it felf at
' the Sun, it conceives the fervent Love of
' things above ; becomes aerial, turns it felf
' to the Sun, and returns to its firft Prin-
' ciple a-new.'

' Repentance is moft defervedly plac'd a-
' mong the Virtues, faid *Saturn* ; for tho
' it be the Daughter of its Father *Error*,
' and of its Mother *Iniquity*, 'tis neverthelefs
' like the Vermilion Rofe, which grows upon
' the black and pungent Thorns ; 'tis like

' a

' a lucid and fhining Spark that flies out of
' the black and hard Flint, which towers on
' high, and tends to its kindred Sun.' 'Well
' provided, well determin'd, faid the whole
' Council of the Gods. Let *Repentance* have
' a Seat among the Virtues, let it be one of
' the celeftial Deities.'

At this general Vote, before any thing
was propos'd about *Caffiopeia*, the furious
Mars rais'd his Voice, and faid; ' Let none
' pretend, O ye Gods, to take from my war-
' like *Spain* this vain-glorious, haughty, and
' imperious Matron, who was not contented
' to mount to Heaven without carrying her
' Chair and Canopy of State along with her.
' I will have you to determine that fhe fo-
' journ there, becaufe fhe has the Manners
' of that Country, and appears to have been
' born, nurs'd, and brought up there; if it
' feem good to the Almighty Thunderer, and
' if the reft of you would not difpleafe me,
' and run the hazard of fuffering the like
' with Intereft, when you fhall have occa-
' fion to come thro my hands.' *Momus* anfwer'd, ' Let none pretend to take away Ar-
' rogance, and this Woman who is the live-
' ly Image of Arrogance, from Signor *Bravo*
' Captain of the Squadrons.' To which
Mars reply'd, ' With this Sword I will make
' not only you, poor Rafcal, know that you
' have no other Virtue or Strength, than that
' of a rotten infipid Tongue, but likewife
' any other (except *Jupiter*, becaufe he is

L 3 ' Father

'Father of us all) who fays there is no
'Beauty, Glory, Majefty, Magnanimity,
'and Force worthy the Protection of the
'Shield of *Mars*, under what you call *Boaft-*
'*ing* ; the Affronts againft which are un-
'worthy to be reveng'd by this horrible
'Point, which has been us'd to keep both
'Gods and Men in order.' 'Keep it then,
'in the Devil's name, anfwer'd *Momus*; for
'there is not one of us fo whimfical and
'fenflefs, as to keep one of thofe Serpents,
'and tempeftuous Beafts, to vex our felves
'withal.' 'Don't fall into a Paffion, *Mars*,
'don't run mad, *Momus*, faid the benign
'Protopaient. This not being a matter of
'very great importance, it may be eafily and
'freely gianted to you who are the God of
'War : If we are oblig'd, in fpight of our
'teeth, to bear with the Whoredoms, Adul-
'teries, Robberies, Ufurpations, and Affaf
'finations which you commit in fo great
'number, by the fole Authority of your fla-
'ming Sword; go then, with my Confent,
'and that of all the reft of the Gods, and
'make what ufe you pleafe of your luftful
'Drab; only let her no longer remain heie
'in the middle of the Stars, among fo many
'virtuous Deities. Let her go below with
'her Chair, and take *Boafting* with her, and
'yield the place to *Simplicity*; which declines
'from the right Hand of Oftentation that
'makes a fhew of more than fhe poffeffes,
'and from the left Hand of Diffimulation,
                                    'which

' which hides and pretends fhe has not that
' which fhe has, and fhews lefs than fhe
' poffeffes. This Hand-maid of Truth ought
' not to travel far abroad from her Queen,
' tho fometimes the Goddefs *Neceffity* con-
' ftrains her to decline towards Diffimula-
' tion, to the end that Simplicity and Truth
' may not be inculcated, or to fhun fome
' other Inconvenience. This being done by
' her not without Method and Order, may
' therefore be very well done without Error
' or Vice.'

When *Simplicity* went to take her place,
fhe appear'd with a fure and fteddy Gate;
Boafting and *Diffimulation*, on the contrary,
walk'd not without fear, as their fufpicious
Steps and fearful Afpect fhew'd. The Afpect
of Simplicity pleas'd all the Gods, for by
her Uniformity, fhe fome way reprefents,
and has the fimilitude of the Divine Countenance. Her Countenance is lovely; it never changes, and therefore for the fame reafon that fhe pleafes at firft, fhe will always
pleafe; and fhe ceafes to be loved, not from
any Defect of her own, but from that of
another. But *Boafting*, which pleafes by pretending to poffefs more than fhe really does
when fhe comes to be known, not only eafily
incurs Difpleafure, but likewife fometimes
Contempt. In like manner, even when *Diffimulation* comes to be known to be other
than what fhe gave out her felf to be, yet
fhe will not be eafily hated by them to

L 4 whom

whom she was first acceptable.   Both the
one and the other of these then was esteem'd
unworthy of Heaven, and of being united
to her that uses to sit between them, but
not far from Dissimulation, which even the
Gods are forc'd to use at times.   For sometimes Prudence hides the Truth with her
Garments, in order to escape Envy, Blame
and Outrage.

Saul. It is true, and very well, *Sophia.*
And the *Ferrareze* Poet hath shewn, not
without the Spirit of Truth, that Dissimulation is sometimes convenient for Men, provided it be not inconvenient for the Gods.
How much soever Dissimulation is for the
most part condemn'd, and thought to be a
token of a bad Disposition; yet it has been
found upon a great many occasions to have
produc'd manifest Advantages : it has prevented Losses, Inconveniences, and Death.
We do not always converse with Friends in
this obscure and mortal Life, which is full of
Envy.   But I would know, *Sophia*, in what
sense you mean that *Simplicity* has the Like-
ness of the Divine Countenance?

Soph. In that it can add nothing to its
Being by boasting, nor take any thing from
it by dissembling.   And this proceeds from
its want of Knowledg or Apprehension of
it self: For what is most simple can never
understand it self, unless it would be some
other thing.   For what feels and beholds it
self, does in a certain manner multiply it
self,

felf, and (to fay better) diverfifies it felf;
becaufe it makes it felf both Object and
Power, both intelligent and intelligible: For
in the Act of Intelligence, many things concur in one. And therefore that moft fimple Intelligence is not faid to underftand it-
felf, as if it had a reflex Act of Intelligent
and Intelligible; but becaufe 'tis a moft abfolute and moft fimple Light · It can only
be faid then to underftand it felf negatively,
inafmuch as it cannot be hid from it felf.
Simplicity then, inafmuch as it apprehends
not, nor comments on its own Effence, is underftood to have the Divine Similitude:
From which vain-glorious Boafting is infinitely diftant, but ftudious Diffimulation not
fo far, to which *Jupiter* gives fometimes a
permiffion to be prefent in Heaven, and yet
not as a Goddefs, but as the Hand-maid of
Prudence, and Shield of *Truth*.

Saul. Let us now fee what is become of
Perfeus, and his Place?

Soph. ' What will you do, *Jupiter*, with
' this Baftard of yours, which you begot on
' *Danae?* faid *Momus*.' *Jupiter* anfwer'd,
' Let him be gone (if it pleafe all this Se-
' nate) for I think there is fome new *Medu-*
' *fa* on Earth, which, no lefs than fhe of old
' time, is able by her Afpect to turn every
' one fhe looks on into Flint. Let him go,
' not as fent by a new *Polydectes*, but as com-
' miffion'd by *Jupiter* and the whole heaven-
' ly Senate: And let him try if by the fame
' Art

' Art he can overcome this Monſter, which
' is as much more horrible than the other,
' as 'tis later.' At this *Minerva* roſe up, and
ſaid : ' And I, for my ſhaie, ſhall not fail to
' fit him with a convenient Shield of Chry-
' ſtal, by which he may blind the Eyes of
' the *Phorcides*, Keepers of the *Gorgons*. And
' I will aſſiſt him in Perſon, till ſuch time as
' he ſhall have ſever'd the Head of this *Me-*
' *duſa* from her Body.' ' That will be very
' well done of you my Daughter, ſaid *Jupi-*
' *ter*, and I lay this Charge upon you, which
' I expect you will execute with all diligence.
' But I would not have you, to the great da-
' mage of the poor People, ſuffer new Ser-
' pents to be generated in the Earth, of the
' Drops of Blood which flow from her open'd
' Veins. Therefore when he is mounted on
' *Pegaſus*, which ſhall come out of her fruit-
' ful Body, let him roam (in the mean time
' ſtopping the Flux of Blood) not thro *Africk*,
' where he may be made Captive by ſome
' wicked *Andromeda* (by whom, tho bound in
' Chains of Iron, he may become bound in
' Chains of Diamond) but let him with his
' wing'd Palfrey run to my *Europa*, and there
' find out thoſe proud *Atlantus*'s, Enemies of
' the Progeny of *Jupiter*, who will be afraid
' he is come to take away the Golden Apples,
' which they keep hid under the Cuſtody,
' and within the Incloſures of Avarice and
' Ambition. Let him look for more gene-
' rous and moie beautiful *Andromeda*'s, who
' are

' are bound by the Violence of falſe Reli-
' gion, and expos'd to Sea-Monſters. Let
' him look if any violent *Phineus*, ſupported
' by the multitude of his pernicious Seɪvants,
' uſurps the Fruits of the Induſtry and La-
' bours of others: If any number of un-
' grateful, obſtinate and incredulous *Poly-*
' *deftes* preſides over them. Let him ſhow
' himſelf bold to all, from within his Glaſs,
' and preſent that part to their Eyes where
' they may view his ugly Image; from which
' horrid Aſpeft may every perverſe Senſe,
' Motion and Life be deſtroy'd.' All very
' well order'd, ſaid the Gods, for 'tis conve-
' nient that *Perſeus*, with his luminous Glaſs
' of Doftrine, and the abominable Piſture of
' Schiſm and Hereſy, ſhould drive a Nail in-
' to the pernicious Conſciences of Malefac-
' tors, and obſtinate Minds, and take away
' the Works of the Tongue, Hand and Senſe;
' and this ɪn conjunftion and company with
' *Hercules*, who by the Arm of Juſtice, and
' Rod of Judgment, is made the Subduer
' of corporeal Forces.'

Saul. Come now, *Sophia*, and ɪnform me
what is ordaɪn'd to ſucceed in the Place
which he left.

Soph. A Vɪrtue in Habit and Mein, very
like what is call'd Diligence, or Carefulneſs,
which hath, and hath had Labour and Wea-
rɪneſs for a Companion, in vɪrtue of which
this *Perſeus* was *Perſeus*, and *Hercules Hercʋ-*
les, and every ſtrong laborɪous Perſon ɪs ſtɪong
and

and laborious. By which the Great Grand-
child of *Abantes* depriv'd the *Phorcydes* of
Sight, took away the Head from *Medusa*, the
wing'd Palfrey from the headless Trunk, the
sacred Apples from the Son of *Clymene* and *Ja-*
petus, the Daughter of *Cepheus* and *Andro-*
meda from the Whale; defended his Wife
from his Rival, took the Kingdom from *Pre-*
tus, and restor'd it to *Crisius* his Brother, reveng'd himself on the ungrateful and barbarous King of the *Seriphian* Island.   By
which, I say, all Vigilance is overcome, all
adverse Occasion is cut off, all Roads and
Accesses are made easy, all Treasures are acquir'd, all Force subdu'd, all Slavery remov'd, all Desires obtain'd, all Possessions
defended, all Havens arriv'd at, all Adversa-
ries overthrown, all Friends rais'd, all Injuries reveng'd; and, in fine, all Designs compass'd.   *Jupiter* then order'd (and this Order
was approv'd by all the Gods) that the laborious and diligent *Solicitude* or *Carefulness*
should present her self.   And behold she appear'd fitted with the wing'd Shoes of Divine Impetus, with which she tramples the
popular *Summum Bonum*, spurns at the flat-
tering Caresses of Pleasures, which like so
many ensnaring Syrens, endeavour to retard
her from the Course of Work which she is
in search of and waits for; having fix'd to
her left Hand the resplendent Shield of her
Fervour, which confounds the Eyes of the
lazy and slothful with stupid Wonder, hold

ing

ing in her right the Serpentine Hair of pernicious Thoughts, under which lies that horrible Head, whose Face stupifies, and turns
into Stone all that it fixes its Eyes upon; out
of which flow a thousand Passions of Disdain, Anger, Fear, Terror, Abhorrence,
Wonder, Melancholy, and disfigur'd mourn-
ful Repentance, mounted upon the wing'd
Horse of studious Perseverance; by which
she arrives at whatever she sets her Mind
upon, overcoming the Heighth of the steep
Hill, and the Retardment of the low Valley,
the Force of the rapid River, and the Ram-
parts of the thickest Hedg, and the highest
and strongest Walls.

Being come then into the Presence of the
most sacred Senate, she heard these words
from the mighty President: ' I bestow upon
' thee, O *Diligence*, this noble Space in Hea-
' ven, because thou art she who feeds gene-
' rous Minds with Labour. Mount, over-
' come, and pass with Courage all craggy
' and rugged Mountains. Kindle thy Affec-
' tions so, that thou may'st not only resist
' and conquer thy self, but moreover that
' thou may'st have no Sense of thy Difficulty,
' no Uneasiness after Labour, for Labour
' ought not to be Labour to it self, more
' than Weight can be Weight to it self.
' Therefore thou shalt not be worthy La-
' bour, if thou dost not so overcome thy self,
' as not to esteem thy self what Labour is;
' since whensoever thou hast a Sense of thy
' self,

' felf, thou canft not be fupeiiour to thy felf
' but if thou art not deprefs'd, thou art at
' leaft fupprefs'd by thy felf. The higheft
' Perfection confifts in not being fenfible of
' Labour, and Wearinefs and Pain, when
' Labour and Pain are born. Thou muft o-
' vercome thy felf with that Senfe of Plea-
' fure, which does not feel Pleafure, that
' Pleafure, I fay, which if it was naturally
' good, thou fhouldft not fee defpis'd by ma-
' ny as the Principle of Difeafes, Poverty
' and Reproach. But thou Labour, be thou
' Pleafure in noble Works, and not Labour to
' thy felf. Be thou, I fay, one and the fame
' thing with that ; which is fo far from be-
' ing a Pleafure to it felf without thefe
' Works and virtuous Acts, that it is intole-
' rable Labour. Thou then, if thou art a
' Virtue, do not bufy thy felf about bafe
' things, frivolous things, or vain things.
' If thou wouldft be under the Vertical
' Point of the fublime Pole of Truth, pafs
' this *Appenine*, mount thefe *Alps*, ford this
' rocky Ocean, go over thefe rigorous *Ri-*
' *phean* Mountains, and this barren and fro-
' zen *Caucafus* ; penetrate inacceffible Preci-
' pices, and enter into that happy Circle
' where is perpetual Light, and where Dark-
' nefs and Cold never come ; but there is a
' perpetual Temperament of Heat, an eter-
' nal Morning or Day.'

' Go then thou Goddefs *Carefulnefs*, or *La-*
' *bour*, and I will, faid *Jupiter*, caufe *Difficul-*
' ty

' *ty* to run before thee, and fly from thee;
' chafe away *Mifhap*, take *Fortune* by the
' Hair, and when it feems good to you, oil
' her Wheel; and when you think it proper,
' ftop her Career. I will make *Health*,
' *Strength* and *Soundnefs* attend thee. Let
' *Diligence* be thy Shield-Bearer, and *Exercife*
' thy Enfign and Standard-Bearer. Let *Ac-*
' *quifition* follow thee, together with her Mu-
' nitions, which are Goods of the Body,
' Goods of the Mind, and, if you will,
' Goods of Fortune : and I order that thefe
' which thou haft acquir'd thy felf, be dearer
' to thee than fuch as thou receiveft from o-
' thers : Like a Mother who loves her own
' Children, the more fhe knows them to be
' hers. I will not have thee to divide thy
' felf, becaufe if thou difmembereft thy felf,
' imploying thy felf partly about the Exer-
' cifes of the Mind, and partly about the La-
' bours of the Body, thou fhalt be defective
' in both ; and if thou give thy felf moft
' to one, thou fhalt excel lefs in the other
' part : If thou inclineft wholly to material
' things, thou fhalt be naught at Intellectuals,
' and *vice verfa.* I order *Occafion* to call thee
' either with a loud Voice, or with a Nod,
' or Silence; or to exhort thee, or allure
' thee, or incite thee, or force thee onward.
' I command *Convenience* and *Inconvenience*
' to advertife thee, when they may hang a-
' bout thy Neck, and when they ought to
' lay down their Burden, as when it is ne-
' ceffary

‘ ceſſary to ſwim over a River. I will make
‘ *Diligence* to remove all Stops and Impedi-
‘ ments, and make *Vigilance* thy Sentinel, to
‘ guard thee on all ſides; that ſo nothing
‘ may approach thee unawares: That *Indi-*
‘ *gence* divert thee from Solicitude and Watch-
‘ fulneſs about Trifles ; the which if ſhe be
‘ not heard by thee, *Repentance* ſhall ſucceed
‘ at laſt, which may make thee know by
‘ Experience, that it is more toilſome to
‘ move empty Arms, than to throw Stones
‘ with the Hands full. Fly ſwiftly with the
‘ Feet of *Diligence*, and make haſte, before a
‘ greater Force intervene, and take away
‘ Liberty, or give Strength and Arms to *Dif-*
‘ *ficulty.*’

 Thus *Solicitude* or *Carefulneſs* having return’d Thanks to *Jupiter*, and the reſt of
the Gods, took her Journy, and ſpoke after
this manner: ‘ Behold I *Labour* move my
‘ Steps, gird my ſelf, and buckle on my Ar-
‘ mour. Begone from me all *Sluggiſhneſs*,
‘ all *Idleneſs*, all *Negligence*, all *careleſs Dum-*
‘ *piſhneſs*, and all *Slowneſs*. Thou my *Induſ-*
‘ *try*, ſet before thy Eyes of Conſideration,
‘ thy Profit, thy End. Render the many
‘ Calumnies of others, the many Fruits of
‘ Malice and Envy, ſalutiferous, as alſo that
‘ reaſonable Fear of thine, which will chaſe
‘ thee from thy native Dwelling, which will
‘ alienate thee from thy Friends, which will
‘ ſet thee at a great Diſtance from thy Coun-
‘ try, and which will baniſh thee to un-
       ‘ friendly

' friendly Countries. My *Induſtry*, make
' this glorious Exile, and travel with me;
' overcome Reſt, overcome native Tranquil-
' lity, Convenience and Peace. What art
' thou doing, *Diligence?* Why do we idle
' away and ſleep out our Time alive, if we
' are to be ſo long idle, and to ſleep ſo long
' in Death? Since if we are to expect another
' Life, or another manner of Being, that
' will not be ours which is ours at preſent,
' for it paſſes away for ever without any
' hopes of a Return. Thou *Hope*, why doſt
' thou not incite, and ſpur me on? Make me
' expect a happy Iſſue from Difficulties, if I
' don't make haſte before the Time, nor give
' over too ſoon; and don't let me reſt with
' promiſing my ſelf to live, but to live well.
' Thou *Zeal*, be thou always my Aſſiſtant,
' that I may never undertake any thing un-
' worthy of a good Deity, and that I may
' not put forth my Hands to ſuch Buſineſs as
' will occaſion greater Buſineſs. O Love of
' Glory! preſent to my Eyes, how bruitiſh
' and baſe it is to be ſolicitous about Security
' in the Entry and Beginning of Buſineſs.
' *Sagacity*, let me not retire, and turn my
' Back upon doubtful and uncertain Matters,
' but make me ſafely leave them by gentle
' degrees. Do thou likewiſe follow me, and
' mingle thy Steps with mine, that ſo my
' Enemies may not find me out, and dart
' their Fury upon me. Do thou lead my
' Steps in ways far diſtant from the Abodes

M ' of

‘ of *Fortune*, becaufe fhe has not long Arms,
‘ and can only imploy thofe who are near
‘ her, and ftirs up none but fuch as are
‘ within her Urn. Thou wilt hinder me
‘ from attempting any thing, which cannot
‘ be conveniently done; and make me more
‘ wary than ftrong in Bufinefs, if thou canft
‘ not make me equally cautious and ftrong.
‘ Make my Labour both hid and manifeft,
‘ manifeft, that every one may not be ob-
‘ lig’d to fearch and inquire after it; hid,
‘ that not many, but very few may find it·
‘ For you very well know, that hidden
‘ things are moft fought after, and that
‘ Thieves defire and covet things moft which
‘ are lock’d up. Befides, what is manifeft
‘ and open becomes cheap, and the open
‘ Cheft is not carefully fearch’d, and what is
‘ not diligently guarded is not efteem’d va-
‘ luable. *Courage*, when Difficulty preffes
‘ hard upon me, do thou hector and refift it
‘ with thy Voice of lively Fervour; not fail
‘ ing to thunder into my Ears this Sentence,

‘ *Tu ne cede malis, fed contra audentior ito.*

‘ Thou *Confultation* wilt inform me when
‘ ’tis convenient to quit, or break off ill-be-
‘ ftow’d Labour; which does not take its
‘ Aim from the Ears and Approbation of vul-
‘ gar and fordid Minds, but from thofe Trea-
‘ fures which are leaft bury’d and difpers’d
‘ by Time, and celebrated and honour’d in
‘ the

‘ the Field of Eternity: That fo it may not
‘ be faid of us, as ’tis faid of the Beetle-flies,
‘ *Meditantur fua Stercora Scarabei.* Thou *Pa-*
‘ *tience,* confirm, fix and adminifter to me
‘ that choice Leifure of thine, which is not
‘ the Sifter of Lazinefs, but Brother of Pa-
‘ tience. Make me decline from Inquietude,
‘ and incline to incurious Solicitude. Suffer
‘ me not to run, where there are dangerous,
‘ infamous and fatal Stumbling-Blocks.
‘ Let me not weigh Anchor, and loofe from
‘ the Shore, when I might be endanger’d by
‘ the infuperable Turbulency of the tempef-
‘ tuous Sea. And allow me *Leifure* to advife
‘ with *Confultation,* which will make me re-
‘ gard my felf in the firft place; fecondly,
‘ my Bufinefs, thirdly, my End, fourthly,
‘ the Circumftances; fifthly, the Time,
‘ fixthly, the Place, feventhly, the Means.
‘ Adminifter me that *Leifure,* by which I
‘ may do finer, better and more excellent
‘ things, than what I leave undone: For in
‘ the Houfe of *Leifure* fits *Counfel,* and there
‘ a happy Life is better confider’d than in a-
‘ ny other part. From thence Occafions are
‘ better feen, from thence one can go to
‘ work with more Vigour and Succefs; for
‘ ’tis impoffible to run well without being
‘ firft well plac’d. Thou *Leifure,* afford me
‘ the Means to be efteem’d lefs idle than all
‘ others; becaufe by thy means I fhall be a-
‘ ble to do Service to the Commonwealth,
‘ and defend my Country better by my

M 2   ‘ Mouth

' Mouth and Advice, than with the Sword,
' Spear and Shield, Soldier, Tribune and
' Emperor. Draw near to me, thou gene-
' rous, heroick and folicitous *Fear*; and by thy
' Inftigation, make me as much afraid to
' perifh from among the Illuftrious, as from
' among the Living. And before Sloth and
' Death deprive me of Hands, let me be fo
' well provided, that they may never be a-
' ble to take away the Glory of my Works.
' *Solicitude*, let the Houfe be finifh'd, before
' the Rain comes. Let the Windows be re-
' pair'd before the North and South Winds
' of flippery and unfettled Winter blow.
' O *Memory* of a well-fpent Life, make old
' Age and Death take me away, before my
' Mind comes to be diforder'd. Let the
' Fear of lofing the Glory acquir'd in Life,
' make old Age and Death not bitter, but
' dear and defirable.'

Saul. This is a moft worthy and honourable *Recipe*, to remedy all Grief and Pain
which old Age brings along with it, and the
importunate Terror of Death, which tyrannizes over all Animals from the Hour they
have the ufe of Senfe. Wherefore *Tanfillus*
of *Nola* faid well, ' Thofe who are not un-
' grateful to Heaven, and who have not been
' cold and unconcern'd about noble Enter
' prizes, enjoy a comfortable State, when
' Snow and Hail fall upon the Hills which
' are cover'd with Herbs and naked Flowers
' Thofe who change their Life and Studies,
' will

' will have no reafon to be forry when their
' Hair and Complexion change. The Huf-
' bandman has no reafon to grieve, when he
' gathers the Fruit of the Ground in its due
' time.'

Soph. Very well faid, *Saulinus*, but it's
time for you to withdraw : for yonder comes
my fo friendly Deity, that fo defirable Grace,
that fo fightly Countenance, fiom the Eaft.

Saul. Well then, my *Sophia*, to moriow at
the ordinary hour (if you pleafe) we'll fee
one another again. And I in the mean time
will go and write over to my felf the excellent things I have heard from you to day,
that fo I may the more eafily recover the memory of your Difcourfe, when I fhall have
occafion for it; and may the more commo-
dioufly communicate your Thoughts to o-
thers.

Soph. What is the matter that he flies towards me more fwiftly than ufual? I fee
him not come according to his ordinary Cuftom, playing with his Wand, and careflefly
beating the liquid Air with his Wings. He
appears to me to be anxioufly bufy. Now
he looks at me, and cafts his Eyes upon me
in fuch a manner, that 'tis evident his Anxiety depends not on any thing which concerns me

Mer. May Fate be always propitious to
you, and the Rage of Time againft you impotent, my pretty lovely Daughtei, Sifter
and Fiiend.

Soph.

Soph. What is the Cause, my pretty God, of this Disorder in your Countenance; altho you are no less liberal towards me, than at other times, of your charming Graces? Why did you come like a Post? And why do you appear to me as if you were in haste to depart and leave me, rather than to stay with me?

Mer. The Reason of this is, that I am sent in all haste by *Jupiter*, to provide a Remedy to the Fire that mad and furious *Discord* has kindled in the *Parthenopian* Kingdom, or in this Kingdom of *Naples*.

Soph. How is that pestiferous *Erynnis* come to this noble Country from beyond the *Alps* and the Sea?

Mer. She was call'd upon by the foolish Ambition, and mad Presumption of some Person; she was invited by very liberal, but no less uncertain Promises, she was mov'd by deceitful Hope; she was attended by doubtful Jealousy, which in the People begets a Disposition to maintain themselves in the same Liberty they have always enjoy'd, and a Fear of entering into a severer Servitude; in the Prince a Suspicion of losing all, for having grasp'd at too much.

Soph. What was the first Original and Beginning of this?

Mer. The great Avarice that is hard at work, under pretext of a Desire to maintain Religion.

Soph. In truth the Pretext is falfe, and if I am not miftaken, inexcufable; becaufe no Caution or Remedy is requir'd, where no Ruin or Danger is threaten'd, while Mens Minds remain the fame as they were, and the Worfhip of that Goddefs continues more firm and entire in thefe than in other Parts.

Mer. But fuppofing it were fo, yet it belongs not to *Avarice*, but to *Prudence* and *Juftice* to apply the Remedy, for that has mov'd People to Fury; and rebellious Minds feem to have taken that occafion, not fo much to defend juft Liberty, as to afpire at unjuft Licentioufnefs, and govern themfelves according to contumacious Luft, to which the beaftly Multitude has always been much inclin'd.

Soph. Tell me (if it be not troublefome to you) what way would *Avarice* apply a Remedy?

Mer. By heightening the Punifhment of Delinquents, in fuch fort, that many innocent, nay even juft Perfons may partake of the Punifhment of one guilty Perfon. And thus the Prince will always become fatter and fatter.

Soph. 'Tis natural that Sheep, who have a Wolf for their Shepherd, fhould be fo chaftis'd, as to be devour'd by him.

Mer. But it may be doubted, if fometimes the Hunger and Rapacity of the Wolf alone, can make them guilty, and it is againft all Law, that the Lambs and the Mother fhould be punifh'd for the Father's Fault.

Soph.

Soph. 'Tis true, there never was such Judgment but among Barbarians, and I believe it obtain'd first among the J—s: For this was so pestilent, leprous, and generally so pernicious a Generation, that it had been better they had died in the Womb than been born. So that to come to our purpose, this was the reason of your Disorder and Confusion, and the Cause why you must leave me so quickly, was it not?

Mer. 'Tis as you say : I was willing to take this Rout, to meet you before I went to those Parts whither I have directed my Flight, that I might not make you wait in vain, and might not be wanting to the Promise I made yesterday. I made some motion to *Jupiter* concerning your Affairs, and I find him more than usual inclin'd to be complaisant towards you. But for these four or five days, and this day among the rest, I have not had Leisure to treat and confer with you about what we are to negotiate with respect to the Instance you know of : Therefore I beg you may have Patience at this time, since it will be better to take *Jupiter* and the Senate in Vacation-time, than in the pickle you may know they must be in at present.

Soph. I am satisfy'd to wait; because the later the Matter is a proposing, the better it may be manag'd. And to tell you the Truth, I in great haste could not satisfy my self (that I might not be wanting in my Duty

ty

ty as to my Promife which I made you to deliver the Requeſt to you this day) becauſe I think Matters ought to be laid open more particularly, than I have done in this Note, which I now give you ; by which you will fee (if you have Leiſure by the way) the Sum of my Complaints.

Mer. I ſhall look into it ; but you will do well to embrace this Opportunity, to make a more ample and diſtinct Memorial, in which every thing may be provided for. Now I will firſt go and raiſe up *Subtilty*, to confound *Force* ; that ſo being join'd to *Deceit*, a Letter of Treachery may be dictated againſt pretended ambitious Rebellion ; by which deceitful Letter, the Maritime Force of the *Turks* may be diverted, and the *Gallick* Fury, which approaches at a great diſtance by Land, may be ſtopt

Thus Boldneſs gives place when Strength is wanting, the People is quieted, the Prince is ſafe, and Fear deſtroys the Thirſt of Ambition and Avarice, without drinking. And hereby at laſt baniſh'd Concord is call'd back, and Peace ſeated in her Chair, by confirming the antient way of Living, and aboliſhing dangerous and ungrateful Novelty.

Soph. Go then, my Deity, and may it pleaſe Fate to accompliſh your Deſigns, that ſo my Enemy War may not diſturb my Repoſe, more than that of others.

The End of the Second Dialogue.

T H E

THE
Third DIALOGUE.

Sophia. IT is not neceſſary, *Saulinus*, to give you a Detail of all the Matters that were inſiſted on by *Labour*, or *Diligence*, or *Solicitude*, or what you pleaſe to call it (for it has more names than I could tell you in an hour) but I will not paſs over in ſilence that which ſucceeded in her place, as ſoon as ſhe with all her Servants and Companions went to take their place where we told you buſy *Perſeus* had his abode.

Saul. Pray let me hear you.

Soph. No ſooner had *Labour* and *Diligence* diſappear'd, but *Idleneſs* and *Sleep*, without Delay or Drowzineſs, ſucceeded them : for the Spur of Ambition knows how to ſtir up and excite all heroick Minds, and even *Sleep* and *Idleneſs* themſelves. Upon which, *Momus* ſaid, ' Deliver us from Evil, *Jupiter*, ' for I evidently ſee, we ſhall not want Em- ' broilments after diſpatching of *Perſeus*, no ' more than after diſpatching *Hercules* ' To which

which *Jupiter* anfwer'd, ' *Idleneſs* would not
' be *Idleneſs*, nor *Sleep Sleep*, if they ſhould
' be too much moleſted by too much Labour
' and Diligence ; for this is remov'd from
' hence as you ſee, and *Sleep* and *Idleneſs* are
' here only by a privative Virtue, which
' conſiſts in the abſence of their Oppoſite and
' Enemy.' ' All will go well, ſaid *Momus*,
' if they do not make us ſo idle and drouzy,
' as to indiſpoſe us this day to conclude what
' is to be done about the chief Buſineſs.'
Idleneſs then began to ſpeak in this manner :
' As Lazineſs, O ye Gods, is ſometimes evil,
' ſo Diligence and Labour is moſtly evil : as
' Idleneſs is for the moſt part convenient and
' good, ſo Labour is good at its own times.
' I do not believe therefore (if there is any
' Juſtice to be found amongſt you) that you
' will deny me equal Honour, if I am not
' to be reckon'd by you leſs deſerving. I do
' not deſpair to make it out to you by Reaſon
' (by means of certain Arguments that I
' have heard alledg'd in the praiſe of Labour,
' Diligence and Buſineſs) that when we ſhall
' be laid in the Ballance of reaſonable Com-
' pariſon, if *Idleneſs* is not found to be equally
' good, yet it will be found to have much
' greater Advantages : ſo that you will not
' only not eſteem it equally a Virtue with
' me, but comparatively a Vice. What is it,
' O ye Gods, that preſerv'd the ſo much
' prais'd Golden Age, that inſtituted and
' maintain'd it, other than the Law of *Idle-*
' *neſs*,

' *neſs,* the Law of Nature? What took it
' away? What juſtled it out of the World
' almoſt irrevocably, other than ambitious
' Solicitude and curious Diligence? Is it not
' that that has diſturb'd Ages, has divided
' the World by Schiſms, and reduc'd it to
' an Iron Age, an Age of Clay and Mud,
' having ſet People upon Wheels, and Whirl-
' pools, and Precipices, after raiſing them to
' Pride and the Love of Novelty, and the
' Luſt of heaping Honours and Glories upon
' a particular ſingle Perſon? He who is
' not unlike all in Subſtance, and who is
' ſometimes below theſe ſame in Dignity and
' Merit, is perhaps ſuperiour to many in
' Malignity and Ill-nature; and thence comes
' to be able to overturn the Laws of Nature,
' to make his own Luſt the Law: who
' makes uſe of a thouſand Complaints, a
' thouſand Diſdains, a thouſand Tricks, a
' thouſand Solicitudes, and a thouſand other
' Companions of proud and oſtentatious La-
' bour; not to name others that lurk under
' the Habit and Cover of theſe, as Subtilty,
' Vain-glory, Contempt of others, Violence,
' Malice, Fiction, and their Retainers, which
' have not appear'd yet before you. ſuch as
' Oppreſſion, Uſurpation, Pain, Torment,
' Fear, Death, which are the Executers and
' Avengers, never of quiet Idleneſs, but al-
' ways of ſolicitous and curious Induſtry,
' Labour, and Diligence, Work, and a thing
' of ſo many names, as ſhe makes her ſelf
' -known

'known by, or rather, as she hides more
'than discovers her self by. All praise the
'fine Age of Gold, in which I made the
'Minds of Men quiet and peaceable, per-
'fectly free from this virtuous Goddess of
'yours. Hunger was the best Sauce to those
'who were contented with Acorns, Apples,
'Chesnuts, Peaches, and the Roots which
'bountiful Nature afforded: And they were
'better nourish'd, better pleas'd, and longer
'preserv'd in Life with such Nourishment,
'than with all the artificial Sauces that In-
'dustry, Study, and their Servants have
'found out; which by imposing upon, and
'delighting the Taste, make Poison seem
'sweet. And thus things that please the Pa-
'late are more sought after, than things that
'comfort the Stomach, and while Men are
'thus intent upon pleasing their Taste, they
'injure their Health, and endanger their Life.
'All magnify the Golden Age, and yet that
'Baggage that put an end to it is esteem'd
'and cry'd up for a Virtue, she that found
'out *Meum* and *Tuum*, she that divided and
'made Properties to this and t'other not
'only of the Earth, which was given in
'common to all its Animals, but also of the
'Sea, and perhaps the Air likewise; she that
'set bounds to our Choice and Pleasure, and
'of what was sufficient for all, has made
'Superfluity to some, and Want to others,
'insomuch that the former, in spight of
'their teeth, surfeit themselves, while the
'latter

‘ latter die of Hunger ; fhe that has pafs’d
‘ the Seas to violate thofe Laws of Nature,
‘ confounding thofe People whom the boun-
‘ tiful Mother diftinguifh’d ; and propaga-
‘ ting Vices from one Generation to another,
‘ becaufe Virtues cannot be fo eafily propa-
‘ gated, unlefs we’ll call thofe Virtues, which
‘ by a certain ’Trick and Cuftom are fo call’d
‘ and believ’d, tho their Effects and Fruits
‘ are condemn’d by all Senfe and natural
‘ Reafon ; fuch as open Knavery and Folly,
‘ the Malignity of ufurping Laws, and of
‘ Poffeffors of *Meum* and *Tuum* ; the ftron-
‘ ger being the moft rightful Poffeffor, and
‘ his being the moft worthy, who is moft
‘ folicitous, moft induftrious, and the firft
‘ Occupant of thofe Gifts and Parts of the
‘ Earth, which Nature, and confequently
‘ God, gives to all indifferently. Shall I be
‘ lefs in favour than *Induftry* ? I who by
‘ my Sweetnefs which flows out of the mouth
‘ of the Voice of Nature, have taught how
‘ to live quiet, peaceable, and contented
‘ with this prefent certain Life ; and to re-
‘ ceive with grateful Affection and thankful
‘ Hand, the Sweetnefs which Nature offers,
‘ and beftows upon us ; and not like un
‘ grateful and unacknowledging Wretches
‘ deny what fhe gives us, and dictates to us,
‘ becaufe God, the Author of Nature, gives
‘ and commands us the fame, and would like-
‘ wife pronounce us ungrateful ? Shall fhe,
‘ I fay, have more Favour than I ? She
‘ that’s

' that's rebellious and deaf to Counſel, ob-
' ſtinate and peeviſh againſt the Gifts of
' Nature, that applies her Thoughts and
' Hands to artificial Works and Machina-
' tions, by which the World is corrupted,
' and the Law of our Mother perverted ?
' Don't you hear how that Age laments thoſe
' Evils which the World is too late convinc'd
' of in theſe times (that Age in which I
' made Mankind pleas'd and contented) and
' abominates the preſent Age with loud La-
' mentations and Cries, in which Solicitude
' and induſtrious Labour diſturbs all with
' the Spur of ambitious Honour, under pre-
' tence of keeping all things in * order?
' O ſweet Age of Gold! not becauſe Rivers
' flow'd with Milk, and the Woods dropt
' Honey ; not becauſe the uncultivated
' Ground gave its Fruits ; not becauſe the
' gloomy Clouds did not then ſpread a Veil,
' and an eternal Spring ſmil'd, the Winter
' ſhin'd, and the Heavens gave Heat with a
' ſerene and warm Light, nor becauſe the
' foreign Pine brought neither War nor Mer-
' chandize to ſtranger Shores : but only be-
' cauſe that vain and empty Name, that Idol
' of Error and Deceit, that Idol which was
' afterwards call'd *Honour* by the mad Vul-
' gar, and which is the great Tyrant of our
' Nature, did not then mix its Uneaſineſs

---

* *Vid.* Fanſhaw's *Paſtor Fido, pag.* 163. *of the Edition in quarto.*

' and

‘ and Trouble amongſt the glad **Sweetneſſes**
‘ of the amorous Flock ; nor was its hard
‘ Law known to the Souls accuſtom’d to Li-
‘ berty ; but the golden and happy Law
‘ which Nature engrav’d, *SI LIBET, LI-*
‘ *CET.*

‘ This Induſtry that envies the Quiet and
‘ Happineſs, or rather Shadow of Pleaſure,
‘ that we might take in our own Being, hav-
‘ ing ſet bounds to Copulation, to Food, and
‘ Sleep, (from whence we muſt not only be
‘ leſs pleas’d, but moreover, more griev’d
‘ and tormented) makes the Gift of Nature
‘ become a Theft ; and would have us deſpiſe
‘ what is fine, ſweet and good, and eſteem
‘ what is evil, bitter, and worthleſs. She ſe-
‘ duces the World to leave the certain pre-
‘ ſent Good it has, and to be buſy’d and tor-
‘ tur’d for a Shadow of future Glory. I
‘ come from all the Corners of the internal
‘ Edifice, to exhort the World to embrace
‘ that which Truth ſhows by as many Glaſ-
‘ ſes as there are Stars in Heaven, and that
‘ which Nature inculcates with as many
‘ Tongues and Voices, as there are pleaſant
‘ and agreeable Objeꞓts   * Leave the Sha-
‘ dow, and embrace the Subſtance . Change
‘ not the preſent for the future. You are
‘ the Dog in the Fable, that let the Meat fall
‘ into the River while he deſir’d the Shadow
‘ of that which he had in his mouth.   There

---

* *Vid.* Taſo

‘ was

' was never yet any wife and well-advis'd
' Perfon that loft one Good in order to get
' another. Why do you go fo far off to
' feek a Paradife, when you have one in
' your felves? Whoever neglects a Good in
' this World, muft not expect to get one in
' another; for Heaven will difdain to give
' a fecond Good to one who did not value
' the firft: and thus thinking to raife your
' felves, you fink to the bottom, and for-
' faking Pleafures, you condemn your felves
' to Pains; and by an eternal Cheat, you
' fix your felves in Hell by defiring Heaven.'

Here *Momus* anfwer'd, and faid, That the
Council had not fo much Leifure as to anfwer particulaily to every one of the Reafons which *Idlenefs* or Leifure had fram'd and
fet in order, out of the abundance of Leifure; but that for the prefent it might
make ufe of its Being, and attend for three
or four days: for peihaps the Gods would
find themfelves at leifure in that time, to
determine fomewhat in its favour, which at
prefent is impoffible.

Idlenefs or Leifure reply'd, ' Allow me,
' *Momus*, to bring one other couple of Ar-
' guments, in no more Terms than in the
' form of a couple of Syllogifms, more effi-
' cacious in Matter than Form. The firft of
' which is this: *Jupiter* gave me as a Com-
' panion to the firft Father of Men fo long
' as he was good, and to the firft Mother of
' Women whilft fhe was good; but when
N   ' they

' they became evil, *Jupiter* call'd her to the
' Man's Company, that so he might make
' her Belly sweat, and his Brow ake.'

Saul. It should be his Brow sweat, and
her Belly ake.

Soph. ' Now consider, ye Gods, said *Idle-*
' *ness*, the Conclusion that hangs on my being
' declar'd Companion to Innocence, and La-
' bour's being the Companion of Sin. For
' if Like sorts with Like, Good with Good,
' I am a Virtue, and she a Vice ; and by
' consequence, I am worthy, and she un-
' worthy of such a Seat. The second Syllo-
' gism is this : The Gods are Gods, because
' they are most happy, they are happy
' because they have no Care nor Labour ;
' those who do not move nor change, have
' no Care nor Labour, and those are espe-
' cially such as are idle : and therefore the
' Gods are Gods because they are idle.'

Saul. What said *Momus* to that ?

Soph. He said, that having learnt his Lo-
gicks from *Aristotle*, he had not learnt to answer Arguments *in quarta figura*.

Saul. And what said *Jupiter* ?

Soph. That of all that *Idleness* had said,
and he had heard, he remember'd nothing
but the last Reason about being Companion
to the good Man and Woman : concerning
which he return'd, that Horses are not Asses,
for being in Asses Company, nor Sheep Goats,
for being among Goats. And he added, the
Gods had given Men Understanding and
Hands,

Hands, and had made them like unto themselves, in giving them Faculties above other Animals; which confifts not only in acting according to Nature and Order, but likewife without Laws, that fo they might form, and be able to form other Natures, other Methods by their Knowledg; and might make ufe of the Earth with that Liberty, without which they could not be reckon'd to have the faid Similitude. Certainly when Liberty becomes idle, it will be fruftraneous and vain, as the Eye that fees not, and the Hand that handles not, are ufelefs. And therefore Providence hath determin'd that it be employ'd in Action by the Hands, and in Contemplation by the Intellect; that fo it may not contemplate without Action, nor act without Contemplation. Therefore in the Golden Age Men were not more virtuous, than the Beafts are at prefent virtuous, and perhaps they were more ftupid than many of the Beafts.

Now Difficulties fpringing, and Neceffities arifing among them thro Emulation of Divine Acts, and Adaptation of fpiritual Affections; Wits are fharpen'd, Arts difcover'd, and new Inventions and wonderful Difcoveries are perpetually from day to day rais'd by means of Poverty, out of the Profundity of the human Underftanding. From whence always more and more removing themfelves from the brutal Condition, by folicitous and urgent Occupations, they approach the more,

on

on the other fide, to the Divine Being. You
ought not to be furpriz'd that Injuftice and
Wickednefs arifes together with Induftry,
for if Oxen and Apes had as much Skill and
Knowledg as Men, they would have the
fame Apprehenfions, the fame Affections, and
the fame Vices. Thus among Men, thofe
who have much of the Afs, the Ox, or the
Hog, are not infected with fo criminal Vices.
But they are not therefore more virtuous, except inafmuch as Beafts are more virtuous
than they, for not having fo great Vices as
they. But we do not praife the Virtue of
Continence in a Sow a brimming, that is
fatisfy'd with one Boar, and once only in a
year, but in a Lady who is not only folicited once a year for the Bufinefs of Generation, but likewife by her own Fancy, which
often reprefents to it felf Pleafure; befides,
that fhe is her felf the End of her own Actions. Moreover, we do not much praife
the Continence of a Sow or Boar, which by
Stupidity or Hardnefs of Complexion is rarely, and with but little fenfe folicited to Luft,
neither that of one that is cold, fpiritlefs,
and decrepid: but we ought to confider Continence that is truly Continence, and truly a
Virtue in a genteel, well-bred, ingenious and
perfpicacious lively Complexion, as a Virtue.
And therefore, generally fpeaking, 'tis no
Virtue in *Germany*, pretty much a Virtue in
France, more fo in *Italy*, and moft of all in
Sybia. Wherefore if you confider more deep-
ly,

ly, *Socrates* was so far from discovering any
Fault in himself, that he rather prais'd himself so much the more for Continence, when
he approv'd the Judgment of the Physiogno-
mist about his filthy Love of Boys. If therefore you consider, *Idleness*, what ought to be
consider'd in this matter, you'll find that in
your Golden Age Men were not therefore
virtuous, because they were not so vicious as
at present; there being a great difference betwixt not being vicious, and being virtuous;
and the one does not so easily follow from the
other, considering that Virtues are not the
same, where Prejudices, Tempers, Disposi-
tions and Complexions are not the same.
Wherefore if you draw your Comparisons
from Idiots and Brutes, the Barbarians and
Savages will be better than us Gods, as not
being branded with the same Vices, because
being much less remarkable for Vices than
we, they will for this reason be much better
likewise. And therefore you *Idleness* and
Sleep, with your Golden Age, may sometimes
and in some manner be justly esteem'd no
Vices; but never, in any manner, can you
be reckon'd Virtues. When therefore, thou
Sleep ceasest to be *Sleep*, and thou *Idleness* shalt
become full of Business, you shall then be
number'd among the Virtues, and exalted
with them.

Here *Sleep* made a little step forward, and
rub'd her Eyes at the same time, that she
might say some little thing as well as others,

and

and lay fome little matter before the Senate, that fhe might not appear to have come in vain. When *Momus* faw her thus fweetly and gently advance, ravifh'd with the Grace and Charms of the Goddefs *Ofcitation*, which preceded her as the Morning does the Sun, juft ready to make the Prologue, and not daring to difcover his Love in prefence of the Gods to this Hand-maid, he made his Careffes to *Sleep* in this manner, (after having breath'd a gentle Sigh) fpeaking like a Scholar, to fhew her the more Reverence and Refpect.

Somne quies rerum, placidissime Somne Deorum,
Pax animi, quem cura fugit, qui corpora duris
Fessa ministeriis, mulces, reparasque labore.

No fooner had the God of Cenfure (who for the reafon already laid down had forgot his Office) begun this Song, but *Sleep* charm'd with fo many Encomiums, and allur'd with the Tone of his Voice, obtain'd a Hearing for Slumber, which fhe had lodg'd in her Breaft, which after having made a fign to the Fumofities which had their refidence in the Stomach, mounted up all together into the Brain, made the Head heavy, and fo laid all the Senfes afleep. Now while *Snorting* founded its Pipes and Baffes within, *Sleep* went ftaggering and trembling, and laid her Head in Lady *Juno*'s Lap: by this bowing of her felf, and her Smock being too fhort (for this Deity always goes in her Smock, without

out

out Drawers) fhe fhow'd her Buttocks, her Bum-hole, and part of fomething elfe to *Momus*, and the reft of the Gods that were on that fide. Upon this occafion, behold *Laughter* comes into the field, which prefenting to the Senate a profpect of a great many little Bones, which were all Teeth, and uttering a great many Sneers, that made a diffonant Mufick, broke off the Thred of *Momus*'s Oration, who not being able to fhew his Refentment againft her, turn'd all his Wrath a-gainft *Sleep* that had provok'd him, by not lending him the leaft Attention, and befides going to offer him Purgatory in a very folemn manner, with *Jacob*'s Bag and Staff, as a fign of greater Difregard to his adulatory and amorous *dicendi genus*. Whence it was perceiv'd that the Gods did not fo much laugh at the Condition of *Sleep*, as for the ftrange Accident that befel him, and becaufe *Sleep* was the Buffoon, and he the Subject of that Comedy: and therefore Indignation covering his Face with a fanguine Veil, he faid, ' Whom does this *Laughter*, before this ' Dormoufe, touch? Who prefented this ri-' diculous Spectacle to your Eyes at fuch a ' diftance?' So that the Goddefs *Poltroonery*, mov'd by the furious Complaint of *Momus*, (a God of no fmall Confideration in Heaven) took him in her Arms, and embrac'd him, and taking him quickly away from thence, led him towards the Hollow of a Mountain, near the *Cimmerii* · and with them went

N 4   their

their three Children, *Morpheus, Icilon,* and *Phantafus*; who all quickly arriv'd at that place where perpetual Exhalations arife out of the Earth, caufing an eternal Twilight in the Air, and dumb Reft keeps one of her Palaces, near the Royal Palace of *Sleep*, before the Court of which is a Garden of Ewe, Beach, Cyprefs, Box and Laurel; in the middle of which is a Fountain deriv'd from a Rivulet, which comes from the rapid Current of the River *Lethe*, which flows out of the darkeft Hell towards the Surface of the Earth, and there difcovers it felf to Heaven. Here they laid the fleepy God in bed, the Boards of which were of Ebony, the Bed fill'd with Down, and the Canopy of a dark grey Colour.

In the mean time, *Laughter* taking leave, went out of the Conclave, or Chamber of Sleep, and the Gods putting their Mouths and Cheeks in due pofture (fome of which were almoft torn in pieces) *Idlenefs*, that remain'd there alone, finding the Judgment of the Gods not very favourable, and defpairing of making her Caufe any better, if her chiefeft Reafons, and thefe almoft all fhe had to offer, were not accepted (of which thofe that remain'd were thrown upon the ground, where, by the violence of the Fall, fome were fcarce alive, others burft, others had their necks broken, and others were quite fhatter'd in pieces) thought every moment a year, till fhe had left the

Com-

Company, left some shameful Disgrace should befal her, as it had done to her Companion; upon which account she was afraid left *Momus* would load her with Censures. But he discovering the Fright she was in for Deeds she was not concern'd in: ' Don't be afraid, ' poor Creature, said he, for I who am ap- ' pointed by Fate the Advocate of the Poor, ' will surely plead thy Cause.' And turning to *Jupiter*, he said, ' By what you have said, ' Father, concerning the Cause of *Idleness*, I ' understand you are not fully inform'd a- ' bout her Essence, her Ministers, her Sub- ' stance, her Court; which if you were fully ' appriz'd of, I very easily persuade my self, ' that if you did not give her a Seat in the ' Stars as *Idleness*, yet at least you would give ' her Lodgings together with *Business*, which ' is call'd and esteem'd her Enemy; with ' whom she may sojourn for ever, without ' their doing any harm to one another.' *Jupiter* answer'd, ' That he wish'd for an Op- ' portunity of justly satisfying *Idleness*, whose ' Caresses both Gods and Mortals are often ' delighted with, and therefore he should be ' very glad to hear *Momus* advance something ' in her Favour.'

' Do you think, *Jupiter*, said he, that ' there is as much Idleness in the House of ' *Idleness*, as in an active Life? Where there ' are so many Gentlemen and Servants who ' rise early in the morning, to wash three ' or four times, with five or seven sorts of
' Water,

' Water, and spend two Hours in curling
' and beautifying their Hair with a hot Iron,
' herein imitating the high and great Provi-
' dence, which examines every Hair in the
' Head, that so they may all grow in their
' due Rank and Order : Where next they set
' their Doublet with so much Diligence, ad-
' just the Plaits of their Crevats with so much
' Sagacity, fasten their Buttons with so much
' Moderation, put on their Sleeves with so
' much Handsomness, cleanse and pare their
' Nails with so much Nicety, join the
' Breeches to the Doublet with so much Jus-
' tice, Prudence and Equity, and tie the
' Knots of their Ribbons with so much Cir-
' cumspection; draw on their Stockings,
' and stretch them with so much Sedulity,
' proportion the Bounds and Confines of the
' Knees of their Breeches, so that they may
' be join'd to the Stockings just at the bow-
' ing of the Knee, with so much Exactness,
' wear strait Garters with so much Patience,
' that so their Stockings may not fall down
' and make Plaits, and so confound the Pro-
' portion of the Legs : Where with great
' straining, Judgment dispenses and discerns,
' that it being inconvenient and unhandsome
' that the Shoe should be made for the Foot,
' the great, distorted, gouty and clumsy
' Foot should, in spight of Nature, be fitted
' to a strait, handsome, clean and genteel
' Shoe; where they move their Legs with
' so much Grace, run over all the Town to
' be

‘ be feen, vifit and entertain the Ladies, make
‘ Balls, cut Capers, Courants, Brawls, and
‘ antick Dances; and when they are weary
‘ of thofe Exercifes, and to fhun the Occa-
‘ fions of doing ill, they fit down to play at
‘ Sitting-Games, leaving off the more labo-
‘ rious and tirefome ones: And in this man-
‘ ner they avoid all Sins, if thefe are not
‘ more than mortal and capital ones. For as
‘ a *Genoefe* Gamefter faid, How can that
‘ Man be faid to have Pride, who having
‘ loft a hundred Crowns with an Earl, fits
‘ down to win four Rials from a Groom?
‘ How can he be faid to be avaritious, who
‘ cannot make a Thoufand Crowns ferve him
‘ eight Days? What Luxury or Concupif-
‘ cence can that Perfon have, who fets his
‘ Heart wholly upon Gaming? How can he
‘ be call’d a paffionate Man, who, for fear
‘ his Comrade fhould leave off the Game,
‘ bears a thoufand Affronts, and with Gen-
‘ tlenefs and Patience anfwers a proud faucy
‘ Coxcomb who is juft before his Nofe?
‘ How can one be call’d an Epicure, who
‘ lays out all his Mony, and applies all his
‘ Care on Exercifes? How can one be faid
‘ to covet the Poffeffions of his Neighbour,
‘ who throws away, and feems to defpife his
‘ own? How can he be faid to be lazy, who
‘ begins at twelve a clock in the day, and
‘ fometimes in the morning, and never gives
‘ over Play till midnight? And do you be-
‘ lieve the Servants are idle in the mean
        ‘ while,

' while, any more than such as muſt aſſiſt
' them, and attend them to the Church,
' Market, Cellar, Kitchin, Stable, Bed and
' Bawdy Houſe? And to let you know, *Ju-*
' *piter*, and you other Gods, that there are
' not wanting in the Houſe of *Idleneſs* learned
' Perſons imploy'd in Study, as well as Per-
' ſons imploy'd in Buſineſs, which we have
' ſpoken of, do you believe that the contem
' plative Life is idle in the Houſe of *Idle-*
' *neſs*, where there are ſo many Gramma
' rians, who diſpute whether the Verb or
' Noun comes firſt? Why the Adjective is
' put ſometimes before, and ſometimes after
' the Subſtantive? Why in ſpeaking ſome
' Conjunctions are put before, as *Et*, and ſome
' put behind, as *Que*? How the *E* and *D*,
' with the addition of an Axis, and the Section
' of *D* thro the middle, make a tolerable Pic-
' ture of that Deity of *Lampſacus*, who thro
' Envy committed Murder on an Aſs? Who
' ought to be eſteem'd the Author of the *Pri-*
' *apeia*, who was the *Mantuan Maro*, or the
' *Sulmonian Naſo*? I omit many other fine Pur-
' poſes like theſe, and more curious. Where
' (*viz. in the Houſe of Idleneſs*) are not wanting
' Logicians, who inquire if *Chryſaorius*, who
' was the Diſciple of *Porphyry*, had a golden
' Mouth by Nature, or Report, or Nick-
' name, If the *Peritermenia* ought to go be-
' fore, or come after, or ſtand before or after
' the Categories *ad libitum*; Whether *indivi-*
' *duum vagum* ought to be reckon'd in the
        ' Num

' Number, and plac'd in the midſt as a ſixth
' *Predicable*, or only be a Shield-Bearer to
' *Species*, or a Train-Bearer to *Genus* · Whe-
' ther after being well-skill'd in Syllogiſtick
' Forms, we ought by the firſt to apply our
' ſelves to the Study of the laſt, in which is
' the compleat Art of Judgment, or rather
'· immediately enter upon the *Topicks*, which
' contain the Perfection of the Art of Inven-
' tion: If 'tis neceſſary to practiſe little
' Quirks, *ad uſum, vel ad fugam, vel ad abu-*
' *ſum* · If the Modes which form the *Modals*
' are four, or forty, or four hundred : not to
' mention a thouſand other pretty Queſtions.
' In which Houſe are Naturaliſts, who doubt
' whether the Knowledg of natural things
' ought to be call'd Science; Whether the
' Subject of Phyſicks is *Ens Mobile*, or *Corpus*
' *Mobile*, *Ens Naturale*, or *Corpus Naturale*.
' Whether Matter has any other than *entita-*
' *tive Act*, in which the Line of Coincidence
' of Phyſical and Mathematical Act conſiſts:
' Whether Creation is a Production out of
' nothing or not: Whether more than one ✗
' ſubſtantial Form can be together, and in-
' numerable ſuch like Queſtions about the
' moſt evident things, which are uſeleſs Inqui-
' ries. In which Houſe Metaphyſicians crack
' their Skulls about the Principle of Indivi-
' duation, about the Principle of *Ens in quan-*
' *tum Ens*, about proving that Arithmetical
' Numbers, and Geometrical Magnitudes are
' not the Subſtance of Things, about Ideas,
      ' whether

‘ whether they have their fubftantial Eſſence
‘ of themſelves; about the ſame and different
‘ Eſſence ſubjectively and objectively; about
‘ Eſſence and Exiſtence; about Accidents
‘ the ſame in number in one and more Sub-
‘ jects, about Equivocation, Univocation
‘ and Analogy of Being; about the Con-
‘ junction of the Intelligences with the ſtarry
‘ Orbs, whether they are there by way of
‘ Soul, or by way of Mover; whether infi-
‘ nite Power can be in finite Magnitude; a-
‘ bout the Unity or Plurality of firſt Movers,
‘ about the Scale of finite or infinite Progreſ-
‘ ſion in ſubordinate Cauſes; and about in-
‘ numerable other ſuch like things, which
‘ diſtract ſo many Cowls, and make ſo ma-
‘ ny Protoſophiſts waſte their Brains and Spi-
‘ rits.’

Here *Jupiter* ſaid, ‘ *Momus*, I believe *Idle-*
‘ *neſs* has brib’d or ſuborn’d you, that you
‘ thus idly ſpend your Time and Pains,
‘ make an end, becauſe we have come to a
‘ good Reſolution in diſpoſing of *Idleneſs.*’
‘ I omit then, ſaid *Momus*, to ſpeak of infi-
‘ nite Numbers of other buſy People, who
‘ are imploy’d in the Houſe of *Idleneſs*; ſuch
‘ as the many Verſifiers, who, in ſpight of the
‘ World, would paſs for Poets, the many
‘ Writers of Fables; the many Tellers of old
‘ Stories, related a thouſand times by a thou-
‘ ſand Perſons, a thouſand times better. I
‘ omit the Algebraiſts, the Squarers of Cir-
‘ cles, Figure-flingers, Methodiſts, Refor-
‘ mers

' mers of Dialecticks, Reſtorers of Ortho-
' graphy, Contemplaters of Life and Death,
' the true Poſt-boys of Paradiſe, new Guides
' to eternal Life newly correctly and reprin-
' ted, with many uſeful Additions, new
' Meſſengers of better Bread, better Fleſh
' and Wine than that of the *Soame, Candy,*
' or *Nola.* I ſpeak not of the fine Specula-
' tions about Fate and Election; about the
' Ubiquibility of a Body; about the Excel-
' lency of the Juſtice of Leeches.'

Here *Minerva* ſaid, ' If you do not ſhut
' this Babler's Mouth, Father, we ſhall
' waſte our time in idle Diſcourſes, and it
' will be impoſſible for us to diſpatch our
' main Work this day.' Therefore *Jupiter*
ſaid to *Momus,* ' I have not time to reaſon
' about thy Ironies. But to come to your
' Buſineſs, *Idleneſs*; I tell you that that Idle-
' neſs, which is laudable and ſtudious, ought
' to ſit in the ſame Chair with *Solicitude,*
' becauſe *Labour* ought to relieve it-ſelf by
' *Idleneſs,* and *Idleneſs* ought to be kept in or-
' der by *Labour.* *Idleneſs* will make *Labour*
' more reaſonable, more expedite, and prompt.
' And as Actions without Premeditation and
' Conſideration are not good, ſo without
' premeditating Leiſure they are nought.
' In like manner a paſſing from *Idleneſs* to
' *Idleneſs* cannot be ſweet and agreeable; for
' *Idleneſs* is never ſweet, but when it pro-
' ceeds from the boſom of *Labour.* There-
' fore I now order that no *Idleneſs* ſhall be
　　　　　　　　　　　　　　' agree-

' agreeable, but that which proceeds from
' and fucceeds to worthy Occupations. I or-
' dain that vile and dull *Idlenefs* fhall be the
' greateft Labour and Wearinefs to a gene-
' rous Mind that can be, if it does not offer
' it-felf after laudable Exercife and Labour.
' I impower you to be as a Lord to old
' Age, and make her very often turn her
' Eyes backward; and if fhe has not left
' worthy Marks and Footfteps, you fhall
' make her uneafy, forrowful, and afraid of
' the approaching Judgment of the inexora-
' ble *Rhadamanthus* · and thus fhe fhall feel
' the Horrors of Death before it comes.'

Saul. *Tanfillo* fpoke well to this purpofe.
'Tis moft certain that Repentance is the
moft deplorable State we can be in, becaufe
we cannot make what is paft prefent : And as
all Repentance brings Torment, that which
is fevereft, and moft outrageous, and gives
an incurable Wound, is when one could
have done much, and yet did nothing.

Soph. ' I will no lefs, faid *Jupiter*, that the
' Succefs of unprofitable Exercifes be dif-
' pleafing, fome of which *Momus* has reci-
' ted, which are found in the Houfe of *Idle-*
' *nefs*; and I will, that the Anger of the
' Gods fall heavy upon fuch bufy *Idlenefs*,
' which has troubled and burden'd the
' World more, than ever any Bufinefs and
' Labour could have done : Such, I fay, as
' would turn all the Excellency and Perfec-
' tion of human Life only into idle Beliefs
‘ and

' and Fancies, while they fo unjuftly under-
' value the Concerns and Works of Juftice;
' which they fay do not render Men better,
' tho they are ever fo manifeft and evident ;
' and fo make flight of Vices and Neglects,
' which they fay do not make Men lefs ac-
' ceptable to the Gods, tho they were even
' worfe than they are. Thou dull and un-
' profitable *Idlenefs*, do not expect that the
' Celeftial Gods will give thee a Houfe in
' Heaven, but, that the Servants of rigo-
' rous and implacable *Pluto* will prepare a
' Lodging for thee in Hell.' I will not relate how lazily *Idlenefs* went on her Journy,
and fcarce knew how to move, tho fhe was
prick'd and fpur'd, till fhe was conftrain'd
by the Goddefs *Neceffity*, which gave her a
great many Kicks ; nor what Lamentations
fhe made when fhe left the Council, becaufe
they would not allow her fome days of
Grace to fet her Affairs in order, before fhe
left their Company.

The Second Part of the Third Dialogue.

THEN *Saturn* earneftly requefted *Jupiter* to make more Difpatch in difpofing of the other Seats, becaufe Night was
drawing on, and that he fhould bend all his
Care on removing and fettling, and as to
what concern'd the Order by which the Vir-

tues

tues and other Deities ought to govern, he
fhould determine againft the next principal
Feftivity, when the Gods fhould agree to af-
femble themfelves, which would be the Vi-
gil of the Feaft of *Pantheon.* To which Propofal all the Gods fignify'd their Affent, by
bowing their Heads, except *Difcord, Preci-
pitancy, Unfeafonablenefs,* and fome others.
' I am of the fame mind alfo,' faid the Almighty Thunderer. ' Come then, faid *Ce-*
' *res,* wheie fhall we fend my *Triptolemus,*
' that Charioteer whom you fee there, him
' whom you imploy'd to carry Bread to
' Men ? Will you allow me to fend him to
' the one and the other *Sicily,* where he has
' his Refidence, and three Temples in that
' Country, which by his Diligence and Care
' were confecrated to me, one in *Apulia,* ano-
' ther in *Calabria,* and the third in *Trinacria*
' it felf?' ' Do what you will, Daughter,
' with your Votary and Servant, faid *Jupi-*
' *ter.* Let *Humanity,* which in our Idiom
' is call'd the Goddefs *Philanthropy,* fucceed
' him if the Gods pleafe, of which this Coach-
' man feems to have been the Type; be-
' fides, 'twas fhe that prompted you, *Ceres,*
' to fend him, and influenc'd him to execute
' youi good Offices towards Mankind.'
' That is certain, faid *Momus,* for 'tis fhe
' who makes fuch good Blood in Men by the
' help of *Bacchus,* and fuch good Flefh by the
' help of *Ceres;* fuch as could not be in the
' time of Chefnuts, Beans and Acorns. *Mi-*
' *fanthropy*

' *santhropy* and *Poverty* fly before her; and as
' is cuſtomary and reaſonable, let *Counſel* be
' the left, and *Aſſiſtance* the right Wheel of
' her Chariot; and let the two meek Dra-
' gons, the Drawers of it, be *Clemency* on the
' left, and *Favour* on the right.'

After this *Momus* propos'd to *Mercury* what
he would do with *Serpentaurus*; for he
thought it was good and convenient to ſend
him to ſome *Marſian* Mountebank, who
could handle ſo great and mighty a Serpent
without Fear or Danger. He ſpoke of the
Serpent likewiſe to radiant *Apollo*, asking whether he would put it in the Service of his Magicians and Poiſoners; that is to ſay, his *Circe's*
and *Medea's*, to execute their Witchcrafts by:
Or whether he would grant it to his Phyſi-
cians, *viz. Æſculapius*, &c. to make *Theriac*
of. He propos'd likewiſe to *Minerva*, whether it could be uſeful to her, to avenge her
on ſome rebellious *Lacoon*. ' Let who will
' take it, ſaid the Great Patriarch, and do
' with it what he will (as well as with *Ophi-*
' *ulcus*) provided they be taken from hence,
' and *Sagacity* ſucceed in their room, which is
' ſeen and admir'd in the Serpent.'

' Let *Sagacity* ſucceed then, ſaid all the
' Gods, ſince ſhe is no leſs worthy of Heaven
' than her Siſter *Prudence* : For *Sagacity* over-
' rules, and puts in order what is to be done
' or left undone, for accompliſhing any De-
' ſign; and *Prudence* firſt knows, and then
' judges, by ſtrength of good Underſtand-

O 2 ' ing,

' ing, what it is; and banishes Stupidity,
' Inconfideration and Dulnefs from Places
' where things are doubtful, or under Deli-
' beration: fhe drinks Knowledg out of the
' Veffels of Wifdom, by which fhe is im-
' pregnated, and brings forth the Acts of
' Prudence.'

' Becaufe I have always been curious to
' know, faid *Momus*, to whom the Arrow
' belong'd, that is, if it was that with
' which *Apollo* kill'd the great *Pytho*; or that
' by which my Lady *Venus* made her little
' graceleſs Son wound the furious *Mars*, who
' in revenge of her Cruelty, fix'd his Poi-
' nard in her Belly to the Hilt, or if it was
' that memorable one, with which *Alcides*
' humbled the Queen of the *Stymphalides*, or
' that other, by which the *Caledonian* Bear
' gave the laſt Stagger, or if it is a Relick or
' Trophy of fome Triumph of the chaſte
' *Diana* let it now come to its own Maſter,
' and fix it felf where he pleafes.'

' Very well, faid *Jupiter*, let it remove
' hence with *Treachery*, *Calumny*, *Detraction*,
' *Envy* and *Malice*. Let good *Attention*, *Ob-
' fervance*, and aiming at a reafonable End,
' fucceed.' He added, ' As to the *Eagle*,
' that Divine Bird, and heroick Type of Em-
' pire, I determine and will as follows, That
' it go and clothe it felf with Fleſh and
' Bones in drunken *Germany*, where it will
' be more celebrated than in any other part, in
' Form, and Figure, and Image, and Simili-
' tude,

'tude, in as many Pictures, as many Sta-
' tues, and as many Arms as there are Stars
' in Heaven, to be feen by the Eyes of con-
' templative *Germany*. It will not be necef-
' fary he carry with him *Ambition, Prefump-*
' *tion, Temerity, Oppreffion, Tyranny,* and o-
' ther Servants of thefe Goddeffes, to a
' Place where they muft all be idle, becaufe
' the Country is fufficiently ftock'd with
' them already; but let them take their
' Flight far from that pleafant lovely Coun-
' try, where their Shields are Plates, their
' Helmets are Pipkins and Kettles, their
' Swords the Thigh-bones of falt Beef, their
' Trumpets Drinking-Glaffes, Pitchers and
' Flaggons; their Drums Barrels and Tuns,
' their Field a Table to drink (I would fay
' eat) at: Where their Fortreffes, Bulwarks
' and Baftions are Cellars, Ale-houfes and
' Brandy-fhops, which are more numerous
' than their Houfes.'

At this *Momus* faid, ' Pardon me, Great
' Father, if I interrupt your Difcourfe. It
' is my Opinion, that thefe menial and at-
' tendant Goddeffes will be there, tho you
' do not fend them; becaufe the Ambition
' of being fuperior to all in making them-
' felves Swine, the Prefumption of the Bel-
' ly, which pretends it receives no lefs from
' above, than it fends the Morfel from above
' to below; the Temerity of the Stomach,
' which in vain endeavours to digeft, what
' it will be oblig'd to vomit up in a moment;

O 3 ' the

‘ the Oppreſſion of the Senſes, and the na-
‘ tural Heat ; the Tyranny of the vegeta-
‘ tive, ſenſitive and intellectual Life, reign
‘ more in this alone than in all the other
‘ Parts of the Globe.’ ‘ It is true, *Momus,*
‘ ſubjoin’d *Mercury*; but ſuch ſort of Tyran-
‘ nies, Temerities, Ambitions, and other
‘ like Cacodemons, and their Cacodemonef-
‘ ſes, are not of the Eagle-kind ; but belong
‘ to Blood-ſuckers, Swine and Gluttons.
‘ But to come to the matter of *Jupiter*’s Sen-
‘ tence, it appears to me to be very prejudi-
‘ cial and injurious to the Condition, Life
‘ and Nature of this Royal Bird . which be-
‘ cauſe it drinks little, and eats and devours
‘ much ; becauſe it has clear and piercing
‘ Eyes ; becauſe it is ſwift in flight ; becauſe
‘ by the Levity of its Wings it flies up to
‘ Heaven, and inhabits dry, ſtony, high and
‘ hard Places , it can have no Agreement or
‘ Accord with a Generation which is always
‘ in theſe Fields ; whoſe great Load of Bree-
‘ ches is likely, by a ſtrong Over-ballance, to
‘ bear them down to the dark and deep Cen-
‘ tre ; and makes them a Generation ſo ſlow
‘ and heavy, not ſo unapt to purſue and fly,
‘ as firm to ſtand their Ground in War ; and
‘ which for the moſt part are ſubject to ſore
‘ Eyes, and which drink incomparably more
‘ than they eat.’

‘ What I have ſaid, I have ſaid, anſwer’d
‘ *Jupiter*. I ſaid it ſhould preſent it ſelf there
‘ in Fleſh and Bones, to behold its Repreſen-

‘ tations,

' tations ; but I do not mean that this should
' be a Prison to it, or that it should not be
' wherever it is in Spirit and in Truth with
' other Reasons, and with the fore-mention'd
' Gods : And let this glorious Seat be left
' to all those Virtues, whose Deputy it may
' be suppos'd to have been ; such as the God-
' dess *Magnanimity*, *Magnificence*, *Generosity*,
' with their Sisters and Waiting-Maids.'

' What shall we do now, said *Neptune*,
' with that *Dolphin* ? If you please, I will
' send it into the Sea of *Marseilles*, from
' whence it may go up the *Rhone*, and return
' again, thus visiting and revisiting the *Del-*
' *phinate* ' ' Let him do so quickly, said *Mo-*
' *mus*; for to tell the Truth, I should think
' it no less ridiculous if any one

' *Delphinum Cœlis appinxit, fluctibus aprum*,

' Than if,

' *Delphinum Sylvis appinxit, fluctibus aprum.*'

' Let it go where *Neptune* pleases, said *Ju-*
' *piter*; and let figurative *Dilection*, *Affabi-*
' *lity*, *Dutifulness*, with their Companions and
' Servants, succeed in its place.' *Minerva*
demanded that the *Pegasean* Horse should
leave the twenty lucid Spots, and Curiosity,
and go to the *Fons Caballinus*, so long muddy'd,
troubled and destroy'd by Cows, Hogs and
Asses, and try if with Hoofs and Teeth he
O 4   ' can

can defend that place from such a nasty Concourse; that so the Muses seeing the Water of the Fountain settled and in good order, they may not disdain to return, and keep their Colleges and Promotions there. And in this place of Heaven shall succeed Divine Fury, Rapture, Enthusiasm, Prophecy, Study, and Knowledg, with their Relations and Servants; from whence the divine Water from above may drop upon Mortals, to wash their Souls, and water their Affections.

Neptune said, ' Let us remove hence, if
' the Gods please, this *Andromeda*, which by
' the hand of Ignorance hath been tied to
' the Rock of Obstinacy, with the Chain of
' perverse Reasons, and false Opinions, and
' waft her over from the Whale of Perdi-
' tion and final Ruin, that swims thro the
' instable and tempestuous Sea: and let us
' commit her to the provident and friendly
' Hands of the careful, laborious, and cir-
' cumspect *Perseus*, who having loosed and
' taken her from thence, may from a disho-
' nourable Captivity promote her to his own
' honourable Acquest: and what shall suc-
' ceed her among the Stars, let *Jove* deter-
' mine.'

The Father of the Gods answer'd, ' I will
' have *Hope* to succeed to that place, because
' there is nothing so hard and difficult, to
' which she does not enflame all those Minds
' that can have any Sense of an End, by an
' Ex-

' Expectation of Fruits worthy of all their
' Works and Labours.'

Pallas anfwer'd, ' Let that moft holy
' Shield of human Breafts, that divine Foun-
' dation of all the Edifices of Goodnefs, that
' moft fecure Shelter of Truth, fucceed : She
' that never diftrufts, in the moft ftrange and
' furprizing Accidents, becaufe fhe feels in
' her felf the Seeds of Self-fufficiency, which
' fhe can never be rob'd of by the moft vio-
' lent fhock : She, in virtue of whom 'tis
' reported, that *Stilpo* got the better even of
' his Enemies Victory ; that *Stilpo,* I fay, who
' efcaping from the Flames that burnt his
' Country, his Houfe, his Wife, Children,
' and Goods to afhes, anfwer'd *Demetrius,*
' That all that was his he carry'd about him,
' becaufe he had with him that Fortitude,
' that Juftice, that Prudence, from which he
' could hope for the greateft Confolation, De-
' liverance, and Suftenance ; and for which
' he could eafily forgo the Sweetnefs and Plea-
' fures of Life '

' Let us leave thefe, faid *Momus,* and come
' quickly to confider what muft be done with
' that Triangle, or *Delta.*' The Spear-bearing
Pallas anfwer'd, ' I think it deferves to be
' put into the Cardinal of *Cufa's* hand, to
' the end he may try whether he can deliver
' the embarafs'd Geometricians from their
' toilfome Search after the Quadrature of the
' Circle ; by regulating the Circle and Tri-
' angle with his divine Principle of Com-
                        ' menfuration,

‘ menfuration, and Coincidence of the grea-
‘ teft and leaft Figures ; that is, of that
‘ which confifts of the leaft, and that which
‘ confifts of the greateft number of Angles
‘ Let this Trigon be join'd with a Circle
‘ that comprehends it, and with another
‘ that it comprehends : and by the Relation
‘ of thefe two Lines (one of which goes
‘ from the Centre to the Point in which the
‘ inner Circle touches the external Triangle,
‘ the other goes from the fame Centre to one
‘ of the Angles of the Triangle) is com-
‘ pleated that Quadrature, that has been fo
‘ long and fo fruitlefly fought for.’

At this, *Minerva* rofe up, and faid ; ‘ But
‘ that I may not feem lefs courteous to the
‘ Mufes than others, I will fend the Geome-
‘ tricians an incomparably greater and better
‘ Gift than this or any other that has been
‘ given hitherto, for which *Nolanus*, to
‘ whom it was firft reveal'd, and by whofe
‘ hands it was fpread among the Multitude,
‘ owes me not one, but a hundred Heca-
‘ tombs. For by virtue of the Contempla-
‘ tion of the Equality that is between *Maxi-*
‘ *mum* and *Minimum*, *Extimum* and *Intimum*,
‘ *Principium* and *Finis*, I fhew him a way that
‘ is more fruitful, more valuable, more open,
‘ and more fure and fafe than any other ;
‘ which not only demonftrates how a Square
‘ is made equal to a Circle, but likewife all
‘ Trigons, Pentagons, Hexagons, as alfo any
‘ kind of Polygon Figure you will, where
‘ Line

' Line is no lefs equal to Line, than Surface
' to Surface, Area to Area, and Body to
' Body in folid Figures.'

Saul. This will be a moft excellent thing,
and an ineftimable Treafure to the Cofmo-
graphers.

Soph. So excellent and valuable, that in
my mind it furpaffes all the Inventions that
belong to Geometry. But on this depends
another, more entire, greater, richer, fhor-
ter, more eafy, more exquifite, and no lefs
certain; which commenfurates any kind of
Polygon Figure by the Line and Surface of
the Circle ; and the Circle by the Line and
Surface of any fort of Polygon.

Saul. Pray tell me the Method immediately.

Soph. Minerva faid to *Mercury*; ' Firft, ac-
' cording to your way, within this Triangle
' I defcribe a Circle, the greateft that can be
' defcrib'd there; then without this Trian-
' gle I defcribe another Circle, the leaft I
' can defcribe, to touch the three Angles of
' the Triangle : from thence I will not go to
' your troublefome Quadrature, but to an
' eafy Trigonifm, fearching for a Triangle
' whofe Line is equal to the Line of a Cir-
' cle ; and another whofe Surface is equal to
' the Surface of a Circle. This fhall be one
' about that middle Triangle, equidiftant
' from that which contains the Circle, and
' that which is contain'd in the Circle. I
' leave it to the Wit of others to compre-
' hend

‘ hend this; ’tis enough that I have ſhewn
‘ the Place of Places. Thus to ſquare the
‘ Circle, ’tis not neceſſary to take a Trian-
‘ gle, but a Quadrangle that is betwixt the
‘ greateſt within and the leaſt without the
‘ Circle. To pentagon the Circle, you muſt
‘ take the middle betwixt the greateſt Pen-
‘ tagon contain’d within the Circle, and the
‘ leaſt that contains the Circle within it.
‘ You may do the ſame in making any ſort
‘ of Figure equal to a Circle in Area and
‘ Compaſs. Thus alſo having found the
‘ Circle of a Square equal to the Circle of
‘ a Triangle, you will find the Square of
‘ this Circle equal to the Triangle of that
‘ other Circle of the ſame Extent with this.’

Saul. Thus, *Sophia,* all Figures may be
made equal to all other Figures, by the help
and relation of a Circle, which you make to
be the Meaſure of Meaſures: that is, if I
would make a Triangle equal to a Quadran
gle, I take the middle betwixt the two added
to the Circle, with the middle between two
Quadrangles added to the ſame Circle, or
one equal to it. If I would have a Square
equal to a Hexagon, I will deſcribe both
the one and the other, without and within a
Circle, and take the middle that is between
both.

Soph. You take the thing right: ſo that
from thence we have not only the Equature
of all Figures to the Circle, but likewiſe of
all other ſorts of Figures to all others, by
means

means of the Circle, always keeping the Equality according to Line and Surface. Thus with very small Confideration and Attention, any Equality and Proportion of any Chord to any Arch, may be taken, whether it be whole, or divided, or augmented after a certain way, till it come to conftitute such a Polygon as either takes in or is taken in by such a Circle. Let us now determine prefently, said *Jupiter*, what we shall place there. *Minerva* anfwer'd, ' 'Tis my Opi-
' nion that Faith and Sincerity (without
' which all Contracts are perplex'd and
' doubtful, all Society diffolv'd, all Fellow-
' fhips deftroy'd) fhould be admitted there.
' You fee what a pafs the World is reduc'd
' to, by a Cuftom that is become a Proverb,
' *That Governours are not oblig'd to keep Faith.*
' Befides, Faith to Infidels and Hereticks is
' not obferv'd. Next, he to whom Faith
' is broken, breaks it. Now what if all
' fhould practife this ? What would the
' World come to, if all the Republicks,
' Kingdoms, Dominions, Families and par-
' ticular Perfons fhould think, they ought
' to be Holy with the Holy, and Perverfe
' with the Perverfe ? And if they fhould
' be excus'd for being wicked, becaufe they
' have a wicked Companion or Neighbour;
' and that we ought not to force our felves
' to be good abfolutely, as if we were Gods,
' but for Convenience and on Occafion fhould
' be like Wolves, Serpents, Bears and poifo-
' nous

' nous Creatures.' The Father faid, ' I will
' have Faith to be the moft celebrated a-
' mong the Virtues ; and if it be not given
' with a Condition of another Faith, it fhall
' never be broken for the Breach of another :
' for 'tis a Law of fome *Jew* or *Saracen*, beaft-
' ly Fellow or Barbarian (not of a *Greek* or
' *Roman*, civil or heroick People) that fome-
' times, and with certain fort of People, on-
' ly for our own Convenience, and an Oc-
' cafion to cheat, it is lawful to pledge our
' Faith, and make it an Inftrument of Ty-
' ranny and Treachery.'

Saul. O *Sophia*, there is no Crime more infamous, wicked, and unworthy of Mercy,
than when one breaks Faith with another,
and one is injur'd by another, by having
trufted him as an honeft Man. ' I will there-
' fore, faid the Almighty Thunderer, that
' this Virtue appear celebrated in Heaven,
' that fo it may be more in efteem on Earth
' for the future. Let her come in the place
' of the Triangle, by which Faith was, and
' is very fitly fignify'd : For a triangular
' Body (as confifting of a leffer number of
' Angles, and the fartheft from a circular
' Body) is harder to be mov'd than any
' other fort of figur'd Body. Thus the Nor-
' thern part of Heaven is purg'd, where there
' were commonly obferv'd three hundred
' and fixty Stars, three greateft of all, eigh-
' teen great, eighty one of a middle fize, a
' hundred and feventy feven little, fifty eight
' leffer,

' leffer, thirteen leaft of all, with one cloudy
' and nine obfcure ones.'

Saul. Now give me a fhort account of
what befel the reft.

Soph. ' Determine, O Father, faid *Momus*,
' what muft be done with that Protoparent of
' the Lambs, he that firft makes the languifh-
' ing Plants fprout out of the Earth, he that
' opens the Year, and beautifies it, and clothes
' the Earth a-new with a flowry leafy Gar-
' ment?' ' Becaufe I am unwilling, faid *Jupi-*
' *ter*, to fend him to thofe of *Calabria, Apulia,*
' or *Campania Felix*, where they are often kill'd
' by the Hardnefs of the Winter; and be-
' caufe I don't think it convenient to fend
' him to the *African* Plains and Hills, where
' he is fcorch'd with too much Heat; I
' think it moft proper to fend him to the
' *Thames*, where there are fo many pretty,
' good, fat, white, and nimble ones; which
' are not monftroufly big, as in the Region
' of *Niger*; nor black, as about *Siler* and *Ophy-*
' *tus*; not lean, as about *Sebetus* and *Sarnus*;
' not mifchievous, as about *Tiber* and *Arnus*;
' not ugly to look on, as about the *Tagus*: for
' that place agrees with the Seafon in which
' he is predominant, the Heavens being more
' temperate there, than any where elfe be-
' yond and on this fide of the Equinoctial:
' Snow and Froft being banifh'd from the
' fubjacent Earth, as well as the exceffive
' Heat of the Sun, which the perpetually
' green and florid Ground witneffes, and fo
' enjoys

‘ enjoys a continual and perpetual Spring.
‘ To which we may add, that being clasp’d
‘ there in the protection of the Arms of the
‘ wide Ocean, he will be safe from Wolves, Li-
‘ ons, Bears, and other fierce Animals, and un-
‘ friendly Powers of *Terra-firma.* And because
‘ this Animal has the Quality of a Prince, of
‘ a Duke, of a Leader ; he has the Quality of
‘ a Shepherd, a Captain, and Guide, as you
‘ see, in Heaven, where all the Signs of this
‘ Girdle in the Firmament run behind him:
‘ And as you see on Earth, that when he
‘ skips, or runs down a Precipice, or turns
‘ aside, or goes forward, the whole Flock
‘ quickly imitates him, agrees with him, and
‘ follows him , so I will have his place sup-
‘ ply’d with virtuous Emulation, Exempla-
‘ riness, and good Agreement, with other
‘ sister and servant Virtues , the contrary to
‘ which are Scandal, bad Example, which
‘ have Prevarication, Alienation, and Wa-
‘ vering for their Servants　their Guide is
‘ Malice, or Ignorance, or both; their Fol-
‘ lower is foolish Credulity, which, you see,
‘ is blind, and gropes its way, fumbling with
‘ the Staff of dark Inquiry, and foolish Per-
‘ suasion: Dulness and Meanness are its con-
‘ stant Companions: Let all these together
‘ leave these Abodes, and go to dwell on
‘ Earth.’

‘ Well order’d, answer’d all the Gods ’
Then *Juno* demanded what he would do
with that Bull of his, that Ox, that Consort

of the holy Manger? *Jupiter* reply'd to her,
' If he will not go near the *Alps*, to the Ri-
' ver *Po*, I say to the Metropolis of *Piemont*,
' where is the delicious City of *Turin*, which
' is denominated from him, as *Bucephala* from
' *Bucephalus*, from the Goats the Islands right
' over against *Parthenope* or *Naples* towards
' the West, *Corveto* from Ravens, *Mirmidonia*
' from the Emmets, *Dauphiny* from the Dol-
' phin, *Aprutio* from the wild Boars, *Ophanto*
' from the Serpents, and *Oxon* from I know
' not what other Species: let him go to the
' next Ram for Company, where (as 'tis
' said, their Flesh is the best in the World,
' because of the Fineness of the Grafs, and
' Delicacy of the Pasture) he will have the
' prettiest Companions that are to be seen in
' the whole remaining Space of Heaven.'

Saturn ask'd about a Successor · To whom
Jupiter answer'd, ' Because this is an Ani-
' mal that can endure much Labour and Fa-
' tigue, and is patiently laborious; I will
' that from this time he be a Type of Pa-
' tience, Tolerance, Sufferance, and Longa-
' nimity; Virtues very necessary to the
' World: and let Anger, Indignation, and
' Fury, that use to accompany this some-
' times touchy Animal, depart from hence,
' tho I'm very little concern'd whether they
' go or stay. Here you see *Anger*, the Daugh-
' ter that is born of the Apprehension of In-
' justice and Injury; and she goes away sor-
' rowful and revengeful, because she thinks

' it

' it infufferable that *Contempt* fhould give
' her a Box on the Ear ; how fhe turns her
' fiery Eyes upon *Jupiter*, *Mars*, *Momus*, and
' all the reft ; how the Hope of Revenge
' waits on her Ear, which comforts her a
' little, and bridles her, fhewing her the fa-
' vour of threatning Poffibility againft Con-
' tempt, Contumely, and difrefpectful Ufage,
' her Provokers. There you fee Impetuofity
' her Brother, who gives her Strength, Si-
' news and Fervour : there Fury her Sifter
' that accompanies her, with her three Daugh-
' ters, Excandefcence, Cruelty, and Mad-
' nefs. O how difficult and painful is it to
' behold and reprefs her! O how hardly is
' fhe concocted and digefted by any of the
' Gods but by thee, O *Saturn!* 'Tis fhe
' that has open Noftrils, a violent Forehead,
' a hard Skull, biting Teeth, poifonous Lips,
' a cutting Tongue, griping Hands, a cough-
' ing Breaft, a fhrill Voice, and a fanguine
' Colour.'

Here *Mars* pleaded in behalf of *Anger*, al-
ledging that fometime, nay moft frequently,
it is a moft neceffary Virtue ; as being one
that favours the Law, ftrengthens Truth
and Judgment, and fharpens the Wit : fhe
opens the road to many notable Virtues,
which peaceable Minds know nothing of.
To whom *Jupiter* : ' At the time, and in the
' manner fhe is a Virtue, let her fubfift and
' ftand among thofe Virtues to which fhe is
' propitious · However, let her never ap-
' proach

' proach Heaven, unlefs Zeal goes before her
' with the Lanthorn of Reafon.'

' And what fhall we do with the feven
' Daughters of *Atlas*, Father, faid *Momus*?'
To whom *Jupiter* ' Let them go with their
' feven Lamps, and give light to that noc-
' turnal midnight holy Wedding ; and let
' them bethink themfelves to go before the
' Gate be fhut, and the Cold, Ice, and Snow
' begin to drop from above : becaufe then it
' will be in vain for them to raife their Voice,
' and knock to have the Gate open'd ; for the
' Porter who keeps the Key will fay, *I don't*
' *know you.* Let them know they fhall be
' foolifh if they have not Oil in their Lamps;
' but if they are always moift and never dry,
' it fhall never happen that they will be
' without the Splendour of deferv'd Praife
' and Glory. And let us plant the Region
' which they leave, with Converfation, Fel-
' lowfhip, Marriage, Confraternity, Church,
' Society, Concord, Convention, Confedera-
' cy, and let them thereto join Friendfhip ,
' for where it is wanting, Contamination,
' Confufion and Diforder rule. And if they
' are not regular and orderly, they are not
' themfelves. For they are never truly found
' (altho very often in name) among wicked
' and debauch'd Wretches : but in effect they
' are Monopolies, Clubs, Parties, Confpira-
' cies, Mobs, and Infurrections, or fome o-
' ther thing of deteftable Effence and Name.
' They are not among unreafonable Men, or

' fuch

' fuch as propofe to themfelves no good End;
' nor where idle Believing and Underftanding
' are the fame thing ; but where the fame
' Action is undertaken about things alike
' underftood. They perfevere among the
' Good, but are fhort and inconftant among
' the Perverfe, fuch as we fpoke of when
' we propos'd Law and Judgment, among
' whom is found no true Concord, becaufe
' they are not bufy'd and employ'd about
' virtuous Actions.'

Saul. Thefe do not agree becaufe they underftand alike, but becaufe they are alike ignorant and wicked, and in not underftanding
by different Reafons : Thefe do not agree in
acting alike to a good End, but in making
fmall account of good Works alike, and e-
fteeming all heroick Actions and Deeds of
no value. But to return to our Bufinefs :
What became of the two little Youths?

Soph. Cupid demanded them for the *Great
Turk. Phœbus* would have had them to be
Pages to fome *Italian* Prince. *Mercury* propos'd, they fhould be Gentlemen of the Bed-
Chamber to the Pope. *Saturn,* that they
fhould be inftead of a Warming-pan to fome
old and great Prelate, or rather to himfelf,
who was cold and decrepid. To whom *Venus* faid, ' But who will be Surety that you,
' Father Grey-beard, will not bite them,
' that you will not eat them, if your Teeth
' could not forbear your own Children, for
' which you were defam'd as a Man-eater?'
' And,

' And, which is worfe, faid *Mercury*, 'tis to
' be fear'd, that in fome of his ftubborn Fits
' of Anger, he will plant the Point of his
' Sickle into their Life. Not to add, that if
' they be allow'd to abide in the Court of
' the Gods, it will not be reafonable, good
' Father, that they fhould be claim'd by
' you, more than by many others no lefs ve-
' nerable, who may claim as good a Right
' to them as you.'

Here *Jupiter* pronounc'd, That he would
not admit into the Court of the Gods *in pofte-
rum*, any Pages or other Servants, who had
not a great deal of Senfe, Difcretion, and
Beard : And that the Lot fhould determine
which of the Gods fhould make a Compli-
ment of them to fome Friend on Earth ;
while fome urg'd, that he fhould determine
that himfelf : But he faid, he would not
create Sufpicion of Partiality in their Minds,
by matters of fo much Jealoufy, left he might
be thought to incline more to one than the
other part of the Contenders.

Saul. Very good Order, to prevent the
Diffenfions that might have faln out upon
their account.

Soph. Venus defir'd that Amity, Love and
Peace might fuceeed, together with their
Witneffes, Familiarity, Kiffing, Embracing,
Careffing, Sporting, and all the Brothers
and Servants, By-Standers and Attendants of
double *Cupid*. All the Gods faid, the Demand was juft. ' Let it be done, faid *Jupiter*.

They

They being next to confider how to difpofe of *Cancer* (which becaufe it appears fcalded by the Burning of Fire, and made red by the Heat of the Sun, it is no otherwife in Heaven than if it was condemn'd to the Pains of Hell) *Juno* demanded, as if it had been her own particular Concern, what the Senate would do with it, the greateft part of whom remitted it to her Pleafure. And fhe faid, that if *Neptune*, the God of the Sea, would allow it, fhe would defire that it might plunge it felf in the *Adriatick* Sea, where there are more Companions for it, than there are Stars in Heaven. Befides that there it fhall be near the moft honourable Republick of *Venice*, which by little and little goes by a retrograde Motion from Eaft to Weft, as if it were a Crab. The great God with the Trident confented to it. And *Jupiter* faid, that inftead of *Cancer* fhall ftand the Tropick of Converfion, Emendation, Repreffion, Retraction, Virtues contrary to evil Progrefs, Obftinacy, and Pertinacioufnefs: And immediately propos'd the Cafe of the *Lion*. ' But ' that fierce Animal, faid he, muft be fure ' not to follow *Cancer*, and make himfelf its ' Companion: for if he goes to *Venice*, he ' will find another there, ftronger than he ' can be, for he can fight not only on Land, ' but likewife on Water, and much better in ' the Air, becaufe he has Wings, is cano- ' niz'd, and a Scholar. And therefore it ' will be more expedient for him to go down
' to

' to the *Lybian* Defarts, where he will find
' Miftreffes and Companions. And it is my
' Opinion, that that Magnanimity, that he-
' roick Generofity, which can pardon Sub-
' jects, compaffionate the Weak and Infirm,
' fubdue Infolence, trample upon Temerity,
' rebuke Prefumption, and vanquifh Pride,
' fhould be tranfported to that place.' ' Ve-
' ry well, faid *Juno,* and the greater part of
' the Confiftory.' I omit to tell you with
what grave, magnificent, and comely Apparatus, and great Train, th s Virtue went off,
for at prefent, becaufe we are ftraiten'd for
time, I would have you fatisfy'd to hear the
principal Heads of the Reformation and Difpofition of the Seats, being to inform you of
all the reft, when I fhall lead you from Seat
to Seat, to fee and examine thefe Courts.

Saul. Very well, my dear *Sophia*; your
moft courteous Promife fatisfies me abun-
dantly : fo I am contented, that you inform
me about the Order and Bounds of other
Seats and Changes, as fhortly as you pleafe.

Soph. The chafte *Lucina, Diana* the Hun-
trefs, demanded what fhould become of the
Virgin. *Jupiter* faid, ' Propofe to her, whe-
' ther fhe will go and be a Priorefs, or Ab-
' befs over her Sifters or Nuns, that are in
' the Convents or Nunneries of *Europe,* I
' fay in fuch places where they are not fcat-
' ter'd and difpers'd by the Plague, or a
' Governefs to the Court-Ladies, to the end
' they may not have an itch to tafte and

' eat

' eat the Fruit before or out of feafon, or
' keep too much Company with my Lords.'
' O, faid *Dictyrnus*, fhe cannot, and fhe fays
' fhe will not by any means return to a place
' from whence fhe has been banifh'd, and
' from whence fhe has been fo often oblig'd
' to fly.' The great Protoparent fubjoin'd,
' Let her then ftand firm in Heaven, and
' take good heed fhe falls not, and fee fhe
' be not defil'd in this place.' *Momus* faid,
' It is my Opinion, that fhe may continue
' pure and clean, if fhe continues at a great
' diftance from reafonable Creatures, Heroes
' and Gods : Therefore let her keep amongft
' the Beafts, as fhe has always hitherto done,
' having on the Weft the moft bold and
' fierce *Lion*, and on the Eaft the poifonous
' *Scorpion*. But I know not now how fhe
' will be, when fhe is fo near to Magnani-
' mity, Amoroufnefs, Generofity, and Vi-
' rility, which may eafily mount and ride
' her, and by reafon of domeftick Contact,
' fomewhat of the magnanimous, amorous,
' generous and manly, may infect her ; and
' from Feminine, make her become Mafcu-
' line, and from a favage mountain God-
' defs, and Deity of Satyrs, Sylvans, and
' Fauns, turn her to a gallant, humane, af-
' fable and hofpitable Deity.'
' Let it be as it ought, faid *Jupiter* ; and
' in the mean while let us join to her Seat,
' Chaftity, Shamefacednefs, Modefty, Con-
' tinence, Decency, which are contrary to
' profti-

' proftituted Luft, boundlefs Incontinency,
' Impudence, Shamelefnefs : by which I
' intend that Virginity fhall be one of the
' Virtues; for of her felf fhe is of no ac-
' count, becaufe of her felf fhe is neither
' Virtue nor Vice, nor contains any Good-
' nefs, Dignity or Merit : And when fhe
' does not ferve commanding Nature, fhe be-
' comes a Fault, Impotence, Stupidity and
' abfolute Folly : And when fhe yields to a-
' ny urgent Reafon, fhe is call'd Continence,
' and has the Being of Virtue, as partaking
' of fuch a Fortitude, and Contempt of Plea-
' fures; which is not vain and ufelefs, but
' improves human Society, and the honeft
' Satisfaction of others.'

 ' What fhall we do with *Libra*, or the *Bal-*
' *lance*, faid *Mercury*?' ' Let it go every
' where, anfwer'd the firft Prefident of the
' Council. Let it go thro Families, that Fa-
' thers may weigh the Inclinations of their
' Sons, whether they turn to Letters, to
' Arms, to Husbandry, to Religion, to Ce-
' libacy, or to Love, for it is foolifh to fet
' Affes to fly, or Hogs to plough. Let it run
' thro Academies and Univerfities, and exa-
' mine if thofe who teach are of a juft
' weight, or too light, or too heavy ; or
' if thofe who prefume to teach in the Chair,
' or by Books, have need to hear and be Stu-
' dents; if the Brain is too light or too hea-
' vy ; if one is fitter to be a Shepherd than
' one of the Flock, or fitter to feed Swine
       ' and

' and Affes than reafonable Creatures.　Let
' it go thro Veftal Edifices, and inftruct both
' the He and She-Inhabitants what Violence
' they do to the Law of Nature, by ano-
' ther which is above, beyond and contrary
' to it, contrary to all Reafon and Duty
' Thro Courts, that fo Offices, Honours, Pla-
' ces, Favours and Exemptions may be di-
' ftributed according to the weight of every
' one's Merit and Dignity, for they who
' underftand not how to govern according to
' Order, deferve not to be made Prefidents
' over Order (tho they often prefide over Or-
' der to the great wrong of Fortune.)　Thro
' Commonwealths, that fo the Burden of
' Adminiftrations may overbalance the Suf-
' ficiency and Capacity of the Subjects ; and
' that Charges be not diftributed according
' to the weight of Degrees in Blood, Nobi-
' lity, Titles and Riches, but according to
' the Virtues which bring forth the Fruits
' of noble Undertakings : by which the Juft
' prefide, the Rich diftribute, the Learned
' teach, the Prudent manage, the Brave fight,
' the Judicious give Counfel, thofe who have
' Authority command.　Let it go thro all
' States, that fo in Contracts of Peace, Con-
' federations and Laws, there may be no
' Prevarication, or declining from Juftice,
' Honefty and common Advantage.　Let it
' attend to the meafure and weight of
' Faith given to and receiv'd from thofe
' with whom Contracts are enter'd into ; and
' in

' in the Undertakings and Affairs of War, let
' it confider in what Equilibrium the Forces
' of both fides ftand : Let it compare what
' is prefent and neceffary with what is future
' and contingent ; the Facility of propofing,
' with the Difficulty of executing ; the Con-
' venience of entering, with the Inconve-
' nience of getting out , the Inconftancy of
' Friends, with the Conftancy of Enemies ;
' the Pleafure of acting offenfively, with the
' Thoughts of acting defenfively , the Eafi-
' nefs of difturbing the Affairs of others,
' with the Difficulty to preferve our own in
' order ; the certain Expence and Lofs of
' our own, with the uncertain Gain and Ac-
' quifition of that of others. Let it go to all
' particular Perfons, that every one may lay
' what he wills in the Ballance againft what
' he knows, what he wills, knows and can,
' againft what he ought ; what he wills,
' knows, can and ought, with that which is,
' that which he does, has and expects.'

Then *Pallas* ask'd, What they would put
in the place of the Ballance ? What fhould
be in the room of *Libra* ? A great many anfwer'd, ' Equity, Juftice, Retribution, rea-
' fonable Diftribution, Favour, Gratitude, a
' good Confcience, knowing of one's felf,
' Refpect due to Superiours, Equanimity due
' to Equals, Goodnefs towards Inferiours,
' Juftice without Rigour towards all ; which
' thruft at Temerity, Ingratitude, Infolence,
' Boldnefs, Arrogance, Difrefpect, Iniquity,
' Injury,

' Injury, and all their Familiars.' ' Good,
' good,' ſaid the whole Conſiſtory.

After which Vote, *Apollo*, with his fine
Hair, rais'd himſelf on his Feet, and ſaid,
' The Hour is come, O ye Gods, in which
' we ought to pronounce Sentence againſt
' that infernal Worm, which was the princi-
' pal Cauſe of the horrible Fall and cruel
' Death of my beloved *Phaeton*, for when
' that poor, miſerable, wavering and fearful
' Charioteer, with his unmanageable Horſes,
' govern'd the Chariot of my eternal Fire,
' this pernicious menacing Monſter came ſo
' right againſt him with the Point of its mor-
' tal Tail, and frighted him ſo out of him-
' ſelf, that he let the Reins fall out of his
' trembling Hands from the Horſes Backs,
' from whence came that ſignal Ruin of
' Heaven, which appears to this day in the
' *Milky Way*; that ſo famous Deſtruction of
' the World, which appears in Aſhes in ma-
' ny Parts; and the ſo very ſhameful Affront
' of my Divinity which follow'd upon it.
' It is even a ſhame that ſuch a Blot ſhould
' have taken up the room of two Signs ſo
' long a time.'

' See then, *Diana*, ſaid *Jupiter*, what you
' will do with this Animal of yours, which
' alive is hurtful, and dead is good for no-
' thing. Permit me, if you pleaſe, to ſend
' it back to *Scio* on Mount *Chelippus*, where
' by my order it was produc'd in ſpight to
' the preſumptuous *Orion*; and let it be there
' reſolv'd

' refolv'd into its firft Principles. With it
' let Fraud, Deceit, Chicane, Guile, perni-
' cious Fiction, Untruth, Perjury and Trea-
' chery depart, and the contrary Virtues fuc-
' ceed; fuch as Sincerity, Performance of
' Promife, Obfervation of Faith, and their
' Sifters, Hand-Maids and Followers.' ' Do
' with it what you pleafe, faid *Momus*; for
' we will not difpute it with you, as we did
' with old *Saturn* about the two Boys.'

Let us quickly fee what we fhall do with
the Son of *Eufchemius,* who thefe feveral
thoufand years has held his Arrow bent in his
Bow, being afraid to fend it away, left he
don't find another; and taking his Aim at
Scorpio, juft at the joining of the Tail with
the Backbone. And indeed as I believe him
too well skill'd and practis'd in taking a
View, or, as they fay, aiming at the Mark,
which is the Butt of the *Sagittary* Art; you
may believe him no lefs expert in the remaining part of drawing, and hitting his
Mark, which makes the other Butt of that
Exercife. I would advife you to fend him,
to get Reputation in the Ifle of *Britain,*
where fuch fort of Gentlemen, fome in Jer-
kins, and fome in plaited Jackets, ufe to celebrate the Feaft of Prince *Arthur,* and Duke
of *Sardica.* But I am afraid left he, wanting the principal word for giving the Signal,
come to difgrace the Trade , for which reafon I wifh you Gods would confider how to
difpofe of him: for to tell the Truth, as I intend,

tend, I don't think him fit for any other
thing but to be a Scare-crow, to keep the
Birds, *verbi gratia*, from Beans and Melons.
' Let him go where he will, said the Great
' Patriarch; but some of you give him the
' best Supply you think fit, and let figurative
' Speculation, Contemplation, Study, Atten-
' tion, Aspiring, Aiming at the best End,
' with their Attendants and Companions,
' succeed in his Place.'

Here *Momus* said, ' What will you do, Fa-
' ther, with that holy, undefil'd and venera-
' ble *Capricorn*? with that divine and sacred
' Foster-Brother of yours? with that our
' strenuous and most heroick Fellow-Soldier,
' against the dangerous Insult of Gigantick
' *Perversity*? That Great Counsellor of War,
' who found a way to dispatch that Enemy,
' who, from his Den in Mount *Taurus*, ap-
' pear'd the formidable Antagonist of the
' Gods in *Egypt*? That worthy Person who
' taught us (for we durst not have had the
' boldness to assault him openly) to trans-
' form our selves into Beasts, that so Art and
' Cunning might supply the Defect of our
' Nature and Force, and gain us an honoura-
' ble Triumph over hostile Powers? But, a-
' las! this Merit is not without some De-
' merit; for this Good is not without some
' mixture of Evil, because perhaps 'tis de-
' creed and ordain'd by Fate, that no Sweet
' should be free from Bitter and Unpleasant,
' or for I don't know what other reason.'

' But

' But pray what Evil, said *Jupiter*, could he
' occasion, which can be said to be mix'd
' with so great a Good? What Dishonour
' could accompany so great a Triumph?
Momus answer'd, ' He was the occasion of
' the *Egyptians* worshipping the live Images
' of Beasts, and adoring us in their Form;
' which made us to be flouted and laugh'd
' at, as I shall tell you.' ' You ought not to
' account this an Evil, *Momus*, said *Jupiter*;
' for you know that Animals and Plants are
' the living Effects of Nature, which Nature,
' you must know, is no other than God in
' Things.'

Saul. Then, *Natura est Deus in Rebus.*

Soph. ' Wherefore, said he, divers living
' Things represent divers Deities, and divers
' Powers; which besides their absolute Be-
' ing, have a Being communicated to all
' Things, according to their Capacity and
' Measure. From whence whole God (yet
' not totally, but in some more, in some less
' excellently) is in all things. Wherefore
' *Mars* is more efficaciously in natural Tra-
' ces, and by way of substance in a Viper or
' Scorpion, nay even in an Onion or Garlick,
' than in any inanimate Picture or Statue.
' In like manner you ought to conceive of
' *Sol*, in a Crocus, a Daffodil, a Turnsole, in
' a Cock, or in a Lion. Thus you ought to
' conceive of each of the Gods by each of
' the Species, under the divers Genus's of
' *Ens*. For as the Divinity descends in a cer-

' tain

' tain manner, inafmuch as it communicates
' it-felf to Nature; fo there is an Afcent
' made to the Divinity by Nature. Thus
' the Life which fhines in natural Things,
' mounts up towards the Life which prefides
' over them.' ' What I was a faying is true,
' reply'd *Momus*; for in truth I fee how the
' wife Men, by thefe means, were able to
' make the Gods familiar, affable and do-
' meftick; how they made them fend Words
' out of Statues, by which they gave Di-
' vine Counfels, Doctrines, Divinations, and
' fupernatural Inftitutions: From whence,
' with magical and divine Rites, they moun-
' ted by the fame Ladder of Nature to the
' very Height of the Divinity, by which
' the Divinity defcended to the very meaneft
' and loweft Things by the Communication
' of it-felf. But what I think moft deplora-
' ble, is, that I fee fome fenflefs and foolifh
' Idolaters, who no more imitate the Excel-
' lency of the *Egyptian* Worfhip, than the
' Shadow partakes of the Nobility of the
' Body; who look for Divinity, without a-
' ny manner of Reafon, in the Excrements
' of dead and inanimate Things; who with-
' al not only fcoff and mock thofe divine
' and fharp-fighted Worfhippers, but like-
' wife us, whom they reckon no better than
' Beafts: And what is worfe than all this,
' they triumph for Joy, to fee their own foo-
' lifh Rites in fo much Reputation, and thofe
' of others vanifh'd and annul'd '

' Let

‘ Let not this trouble you, *Momus*, faid
‘ *Ifis*, fince Fate has ordain’d a Viciffitude of
‘ Darknefs and Light.’ ‘ But the Evil of it
‘ is, anfwer’d *Momus*, that they hold for
‘ certain, they are in the Light.’ *Ifis* reply’d,
‘ That Darknefs would not be Darknefs to
‘ them if they knew it. So then, in oider
‘ to obtain certain Benefits and Gifts from
‘ the Gods, they by the method of profound
‘ Magick made ufe of certain natural things,
‘ in which there was a latent Divinity after
‘ a certain manner, and by which the Divi-
‘ nity was willing and able to communicate
‘ it felf to certain Effects : Wherefore thofe
‘ Ceremonies were not vain Fancies, but live-
‘ ly Words, which reach’d the Ears of the
‘ Gods, of whom as we would be under-
‘ ftood, not by the words of any Language
‘ we may imagine they fpeak, but by the
‘ Voice of natural Effects ; fo by the Acts of
‘ Rites and Ceremonies they endeavour’d to
‘ be underftood by us ; otherwife we fhould
‘ have been as deaf to their Wifhes, as a
‘ *Tartar* to one fpeaking *Greek*, which he ne-
‘ ver heard before. Thofe wife Men knew
‘ that God was in Things, and that the Di-
‘ vinity lay hid in Nature, fhining and dif-
‘ covering it felf differently in different Sub-
‘ jects ; and made them Partakers of it felf,
‘ I mean of Life, Effence, Intellect, by cer-
‘ tain Phyfical Forms in certain Orders , and
‘ fo with the very fame different Orders,
‘ they put themfelves in a Difpofition to re-

Q ‘ ceive

' ceive all thofe Gifts they defir'd : For which
' reafon they facrific'd to *Jupiter Magnanimus*
' by an Eagle, when they got a Victory,
' where Divinity is lodg'd agreeable to that
' Attribute. They facrific'd to *Jupiter* the
' Wife, by a Serpent, for Prudence in the
' Conduct of Affairs : To *Jupiter* Menacing,
' by a Crocodile, againft Treachery ; and fo
' for other innumerable Ends they facrific'd
' by other innumerable Species : which was
' not done without the moft effectual and
' magical Reafon.'

Saul. How can you fay fo, *Sophia*; if *Jupiter*'s Name was not known at the time of the *Egyptian* Worfhips, but was found out a long time after amongft the *Greeks* ?

Soph. The *Greek* Name fhould not ftumble you, *Saulinus*; becaufe I fpeak according to the moft univerfal Cuftom, and becaufe Names, even among the *Greeks*, are only forg'd and tack'd to the Divinity : for every body knows, that *Jupiter* was one of the Kings of *Crete*, a mortal Man, and whofe Body, no lefs than thofe of other Men, is rotten, or reduc'd to Afhes. Nor is it a Myftery or Secret, that Lady *Venus* was of mortal Race, that fhe was a moft delicate Queen, beyond meafure beautiful, kind and liberal, in *Cyprus.* In like manner all the other Gods were known to be Men.

Saul. How then did they worfhip and invoke them ?

Soph. I'll tell you: They did not worſhip *Jupiter* as if he had been the Divinity, but they worſhip'd the Divinity as if it had been in *Jupiter* : for ſeeing excellent Majeſty, Juſtice and Magnanimity in a Man, they preſum'd that there was a magnanimous, juſt and bountiful God within him : and they ordain'd or put in practice the Cuſtom of calling ſuch a God, or at leaſt the Divinity which communicated it ſelf in ſuch a manner, by the name of *Jupiter* ; as Divine Wiſdom came under the name of *Mercury*, a moſt wiſe *Egyptian*, by Interpretation and Manifeſtation. So that this or that Man is only celebrated by the Name and Repreſentation of the Divinity, which came to be communicated to Mankind by the Birth of ſuch a Man, and was underſtood to have finiſh'd the Courſe of its good Works, at its Death or Return to Heaven. Thus the eternal Deities (without any Inconveniency or Injury done to the Truth of the Divine Subſtance) have different Names, in different Times, and different Nations : as you may ſee by manifeſt Hiſtories, That *Paul* of *Tarſus* was call'd *Mercury*, and *Barnabas* of *Galilee* was nam'd *Jupiter*; not that they were believ'd to be the ſame Gods, but becauſe they thought that that Divine Virtue, which was in *Mercury* and *Jupiter* in former times, was now actually preſent in thoſe, from the Eloquence and Perſuaſion of the one, and the good Effects produc'd by the other. Here

then

then is a Proof, that Crocodiles, Cocks, Onions and Turnips were never worſhip'd; but only the Gods, and the Divinity in Crocodiles, Cocks, Onions and Turnips: which Divinity hath, is, and will be preſent in divers Subjeꞓts, however mortal they be, at certain Times and Places, ſucceſſively and all at once; always having regard to the Divinity, as it is near and familiar with theſe things, and as it is moſt high, abſolute in it ſelf, and without habitude or relation to things produc'd. You ſee then how one ſimple Divinity, which is in all things, one ſimple Nature, the Mother and Preſerver of the Univerſe, ſhines forth in divers Subjeꞓts, and aſſumes divers Names, according as it communicates it ſelf diverſly: you ſee how we are oblig'd to aſcend to this one diverſly, by the participation of divers Gifts; otherwiſe we ſhould be like thoſe who endeavour to take up Water in a Net, and catch Fiſh with a Diſh. From hence they conceive that the Life, which informs things according to two principal Reaſons, is owing to the two principal Bodies which are next to our Globe and Maternal Deity, *i. e.* the Sun and Moon Then they conceive Life according to ſeven other Reaſons, deriv'd from the ſeven wandring Stars; to which, as to an original Principle, and fruitful Cauſe, they reduce the Differences of Species in any Genus you pleaſe, ſaying of Plants, of Animals, of Stones, of Influences, and many other ſorts

of

of things, thefe belong to *Saturn*, thefe to *Jupiter*, thefe to *Mars*, thefe and others to this and t'other Planet. Thus alfo of Parts, of Members, of Colours, of Seals, of Characters, of Signs, of Images diftributed into feven Species. But notwithftanding all this, they were not ignorant of the Unity of the Divinity, which is in all things, which as it diffufes and communicates it felf in innumerable ways, fo it has innumerable names, and is fought after by innumerable ways and reafons fuited and appropriated to each of thefe names, whilft it is worfhip'd and honour'd with innumerable Rites, by which we endeavour to obtain innumerable kinds of Favours from it. Wherefore in this is requir'd that Wifdom and Judgment, that Art, Induftry and Ufe of intellectual Light, which is fometimes lefs, and fometimes in greater abundance reveal'd by the intelligible Sun : which Habit is call'd Magick, which as it is converfant about fupernatural Principles, is Divine ; and as it is imploy'd in the Contemplation of Nature, and an Inquiry into its Secrets, is natural ; and it is call'd Middle and Mathematical, as it confifts in Reafons and Acts of the Soul, which is in the Horizon of Corporeal and Spiritual, Spiritual and Intellectual.

But to return to the purpofe from which we digrefs'd : *Ifis* faid to *Momus*, ' That the ' ftupid and fenflefs Idolaters had no reafon ' to laugh at the Magical and Divine Wor-

fhip

' fhip of the *Egyptians*, who contemplated
' the Divinity in all Things, in all Effects, ac-
' cording to the proper Reafons of each;
' and knew, by means of the Species in the
' Womb of Nature, how to receive thofe Be-
' nefits they defir'd of her: which as fhe gives
' Fifh to the Sea and Rivers, favage Crea-
' tures to the Defarts, Metals to the Mines,
' and Fruit to the Trees; fo fhe gives cer-
' tain Lots, Virtues, Fortunes and Impref-
' fions to certain Parts, Animals, Beafts and
' Plants. Wherefore the Divinity in the Sea
' was call'd *Neptune*; in the Sun, *Apollo*, in
' the Earth, *Ceres*, in the Defarts, *Diana*,
' and diverfly in all other Species, which like
' divers Ideas, were divers Deities in Nature;
' who all center'd at laft in one Deity of Dei-
' ties, and Fountain of the Ideas above Na-
' ture.'

Saul. From hence I believe is deriv'd that
Cabala of the *Jews*, the Wifdom of which
(of whatfoever kind it be) hath proceeded
from the *Egyptians*, among whom *Mofes* was
educated. In the firft place it gives an ineffa-
ble Name to the firft Principle, from whence
fecondarily proceed four, which are afterwards refolv'd into twelve, and thefe never
reft till they come to feventy two in a direct
Line, which again go in a direct and oblique
Line till they come to a hundred and forty
four, and fo on by fours and twelves till they
become innumerable, according to the innumerable Species of Things. And in this
manner

manner they name, according to their proper Idioms, by fit names, a God, an Angel, an Intelligence, a Power that presides over one Species; so that in the end, the whole Deity is reduc'd to one Fountain, as all Light to the first and of it self lucid Principle; and the Images which are in divers and numerous Looking-Glasses, as in so many particular Subjects, all center in one formal and ideal Principle, the Fountain of them.

Soph. It is so. So that God consider'd absolutely, has nothing to do with us, but only as he communicates himself by the Effects of Nature, to which he is more nearly ally'd than Nature it self; so that if he is not Nature it self, certainly he is the Nature of Nature, and the Soul of the Soul of the World, if he is not the very Soul it-self. And therefore if they would fit themselves according to special Reasons to receive Assistance from him, they must present themselves before him by the way of orderly Species, as he who wants Bread, goes to the Baker; he who wants Wine, goes to the Wine-Merchant; he who desires Fruit, goes to the Gardiner; he who seeks Knowledg, goes to a Master; and so of all other Things. Insomuch that one Goodness, one Felicity, one absolute Principle of all Riches and Benefits, regards many Reasons, and pours forth its Gifts according to the Exigencies of every particular thing. From hence you may gather how the Wisdom of the *Egyptians,* which

is

is now loft, worſhip'd Crocodiles, Lizards,
Serpents and Onions, and not the Earth, the
Moon, the Sun, and the other Stars of Hea-
ven only.

Which magical and divine Rite (by which
the Divinity communicated it ſelf ſo conveniently to Men) is deplor'd by *Triſmegiſtus*,
where ſpeaking to *Aſclepius*, he ſays, *Do you
ſee*, Aſclepius, *theſe animated Statues, full of
Senſe and Spirit, which perform ſo many and
ſtrange Operations ? Theſe Statues, I ſay, which
prognoſticate and foretell Things to come, which
bring on Infirmities and Diſeaſes, and apply
Cures, which cauſe Joy and Grief, according to
the Merits of human Affections and Bodies?
Don't you know*, Aſclepius, *how that* Egypt *is
the Image of Heaven ; or to ſay better, a Colony
of every thing which is order'd and done in Heaven ? To ſay the Truth, our Country is the Temple of the World. But, alas ! the Time will
come, when* Egypt *ſhall think ſhe has been a religious Worſhipper of the Divinity in vain, becauſe the Divinity returning to Heaven, ſhall
leave* Egypt *forſaken · And this Seat of the Divinity ſhall remain deſolate, and void of all Religion, being baniſh'd from the Preſence of
the Gods, and poſſeſs'd by a ſtrange and barbarous Nation, without Religion, Piety, Law, or
Divine Worſhip. O* Egypt ! Egypt ! *only the
Tales of thy Religions ſhall remain, and ſuch
Tales as ſhall be incredible to future Generations,
to which nothing will be left to tell thy pious
Deeds, but Inſcriptions on Stones, which will tell*
them,

them, *not to the Gods and Men (for Men shall
be dead, and the Gods transmigrated to Heaven)
but to* Scythians *and* Indians, *or such other
savage Natures. Darkness will be prefer'd to
Light, Death will be judg'd better than Life;
no body shall lift his Eyes to Heaven; the Religious shall be thought mad; the Impious shall be
judg'd Prudent; the Furious, Brave; the Worst,
Good. and believe me, capital Punishment shall
be inflicted on him who applies himself to the Religion of the Mind, because there shall be new
Justice, new Laws; there shall be none holy,
none religious; there shall be nothing heard
which is worthy of Heaven, or the Inhabitants
of it. Only pernicious Angels shall remain, who
mingled with Men, shall force the poor Wretches
to the Boldness of committing all Evil, as if
that was Justice; furnishing Matter for Wars,
Rapines, Frauds, and all other things which are
contrary to the Soul, and natural Justice; and
this shall be the Villany, Disorder and Irreligion
of the World. But be assur'd,* Asclepius, *that
when these things shall have come to pass, then
the Lord and Father, God the Governour of the
World, the Omnipotent Overseer, shall certainly
put an end to that Blot, and restore the World
to its antient Face, either by a Deluge of Water,
or Fire, or Diseases, or Pestilence, or other Ministers of his merciful Justice.*

Saul. Let me hear the Sequel of *Isis*'s Discourse with *Momus.*

Soph. As to the Reproachers of the *Egyptian* Worship, she recited that Verse of the
Poet :   Lori-

Loripedem rectus, derideat Æthiopem albus.

' The fenflefs Beafts, and very Brutes laugh
' at us Gods as ador'd in Plants, in Beafts,
' in Stones, and at my *Egyptians* that pay
' their Acknowledgments to us in this fafhion,
' not confidering that the Divinity fhews it
' felf in all things : tho 'tis found and feen
' in the moft abject things, for Ends proxi-
' mate, convenient and neceffary to the di-
' vers Acts of human Life ; and for the moft
' univerfal and excellent End in the greateft
' Things and general Principles ; fince every
' thing, as has been faid, has the Divinity
' latent in it : for it unfolds and communi-
' cates it felf even to the very meaneft, and
' from the very meaneft things, according to
' their Capacity. Without which Prefence,
' nothing fhould have Being ; for that is the
' Effence of Being from the firft to the very
' laft. To what is faid, I add and demand,
' on what account they condemn the *Egyp-*
' *tians* for that in which they themfelves are
' comprehended. And to come to thofe who
' fled from us, or were banifh'd as leprous
' to the Wildernefs , had not they recourfe
' to the *Egyptian* Worfhip in their Neceffity,
' when they were oblig'd to worfhip me in
' the Idol of a golden Calf? Did they not
' in another Neceffity fall down, and bow
' the Knee, and lift up their Hands to *Theuth*
' in form of a brazen Serpent ; and agreeable
' to

' to their innate Ingratitude, after they had
' obtain'd Favour of both the Deities, broke
' both Idols? Afterwards when they had a
' mind to honour and dignify themſelves with
' the names of *Saints, Holy, Bleſſed,* they could
' fall upon no other method to obtain that
' Honour, but by calling themſelves Beaſts:
' As we ſee, when the Father of the twelve
' Tribes gave his Benediction to his Sons, he
' honour'd them with the magnificent Names
' of twelve Beaſts. How often do they call
' their old God, *an awaken'd Lion, a flying Ea-*
' *gle, a burning and conſuming Fire, a loud*
' *Storm, a ſtrong Tempeſt?* And how often
' do their Succeſſors call their young God *a*
' *bleeding Pelican, a ſolitary Sparrow, a ſlain*
' *Lamb?* And thus they name him, thus
' they paint him, and thus they underſtand
' him, where I ſee him in Statue or Image,
' with a Book (I know not if I may ſay)
' in his hand, that none can open or read but
' himſelf. Beſides, all thoſe who are deiſy'd
' for believing in him, are they not denomi-
' nated from him? and do they not glory in
' calling themſelves *his Sheep, his Paſture, his*
' *Stall, his Sheepfold, his Flock?* Not to ſpeak
' of the ſame People's being repreſented by
' *Aſſes,* the *Jewiſh* People by the Mother Aſs,
' and all the Generations that gave credit to
' their Stories, and ſo join'd themſelves to
' them, by the Aſſes Colt. You ſee then
' how thoſe Saints, this elect People, were
' repreſented by ſo poor and vile Beaſts; and
' yet

' yet they laugh at us who are reprefented in
' more honourable, imperious, and ftrong
' ones. Nor need I tell you, that all noble
' and illuftrious Generations, when they had
' a mind to fhew and reprefent their Enter-
' prizes by fit Signs, did it by Eagles, Hawks,
' Kites, Cuckoos, Owls, Bears, Wolves, Ser-
' pents, Horfes, Goats; and becaufe they
' thought fometimes they were fcarce worthy
' to be reprefented by a whole Beaft, behold
' they fhew you a piece of one, a Limb, a
' Head, a Pair of Horns, a Tail, or a P—.
' And don't you believe, that if they could
' transform themfelves into the Subftance of
' fuch Animals, but they would do it very
' willingly? Elfe for what end, think you,
' do they paint them on their Shields; when
' they always carry their Picture and Statue
' along with them? Perhaps you would
' think they would thus fay: This, this
' whofe Image you fee, Spectator, is that
' Beaft that ftands next to him, and painted
' with him; or if you would know what
' this Beaft is, know that it is the Beaft
' whofe Picture you fee drawn, and Name
' written here. How many are there, that
' they may the better appear to be Beafts,
' put on the Skin of a Fox, a Wolf, a Badger,
' a Buck, fo that they do not feem to want
' any thing of fuch Animals but the Tail?
' How many are there, who, to fhew how
' much they have of the Bird, and with
' what Lightnefs they can raife themfelves to
                                    ' the

' the Clouds, adorn their Hats and Caps
' with Feathers?'

Saul., What shall I say of the noble Ladies,
as well those that are truly great, as those
that give out themselves for such? Don't
they put a greater value on Beasts than on
their own Children? If they would speak
out what they think, we have reason to believe, it should be in these or the like words:
*O my Child, who art the Image of my self, and
hast the Figure of a Man; if instead of this thou
hadst the shape of this Rabbit, Puppy, Wezel,
Cat, or Squirrel; (whereas I have now committed thee to this Maid, this poor Nurse, this nasty,
greazy, drunken Slut, who choaking thee with her
rank Smell, being thou must lie with her, may be
the death of thee) I, I should be she that would
carry and hold thee in my Arms, would nurse
thee, comb thee, sing to thee, dandle thee, and
kiss thee, as I do this pretty Creature, which I
will not have to lodge any where but with my self,
nor allow it to be touch'd by any body but my self,
nor stay in any other Chamber, nor lie in any other
Bed but mine. If cruel* Atropos *should bereave
me of it, I would not suffer it to be buried like
thee, but would embalm it, and perfume its Skin;
I would have its Picture in enamel'd Gold, set
with Diamonds, Pearls and Rubies, like a divine
and sacred Relick, that wants both Head and
Feet. When I make a visit in state, I will carry
it with me, and sometimes put it on my Neck,
sometimes bring it to my Face, Nose, Mouth,
sometimes carry it in my Arms, sometimes take*

away

away my Arms, and let it lie at its full length on my Breaft, that fo I may have a full view of it in all its parts. From whence it evidently appears how much more Care and Affection thofe great Ladies have for thefe Beafts, than for their own Children; to fhew how much more noble thofe are than thefe, and confe-quently how much more they are to be re-garded.

Soph. And to turn our Thoughts to more ferious and weighty Reafons; thofe who are, and hold themfelves to be the greateft Prin-ces, (to manifeft by exprefs Marks and Signs their Divine Power and Pre-eminence above others) adorn their Head with a Crown; which is nothing but a figure of fo many Horns, which by a Circle do crown or cor-nute their Heads, and the higher and more raifed they are, they make the more princely Reprefentation, and are a mark of the greater Grandeur. Whence a Duke is jealous if a Marquifs or an Earl has as great a Crown as he: a greater belongs to a King, the greateft to an Emperor, and a Triple Crown belongs to the Pope, as the great and chief Patriarch, who ought to have enough for himfelf and his Companions. The Chief Priefts have always worn a Mitre that rifes with two Horns, the Duke of *Venice* appears with a Horn on the middle of his Head; the *Great Turk* makes his rife out of his Turbant, high and ftrait, in form of a round Pyramid; all which is done to fhew his Grandeur, in

adorning

adorning his Head by the beſt Art he can,
with that beautiful part, which Nature has
beſtow'd upon Beaſts; to ſhew, I mean, that
he has ſomething of the Beaſt about him.
No body, either before or ſince, was ever
able to expreſs this more to the life, than the
Leader and Legiſlator of the *Jewiſh* People;
that *M——*, I mean, who left the Court of
Pharaoh, after having receiv'd his Doctor's
Degrees in all the Sciences of the *Egyptians:*
Who in the number of his Signs ſurpaſs'd all
the Profeſſors in Magick. In what manner
did he ſhew his Excellency, and Abilities for
being a Divine Ambaſſador, and Repreſenter
of the Authority of the God of the *Hebrews?*
Do you think it was by coming down from
Mount *Sinai,* with the great Tables in his
hands, in the form of a ſimple pure Man?
No, no; it was by preſenting himſelf vene-
rable with two great Horns, which branch'd
upon his Forehead, at which awful and ma-
jeſtick Preſence, the Hearts of that vagabond
People fail'd them, ſo that he was oblig'd to
cover his Face with a Veil: and this he did,
that he might not make that divine and more
than human Aſpect become too familiar.

Saul. Thus I hear that the *Great Turk,*
when he does not give a familiar Audience,
has a Veil before him. Thus I have ſeen the
Religious of *Caſtello* in *Genoa,* for a little time
ſhewing a fine Tail veil'd, and making People kiſs it; ſaying, Don't touch it, but kiſs
it; this is the holy Relick of that Bleſſed Aſs
which

which was made worthy to carry our God from Mount *Olivet* to *Jerusalem*; worship it, kiss it, and give Alms; *Centuplum accipietis, & vitam æternam possidebitis.*

Soph Let us leave that, and come to our purpose. By the Law and Decree of that Elect Nation, none is made King, without pouring Oil with a Horn on his Head, and it is order'd that this royal Liquor be pour'd out of the sacred Horn, that the great Dignity of Horns may appear, which preserve, pour out, and beget Royal Majesty. Now if a Piece, a Relick of a dead Beast is in so much Reputation; what must we think of a living and perfectly intire Beast, that does not borrow its Horns, but has them by the eternal Benefit and Kindness of Nature? I pursue my purpose according to *Mosaick* Authority, which in the Law and Scripture never denounces any other Threatning but this, or the like: *Behold my People, thus says our* Jehovah, *I will blunt your Horn, O ye Transgressors of my Precepts. O ye Perverters of my Law, I will bind and break your Horns. I will surely unhorn you to purpose, you wicked Knaves.* Thus for ordinary, he makes no other Promises but this, or the like · *I will surely horn thee by my Faith, by my self I swear, that I will adorn thee with Horns, my chosen People. My faithful People, be thou assured, that thy Horns shall suffer no evil; none of them shall wither. Holy Generation, blessed Sons, I will raise, magnify, and exalt your Horns; for the*

Horns

Horns of the Juſt ought to be exalted. From whence it evidently appears, that in Horns conſiſt Excellence, Splendour, and Power: they are the Enſigns of Heroes, Beaſts, and Men.

Saul. How does it happen then, that one without Reputation, or who has loſt ſome reputed ſort of Honour, is commonly call'd horn'd?

Soph. How comes it that ſome ignorant Swine on ſome occaſions call you Philoſopher; (which, if true, is the moſt honourable Title any Man can have) and call you ſo by way of Affront and Contempt?

Saul. From certain Envy.

Soph. Why do you ſometimes call a Fool, and a Booby, a Philoſopher?

Saul. By a certain Irony.

Soph. So you may underſtand, that they who are, and they who are not honour'd and reſpected, are call'd Horned, from certain Envy and certain Irony. *Iſis* then concluded with *Capricorn,* ' who is not only a celeſtial God, but ' likewiſe worthy of a greater and better Place ' than this is, becauſe he is horned, and be- ' cauſe he is a Beaſt, and moreover becauſe ' he made the Gods become horned and ' Beaſts; which contains in it great Know- ' ledg and Judgment of natural things, and of ' Magick, as it reſpects the divers Reaſons by ' which the divine Form and Subſtance im- ' merſes, expands, and communicates it ſelf ' by all, with all, and from all Subjects. As ' to what the moſt vile Idolaters, even the

R   ' vileſt

' vileſt in all *Greece,* and other parts of the
' World, upbraid *Egypt* with, what has been
' ſaid already is a ſufficient Anſwer; *viz.*
' That if any Indecency is committed in
' Worſhip, which is in ſome manner neceſ-
' ſary, and if they ſinn'd who worſhip'd the
' Deity, that is one, and ſimple, and abſolute
' in it ſelf, multiform and omniform in all
' things, under the forms of living Beaſts,
' living Plants, living Stars, and inſpir'd
' Statues of Stone and Braſs: how incompa-
' rably worſe is that Worſhip, and how much
' more abominably do they ſin, who with-
' out any Advantage or Neceſſity, nay with-
' out any Reaſon or Decency, worſhip Beaſts,
' and worſe than Beaſts, under the Titles,
' Habits and Enſigns of the Divinity?

' The *Egyptians,* as is well known to the
' Wiſe, aſcended from theſe natural external
' Forms of living Beaſts and Plants; and, as
' their Succeſs ſhews, penetrated to the Di-
' vinity. But thoſe from the magnificent
' external Habits of their Idols, adorning the
' Heads of ſome of them with the golden
' Rays of *Apollo,* others with the Gracetul-
' neſs of *Ceres,* others with the Purity of
' *Diana,* others with an Eagle, and others
' with the Scepter and Thunder of *Jupiter*
' in their hand, thus, I ſay, they deſcend af-
' terwards to worſhip thoſe for Gods in Sub-
' ſtance, who have ſcaice ſo much Senſe and
' Spirit as our Beaſts: for in the end their
' Adoration terminates in mortal Men, and
                                          ' theſe

' thefe the moft infamous, foolifh, contemp-
' tible, fanatick, difhonourable, unfortunate,
' and infpir'd by bad and perverfe *Genii*;
' without Senfe, without Eloquence, with-
' out any manner of Virtue; who alive were
' good for nothing for themfelves, and dead
' can be no better either for themfelves or for
' another. And altho by their means the
' Dignity of Mankind is fo polluted and de-
' fil'd, that in place of Science, they have
' imbib'd Ignorance that is more than bru-
' tal; from whence they are come to be go-
' vern'd without civil Juftice and Law . yet
' this has not happen'd by their Prudence and
' good Management, but becaufe Fate gives
' Time and Viciffitude to Darknefs.' And
turning to *Jupiter*, fhe added thefe words:
' I am heartily forry for you, Father, on the
' account of many Beafts, which for this
' reafon, that they are Beafts, you have
' judg'd unworthy of Heaven, notwith-
' ftanding, as I have demonftrated, their
' Dignity is fo great.'

To whom the Almighty Thunderer : ' You
' are miftaken, Daughter, if you think 'tis
' becaufe they are Beafts. If the Gods had
' difdain'd being Beafts, fuch and fo many
' Metamorphofes fhould not have happen'd :
' But it being neither poffible nor convenient
' they fhould remain in hypoftatical Sub-
' ftance, I will have them remain there in
' Picture, which may be a fignificative Index
' and Figure of the Virtues that are efta-

R 2   ' blifh'd

' blifh'd in thofe places. And however fome
' of them may have the exprefs Signification
' of Vice, by being Animals difpos'd to re-
' venge themfelves againft Human Kind, yet
' they are not without Divine Virtue in ano-
' ther manner very favourable both to that
' and other Species, for nothing is abfolute-
' ly, but only in a certain refpect evil, as
' the Bear, the Scorpion, and others. By
' this I do not mean to go againft our De-
' fign, but only to carry it on in the manner
' I have been able to penetrate. Therefore
' I do not care that Truth fhould be under
' the Figure and Name of a Bear, Magna-
' nimity under that of the Eagle, Philan-
' thropy under that of the Dolphin, and fo
' of others. And to come to the bufinefs of
' your *Capricorn*, you know what I faid from
' the beginning, when I made an Enumera-
' tion of fuch as ought to leave Heaven;
' and I believe you remember, he was one
' of thofe I excepted. Let him therefore en-
' joy his Seat as well for the Reafons you
' have produc'd, as for many other of no lefs
' importance that might be alledg'd : and
' with him let Liberty of Spirit, on worthy
' accounts, fojourn ; to which fometimes Mo-
' nachifm, (I don't mean that of Coxcombs)
' Hermitage, and Solitude fometimes contri-
' bute, that commonly beget that Divine
' Seal of good Contraction.'

After this, *Thetis* demanded what he would
do with *Apinius*. ' Let him go among
        ' Men,

' Men, anfwer'd *Jupiter*, and folve that
' Queftion about the Deluge, and declare
' how it could be general, by opening all
' the Cataracts of Heaven, and let him hin-
' der it to be believ'd any longer that it was
' only particular, tho it be impoffible that
' the Water both of the Sea and Rivers
' fhould cover both Hemifpheres, or even fo
' much as any one of them. Next let him
' difcover how this Reparation of Mankind
' fwallow'd up by the Waters, was from our
' *Olympus* in *Greece*, and not from the Moun-
' tains of *Armenia*, or *Mongibello* in *Sicily*, or
' any other part. Moreover, that the Ge-
' nerations of Men are found in divers Con-
' tinents, not after the manner that other
' Species of Animals proceed from the
' Womb of Nature; but by force of Tranf-
' fretation, and by virtue of Navigation,
' being carry'd, *verbi gratia*, in thofe Ships,
' which were before the firft was made: For,
' to lay other wicked Reafons afide, as to
' the *Greeks*, *Druids*, and Tables of *Mercury*,
' which reckon up more than twenty thou-
' fand Years (I don't mean Lunar Years, as
' certain poor Gloffators do, but thofe Years
' that are as round as a Ring, which rec-
' kon from Winter to Winter, from Spring to
' Spring, from Autumn to Autumn, and from
' one Summer to another) there is lately
' difcover'd a New Part of the Earth, which
' they call a New World, where they have
' Memoirs and Records of above ten thou-

R 3 ' fand

' fand Years, which, as I tell you, are entire
' and round ; for their four Months are the
' four Seafons ; and becaufe their Years were
' divided into fewer Months, they were
' therefore divided into greater ones. But
' let him (to avoid the Inconveniences which
' you may confider by your felves) fet about
' maintaining this Belief dextroufly, by fine-
' ly accommodating thefe Years, and what
' he cannot excufe or put a meaning upon,
' let him boldly deny, faying that one is ob-
' lig'd to believe the Gods (whofe Letters-
' Patent, and Bulls he fhall carry) rather
' than Men who are all Lyars.'

Here *Momus* faid, ' I think it better to
' fhift off the Difficulty with faying, *verbi*
' *gratia*, that the Inhabitants of that *Terra*
' *Nova* are not a part of human Race ; be-
' caufe they are not Men, tho in Members,
' Figure and Brain they are very like them,
' and in many Circumftances fhew them-
' felves wifer, and lefs ignorant in their Car-
' riage towards their Gods.' *Mercury* anfwer'd, ' That that was too hard to digeft.
' In my mind we may eafily take off the
' difficulty as to what concerns the Memoirs
' of Times, by making fome Years greater,
' and others leffer. But I think it proper
' and convenient to find out fome handfome
' way of tranfporting Men, by fome Blaft
' of Wind, or fome Paffage of Whales, that
' have fwallow'd Perfons in one Country,
' and gone to fpue them alive in other Parts,
' and

' and upon other Continents: otherwife we
' *Grecian* Gods fhall be confounded; for it
' will be faid that you, *Jupiter*, are not the
' Reftorer of all Men by *Deucalion*'s means,
' but only of a certain part.' ' Of this, and
' the manner of proceeding, we fhall fpeak
' at more leifure, faid *Jupiter*.' He added
likewife to his Commiffion, that he muft
give his Determination in this Controverfy;
viz. Whether he was always hitherto reckon'd in Heaven the Father of the *Greeks*, or
Hebrews, or *Egyptians*, or others; and whether his Name was *Deucalion*, or *Noimus*, or
Otrius, or *Ofiris*. Finally, that he muft determine whether he is that Patriarch *Noah*,
who being drunk with Wine, fhew'd his Sons
the organick Principle of their Generation,
to inform them at one view wherein confifted
the reftorative Principle of that Generation
that was fwallow'd up by the Abyfs of the
great Cataclifm; when his two Sons went
backwards, and caft a Garment over their
Father's Nakednefs: or if he is that *Deucalion* of *Theffaly*, to whom, together with his
Wife *Pyrrha*, was fhewn the Principle of human Reparation on the Stones, which they
threw over their fhoulders on the naked Belly
of Mother Earth. And let him tell which
of thefe two Stories is true, and which falfe,
fince they cannot both be true Hiftory · And
if they are both Fables, which is the Mother,
and which the Daughter, and let him try if
he can reduce them to a Metaphor of fome

R 4   Truth

Truth worthy to be kept secret. But let not him infer that the Sufficiency of *Chaldaick* Magick proceeds and is deriv'd from the *Jewish Cabala* · for the *Jews* are without doubt the Excrements of *Egypt*; and no Man could ever pretend with any probability that the *Egyptians* borrow'd any Principle good or bad from the *Hebrews*. From whence we *Greeks* own *Egypt*, the grand Monarchy of Letters and Nobility, to be the Parent of our Fables, Metaphors, and Learning , and not that Generation that never had one inch of ground, that was their own either naturally or by civil Justice : whence we may upon sufficient grounds conclude, that they are not naturally, nor never were long by the Violence of Fortune, any part of the World.

Saul. Let us suppose this to be said by *Jupiter ex invidia* ; since they are deservedly call'd by others, and call themselves *Holy*, for being a celestial and divine, rather than an earthly and human Race; and not having an honourable place in this World, they are by the Angels approved Heirs of the next : which is so much the more worthy and happy, by how much there is no Man either great or small, wise or foolish, that cannot by the Power either of Election or Fate acquire, and most certainly hold it for his own.

Soph. Let us keep close to our purpose, *Saulinus.*

Saul.

Saul. Then tell me what *Jupiter* would have succeed to this place.

Soph. Temperance, Civility, Urbanity : dispatching Intemperance, Excess, Asperity, Savageness, Barbarity.

Saul. How comes Temperance, *Sophia*, to obtain the Seat with Urbanity ?

Soph. Just as the Mother may dwell with the Daughter : for by Intemperance in sensual and intellectual Affections, Families, Commonwealths, Civil Societies, and the World are dissolv'd, disorder'd, destroy'd and drown'd. Temperance is that which reforms all, as I shall inform you when we come to visit these Habitations.

Saul. 'Tis well.

Soph. Now to come to the Fishes: The beautiful Mother of *Cupid* rais'd her self on her feet, and said ; ' I recommend to you with
' all my heart, by the Good you mean me,
' and the Love you bear me, these my God-
' fathers, who on the Banks of the River *Eu-*
' *phrates* laid that great Egg, which hatch'd
' by a Dove brought forth my Mercy.' ' Let
' them return then from whence they came,
' said *Jupiter*, and let it suffice them to have
' been here so long a time; and let this Pri-
' vilege be confirm'd to them, that the *Sy-*
' *rians* may not eat them under pain of Ex-
' communication : and let them take care
' that some new Captain *Mercury* don't come,
' and by taking away the inward Eggs, form
' some Metaphor of new Mercy to restore
' Sight

'Sight to some blind Person: for I would
'not have *Cupid*'s Eyes open'd; since if he
'shoots so even when blind, and wounds
'whoever he pleases, what think you would
'he do if he had clear Eyes? Let them go
'there then, and remain in the Brain for the
'reason I have said. You see there how *Si-*
'*lence* or *Taciturnity* goes to take its place, in
'the form that the Image of the Box, with
'the Index at its mouth, appear'd in *Egypt*
'and *Greece.* Now let it pass, and don't
'speak to it, nor ask it any Questions. You
'see on the other side *Prattle, Garrulity,* and
'*Loquacity,* with their Servants, Waiting-
'Maids and Assistants, fly off.' *Momus* sub
join'd, 'Let that Head of Hair, call'd *Bere-*
'*nice*'s Hair, be gone in an ill hour; and let
'*Thessalus* carry it to the Earth, and sell it to
'some bald Princess.' 'Very well, answer'd
'*Jupiter.*'

Now you see the Space of the Zodiac is
purg'd, from which are taken three hundred
and forty six notable Stars: Five of the first
magnitude, nine great ones, sixty four middle ones, a hundred and thirty three little
ones, a hundred and five lesser ones, twenty
seven of the least size, and three cloudy ones.

The

The Third Part of the Third Dialogue.

'NOW the third Part of Heaven comes
' to be difpatch'd, faid the Great Thun-
' derer, the Part call'd the South, call'd the
' Meridional: Where firft of all, *Neptune*,
' your huge monftrous Animal prefents it-
' felf.' 'The Whale, faid *Momus*; if it is
' not that which ferv'd for a Galley, a Litter,
' or a Tabernacle to the Prophet of *Niniveh*,
' and he on the other hand to it for Food,
' Phyfick and a Vomit; if it is not the Tro-
' phy of *Perfeus*'s Triumph; if it is not the
' Protoparent of *Jannes* and *Jambres*; if it is
' not the huge Beaft of *Cola Catanzano*, when
' he went down to Hell; I (tho I be one of
' the chief Secretaries of the Celeftial Com-
' monwealth) know not in the Devil's name
' what it can be. Let it go (if it pleafe *Ju-*
' *piter*) to *Theffalonica*, and fee if it can ferve
' for fome pretty Story to the accurs'd Na-
' tion and People of the Goddefs *Perdition*.
' And becaufe when this Animal difcovers
' it-felf above the high boiling and tempef-
' tuous Sea, it declares the future Tranquilli-
' ty and Calmnefs (if not the fame day, yet
' fome of the following days) therefore it is
' my Judgment, that it ought to be a good
' Type of Tranquillity of Mind.'

' It

' It is good, said *Jupiter*, that this noble
' Virtue, call'd Tranquillity of Mind, ſhould
' appear in Heaven, if it be that which ſet-
' tles Men againſt worldly Inſtability, which
' renders them conſtant againſt the Injuries of
' Fortune, keeps them remote from the Care
' of Adminiſtrations, preſerves them free
' from the Itch of Novelty, keeps them from
' being troubleſome to their Enemies, and
' burdenſome to their Friends, and in no
' wiſe ſubjects them to Vain-Glory; per-
' plexes them not by variety of Accidents,
' not lets them ſhrink at the Apprehenſions
' of Death.' Next *Neptune* ask'd, What will
you do, O ye Gods, with my Favourite, my
pretty Minion, with that *Orion* I mean, who
makes the Heavens, as the Etymologiſts ſay,
urinate or piſs for fear? Here *Momus* anſwer'd, ' Let me propoſe my Opinion, O ye
' Gods: As the Proverb of *Naples* ſays, *Ne*
' *e caſcato il maccarone dentro il formagio*, The
' *Maccaroon is fallen into the Cheeſe* Becauſe
' he can do Wonders, and, as *Neptune* knows,
' can walk upon the Waves of the Sea with-
' out ſinking, or wetting his Feet, and con-
' ſequently can likewiſe do a great many o-
' ther pretty Tricks; let us ſend him among
' Men, and let us order him to teach them
' every thing which he pleaſes, making them
' believe that white is black, and that hu-
' man Underſtanding, when it thinks it ſees
' beſt, is mere Blindneſs; and that what ap-
' pears to Reaſon good, excellent and choice,
' is

' is bafe, wicked and extremely evil: That
' Nature is a whorifh Baggage; that natu-
' ral Law is Knavery; that Nature and the
' Divinity cannot concur to the fame good
' end; that the Juftice of the one is not fub-
' ordinate to the Juftice of the other, but
' are things as contrary to one another, as
' Light is to Darknefs; that the entire Divi-
' nity is Mother of the *Greeks*, and is like a
' hard Stepmother to all other Generations,
' whence none can be acceptable to the Gods
' but by becoming *Greeks*. For the greateft
' Ruffian or Poltroon who liv'd in *Greece*, as
' being ally'd to the Generation of the Gods,
' is incomparably better than the moft Juft
' and Magnanimous, who could come from
' *Rome* at the time when it was a Common-
' wealth, or than any other Generation,
' however preferable in Manners, Sciences,
' Valour, Judgment, Beauty and Authority;
' becaufe thefe are natural Gifts, and there-
' fore defpis'd by the Gods, and left to thofe
' who are not capable of greater Privileges;
' that is, thofe fupernatural ones which the
' Divinity gives, fuch as dancing on the
' Waters, making Lobfters fing Ballads,
' Cripples cut Capers, and Moles fee without
' Spectacles, and other fuch fine Gallantries
' without number. Let him perfuade with-
' al, that all Philofophy, all Contemplation,
' and all Magick, which may make them
' like us, is nothing but *Bagatelle* That all
' heroick Acts are nothing but Knight-Erran-
' try

' try: That Ignorance is the fineft Science
' in the World, becaufe it is acquir'd with-
' out Labour and Pains, and keeps the
' Mind free from Melancholy. Hereby per-
' haps he may reclaim and reftore the Wor-
' fhip and Honour which we have loft, nay
' and advance it, by making our Loobies be
' efteem'd Gods, provided they are *Greeks,*
' or naturaliz'd fuch. But it is not with-
' out Apprehenfions of bad Confequences
' that I give you this Counfel, O ye Gods ;
' becaufe fome Fly buzzes in my Ears, that
' *Orion* having the Ball at his Foot, may keep
' it for himfelf, and give out that the Great
' *Jupiter* is not *Jupiter*, but that *Orion* is *Ju-*
' *piter*, and that all the Gods are mere Chi-
' mera's and Whimfies : and therefore I
' think it convenient that we fhould not, *per*
' *fas & nefas*, as they fay, permit him to
' fhow his Legerdemain and flight-of-hand
' Tricks, left he fhould by this means become
' our Superiour in Reputation.'

　Here the wife *Minerva* anfwer'd, ' I don't
' know, *Momus*, what you mean by thefe
' Words, why you give thefe Counfels, and
' why you lay before us thefe Cautions. I
' believe your Difcourfe is ironical, becaufe I
' don't reckon you fuch a Fool, as to think
' the Gods beg Reputation among Men by
' fo mean Arts; and (as to what concerns
' thefe Impoftors) that their falfe Reputa-
' tion, which is founded upon the Igno-
' rance and Brutality of thofe who efteem
　　　　　　　　　　　　　　' and

' and value them, is rather for their Ho-
' nour, than a Confirmation of their Indig-
' nity and extreme Diſgrace. It greatly
' concerns Truth, which is Preſident, and the
' Eye of the Divinity, that there ſhould be one
' good and worthy, tho no Mortal ſhould know
' it; and that another ſhould come, and be
' falſly eſteem'd a God by all Mortals, and
' yet that thereby there ſhall no Honour be
' added to him, becauſe he only becomes the
' Inſtrument of Fate, and the Index by
' which the Unworthineſs and Folly of thoſe
' who eſteem him appears ſo much the grea-
' ter, by how much the more he is vile, ig-
' noble and abject. If therefore not only
' *Orion,* who is a *Greek,* and a Perſon of
' ſome Worth, but even one of the moſt con-
' temptible and ſtinking Generation in the
' World, of the baſeſt and moſt abject Na-
' ture and Mind, ſhould be worſhip'd for
' *Jupiter*; certainly *Jupiter* will never be de-
' ſpis'd in him, nor he honour'd in *Jupiter*;
' ſince he only obtain'd that Place and
' Throne *incognito* and in Maſquerade; but
' others will rather be vilify'd and diſgrac'd
' in him. Never therefore can a Vagabond
' Pretender be capable of Honour for this,
' that by the Miniſtry of wicked Genii, he
' ſerves for the Mock and Ridicule of blind
' Mortals.' ' Now hear, ſaid *Jupiter,* what I
' determine concerning him, to avoid all
' poſſible Scandal for the future: It is my
' Pleaſure that he go down to-rights, and I
' command

' command him to lose all the Virtue and
' Power of doing Bagatels, Impostures, fine
' Tricks and Knacks, and other strange
' Pranks which serve for nothing, because I
' would not have him able by these to de-
' stroy all that Excellence and Dignity which
' is found, and consists in things necessary to
' the Common Weal of the World, which
' I perceive is very easily cheated and de-
' ceiv'd, and consequently inclin'd to Foole-
' ries, and prone to all Corruption and Base-
' ness. Wherefore I will not have our Re-
' putation subsist, and stand at the discre-
' tion of him, or any like him : For if a foo-
' lish King should be so senseless as to put so
' much Power and Authority into the hands
' of a generous Captain and General, as to
' put him in a Capacity to make him supe-
' riour to himself (which yet may be done
' without prejudice to the Kingdom, which
' may perhaps be as well, if not better, go-
' vern'd by the Captain than the King ;) how
' much more senseless and worthy of Correc-
' tion should he be, if he should place or
' leave in the same Authority an abject, vile
' and ignorant Man, by whom every thing
' should be vilify'd, spoil'd, confounded and
' turn'd upside down; who should put Ig-
' norance in the room of Knowledg, bring
' Worth into Contempt, and Villany in Re-
' putation?'

' Let him be gone quickly, said *Minerva*,
' and be succeeded by Industry, warlike
' Exercise,

' Exercife, military Art, by which Peace
' and Authority are maintain'd, and Barba-
' rians are attack'd, overcome, and reduc'd
' to civil Life and human Society. Let in-
' human Laws, impure Worfhips, beaftly
' Religions, and cruel Sacrifices be annul'd.
' for to effect all this, my Wifdom, without
' the Point of my Launce, will not be al-
' ways fufficient, becaufe the multitude of
' vile, ignoraht, and profligate Wretches al-
' ways prevails over the few Wife and few
' Good ; by how much thefe Villanies are
' ftrongly rooted, widely fpread, and greatly
' multiply'd in the World.'

To whom *Jupiter* anfwer'd, ' *Wifdom*, my
' Daughter, is fufficient againft thefe laft
' things, which wither and decay of them-
' felves, and which are devour'd and digefted
' by Time, as things that ftand upon a brittle
' Foundation.' ' But in this juncture, faid
' *Pallas*, it is neceffary to refift and repulfe
' them, left they deftroy us before we can
' reform them.'

' We come now, faid *Jupiter*, to the Ri-
' ver *Eridanus*, which I know not how to
' treat of, it being both in Heaven and in
' Earth, while other things that we have un-
' der confideration may leave the Earth, and
' take poffeffion of Heaven. Now it does
' not appear neceffary to give, but conve-
' nient to take away fome place from this
' River, which is both here and there, both
' within and without, both high and low,

S   ' both

'both celeftial and terreftrial, and which is
'yonder in *Italy*, and here in the Southern
'Region.'

'Therefore, faid *Momus*, fince the River
'*Eridanus* has this Property, as to be hypo-
'thetically and perfonally in feveral places
'at once, it feems worthy of our Power and
'Wifdom to make it be wherever it is ima-
'gin'd, nam'd, call'd upon, or rever'd: All
'which may be done with fmall Charges,
'no Intereft, and perhaps not without con-
'fiderable Profit. But let us grant it this
'Privilege, that whofoever eats of its ima-
'gin'd, nam'd, call'd upon, or rever'd Fifh,
'be, *verbi gratia*, as if he had not eat; he
'likewife that drinks of its Water, be as if
'he had not drank, he alfo that has it in his
'Brain, be as one that has no Brains at all:
'he in like manner that has the Company of
'its Nereids and Nymphs, be no lefs alone,
'than one who is befides himfelf.'

'Very well, faid *Jupiter*, there is no harm
'in all this; fince others will not be without
'Meat, without Drink, without fomething
'in their Brain, and without Company, tho
'this Man will have this Meat, and Drink,
'this thing in his Brain, and this Company
'only in Imagination, in Name, in Wifh,
'and in Reverence. Therefore let it be as
'*Momus* propofes, and as I fee all the reft
'confent to. So then let *Eridanus* be in
'Heaven, but no otherwife than in Belief and
'Imagination, which will not hinder any
'other

' other thing from being in the very fame
' place, which we fhall determine one of thefe
' days; becaufe we muft confider of this Seat,
' as we did of that of *Urfa Major.* Let us
' now provide concerning the Hare, which
' I will make the Type of Fear by the Con-
' templation of Death; and alfo, as much
' as may be, of Hope and Confidence, which
' are contrary to Fear; becaufe both the one
' and the other are in a certain manner Vir-
' tues, or at leaft the Matter of Virtues, if
' they are the Daughters of Confideration,
' and Servants of Prudence: But vain Fear,
' Cowardice, and Defpair, let them go be-
' low with the Hare, to caufe a true Hell of
' Punifhments to ftupid and ignorant Minds.
' Let there be no place fo fecret in which
' this falfe Sufpicion may not enter, together
' with the blind Terror of Death, opening
' the Gates of the remoteft Dwellings by
' means of the falfe Apprehenfions that foolifh
' Faith and blind Credulity bring forth, nou-
' rifh, and maintain. But let them not ap-
' proach, unlefs with baffled Force, where
' the impregnable Walls of true philofophi-
' cal Contemplation furround, where the
' Quiet of Life remains fortify'd, and is out
' of the reach of Danger, where Truth is
' open, where the Neceffity of the Eternity
' of all Subftances is maintain'd; where there
' ought to be no Fear, but of being rob'd
' of human Perfection, and Juftice, which

S 2 ' confifts

' confifts in a Conformity to the fupreme
' and unerring Nature.'

Here *Momus* faid, ' I would have every
' one that eats this Hare become beautiful :
' Let us ordain then, that every one who
' eats this celeftial Animal, whether Male or
' Female, from ugly become fair ; from dif-
' agreeable, agreeable ; fiom cruel and un-
' peaceable, peaceable and gentle ; and blef-
' fed be the Stomach and Guts, that receive,
' digeft, and turn it into Nourifhment.'
' Yes, faid *Diana* ; but I will not have the
' Seed of my Hare loft.' ' Oh! I'll tell you
' a way, faid *Momus*, how the whole World
' may both eat and drink, tho there be no-
' thing eat or drank of it, tho there be no
' Teeth to grind, no Hand to touch, no Eye
' to fee ; and, which is more, no Place to re-
' ceive what is both eat and drank.' ' We
' fhall fpeak of this afterwards, faid *Jupiter.*
' We are now come to that Cur that purfues
' her, and catches her *in fpiritu* ; and for fear
' of lofing matter for Chafe, in many Cen-
' turies of Years, the Hour of catching her
' *in veritate* is not come, and fo long a time
' he goes barking after her, pretending to
' take a Leap at her.'

' This is what I have always been con-
' cern'd for, and lamented, Father, faid *Mo-*
' *mus* ; that you fhould have made fuch a
' flip, as to fend that Maftiff in chafe of the
' *Theban* Wolf, and then haul him up to Hea-
' ven, and place him juft at the Hare's Tail,

' as

' as if he had been one of her Young, and let
' the Wolf remain on Earth, metamorphos'd
' into a Stone.'

' *Quod scripsi, scripsi*, said *Jupiter*.' ' And
' this, said *Momus*, is the mischief on't, that
' *Jupiter*'s Pleasure goes for Justice, and his
' Determination for a fatal Decree; to ma-
' nifest that he has absolute Authority, and
' that it may not be thought that he confesses
' himself guilty or capable of an Error, as
' the other Gods do, who sometimes repent,
' sometimes retract, and sometimes correct
' their Mistake, having some grains of Dif-
' cretion.' ' And what would you have us
' to do now, *Momus*, said *Jupiter*, you who
' from a particular would infer a general Sen-
' tence ?' *Momus* excus'd himself, that he
only infer'd in general *in specie*, that is, in
like things; not *in genere*, that is, in all
things.

Saul. The Conclusion is good : for where
it is otherwise, there is not the like.

Soph. But he subjoin'd : ' Therefore, Ho-
' ly Father, since you have so much Power,
' as to make Earth Heaven, and Stone
' Bread, and Bread some other thing; final-
' ly, since you can do what is not, nor can-
' not be done ; make the Art of Hunting,
' which is a Princely Madness, a Royal Fol-
' ly, and an Imperial Fury, to become
' Virtue, Religion, Sanctity , and let it be
' a great Honour for one to be a Butcher,
' by killing, flaying, ungutting, and quar-
' tering

S 3

' tering a wild Beaſt. Tho it would better
' become *Diana* to make this Requeſt to
' you, neverthelefs I do it, becauſe it is ſome-
' times more decent, in the caſe of begging
' Favours and Dignities, that another ſhould
' interpoſe, rather than the Perſon concern'd
' introduce, preſent, and propoſe the mat-
' ter , ſince otherwiſe a Denial would be
' more diſhonourable, and a Grant leſs grace-
' ful.' *Jupiter,* anſwer'd, ' Altho being a
' Butcher ought to be eſteem'd an Art and
' Exerciſe more vile than being a Hangman
' (as is common in ſome parts of *Germany)*
' becauſe the Hangman's Employment is to
' handle human Members, and ſometimes to
' be ſubſervient to Juſtice ; the Butcher's
' Employment is in handling the Members
' of a poor Beaſt, always adminiſtring to an
' irregular and diſorderly Appetite, which is
' not ſatisfy'd with the Food that Nature
' has provided, and that is moſt agreeable
' to the Complexion and Life of Man (I
' omit other more weighty Reaſons :) ſo the
' being a Hunter is an Art and Exerciſe no
' leſs ignoble and vile than being a Butcher,
' for the wild Beaſt is no leſs a Beaſt than the
' domeſtick and field Animal. It is my
' Will and Pleaſure (in order to preſerve
' my Daughter *Diana's* Reputation and good
' Name clear) and I ordain, that to be a
' Butcher of Men ſhall be infamous, to be
' a Butcher, *id eſt,* a Hangman of domeſtick
' Animals, ſhall be a vile thing, but to be
                                          ' Hang

' Hangman of wild Beasts, shall be Honour,
' Reputation and Glory.'

' An Order, said *Momus*, agreeable to *Ju-*
' *piter*, not when he is stationary or direct,
' but when he is retrograde. I must own I
' was amaz'd, when I saw those Priests of
' *Diana* (after having kill'd a Deer, a Kid,
' a Hart, a Boar, or any other of that kind)
' falling down on their knees, uncovering
' their Head, and lifting up their Hands to-
' wards the Stars, and then cutting off the
' Head with their Scymetar, and next pul-
' ling out the Heart, before they touch'd any
' of the Members; and thus successively em-
' ploying a little Knife with a divine Reve-
' rence, and proceeding from one thing to
' another till they came to perform their
' other Ceremonies. From whence it may
' appear, with what Religion and pious Cir-
' cumstances, he alone, who admits of no
' Companions in that Affair, can dispatch
' the Beast; leaving the By-standers to be-
' hold with a certain Reverence, and feign'd
' Amazement: And while he is the only
' Hangman among them all, he reckons him-
' self the only High-Priest, to whom it be-
' longs to carry the *Semhamphorash*, or High
' Priest's Garment, and who alone may set
' his foot in the Holy of Holies. But the
' evil on't is, that it often happens, that
' whilst those *Actæons* pursue the Harts in the
' Woods, they are converted into domestick
' Harts by their *Diana's* at home blowing on

' their

' their Face after a magical way, and throw-
' ing Water out of the Font upon them, and
' saying three times,

Si videbas feram,
Tu currebas cum ea,
Me, quæ jam tecum eram,
Spectes in Galilæa.

' Or enchanting them in this other manner
' *You have left your House, and pursu'd the*
' *Beast, and run after it with so much Diligence,*
' *that you have made your self a Companion*
' *with it in Substance.* Amen.

 ' Thus then, concluded *Jupiter,* I ordain
' Hunting to be a Virtue. both because of
' what *Isis* propos'd with respect to Beasts,
' and also because these same Hunters make
' themselves Harts, Boars, wild Beasts, and
' Brutes, with so much Diligence, Vigilance,
' and religious Worship. Let it be, I say,
' so heroick a Virtue, that when a Prince
' pursues a Doe, a Hare, a Hart, or any o-
' ther wild Beast, he imagine that the Ene-
' my's Legions run before him : when he
' shall have taken any thing, let him ima-
' gine that he has taken that Prince or Ty-
' rant prisoner, whom he fear'd most . from
' whence he shall have good reason to per-
' form those fine Ceremonies, and render
' those warm Thanks, and offer to Heaven
' those pretty and most holy Trinkets.'

' You

' You have provided a good Poſt for the
' hunting Dog, ſaid *Momus*; and I think it
' will be beſt to ſend him into *Corſica* or *Eng-*
' *land*. And I think he ſhould be ſucceeded
' by Preaching of the Truth, Tyrannicide,
' Zeal for one's Country and Family, Vigi-
' lance, Protection and Care of the Com-
' monwealth. Now, ſaid he, what ſhall
' we do with the little Bitch?' At which
fair *Venus* ſtood up, and ask'd her as a Favour from the Gods; becauſe ſometimes ſhe
and her Maids at their ſpare hours were diverted with her wanton Motions, with her
licking their Lips, and with the pretty wagging of her Tail. ' Well, ſaid *Jupiter*; but
' look, my Daughter, that Flattery and Adu-
' lation which are ſo much lov'd, as well as
' Zeal and Contempt, which are ſo much ha-
' ted, depart with her. For in that place
' I will have Familiarity, Affability, Placa-
' bility, Gratitude. ſimple Obſequiouſneſs,
' and loving Servitude' ' Do with the reſt,
' anſwer'd the Beautiful Goddeſs, as you will;
' for without theſe Bitches Courts cannot
' live happily, nor can they perſevere and
' continue virtuouſly, without theſe Virtues
' which you have recounted.'

The Goddeſs of *Paphus* had no ſooner
clos'd her mouth, but *Minerva* open'd hers,
ſaying, ' What do you deſtine to my fine
' Manufacture, that vagabond Palace, that
' moving Houſe, that Shop or Ware-houſe,
' that wandring wild Beaſt, that true Whale
                                        ' which

' which fwallows up living found Bodies in
' one place, and then goes and fpues them
' up on the moft diftant Shores, and oppofite,
' contrary, and different Coafts of the Sea?'
' Let it go, faid a great many Gods, with
' abominable Avarice, vile and precipitate
' Merchandizing, defperate Piracy, Plun-
' dering, Chicane, Ufury, and its other wic-
' ked Hand-Maids, Servants, and Atten-
' dants. And let Liberality, Munificence,
' Noblenefs of Mind, Communicativenefs,
' Readinefs to do Services, and their worthy
' Minifters and Servants, fucceed.'

' It is necessary, faid *Minerva*, that it be
' granted and appropriated to fome-body.'
' Do with it what you pleafe, faid *Jupiter.*'
' Then faid fhe, let it ferve fome folicitous
' *Portuguefe*, or curious and covetous *Briton*,
' that fo with it they may go and difcover
' other Countries and other Regions towards
' the *Weft-Indies*, where the fharp-fighted
' *Genoefe* has made no Difcoveries, and the
' tenacious and ftiptick *Spaniard* has not fet
' his foot: and thus fucceffively, for the fu-
' ture, let it ferve the moft curious, folici-
' tous and diligent Searcher of new Conti-
' nents and Lands.'

Minerva having ended her Difcourfe, the
gloomy, reftive, and melancholy *Saturn* began to fpeak ; faying, ' It is my Opinion, O
' ye Gods, that among fuch as are referv'd
' in Heaven (with the *Affes, Capricorn*, and
' the *Virgin)* fhould be this Hydra, this an-
' cient

' cient and great Serpent, which moſt deſer-
' vedly poſſeſſes the heavenly Dominion; as
' being he that vindicated us from the Affront
' of the bold and curious *Prometheus*, who was
' not ſo much a Friend to our Glory, as too af-
' fectionate to Men, whom he would have by
' the Privilege and Prerogative of Immorta-
' lity, to be like and equal to us. This was
' that ſagacious, diſcerning, prudent, ſly,
' and cunning Animal, and more ſubtile than
' any the Earth produces: who when *Pro-*
' *metheus* had ſuborn'd my Son, your Bro-
' ther, and Father *Jupiter*, to give him thoſe
' Jars and Barrels full of eternal Life; it
' happen'd that carrying theſe Barrels to
' Men upon an Aſs, the Aſs (going a pretty
' way before its Leader) ſcorch'd by the Sun,
' burnt with Heat, and overcome with Fa-
' tigue, finding its Lungs dry'd up with
' Thirſt, was invited by it to a Well, which
' being a little deep and hollow (ſo that the
' Water was two or three hand-breadths be-
' low the Brink) the Aſs was forc'd to ſtoop
' and bow it ſelf in order to touch the liquid
' Surface with its Lips; ſo that the Barrels
' fell off of its Back, the Jars burſt, eternal
' Life was ſpilt and ſcatter'd on the ground,
' and on that Mud and Graſs which ſurroun-
' ded the Well: and this Serpent gather'd
' up ſome Particles of it for it ſelf. *Prome-*
' *theus* was confounded, Men remain'd un-
' der the ſad Condition of Mortality, and
' the Aſs became their perpetual Scorn and
                                    ' Enemy,

' Enemy, condemn'd by Mankind, with *Ju-*
' *piter's* Confent, to eternal Labour and Toil,
' to the worſt ſort of Meat that could be
' found, and to the Reward of many and
' heavy Blows Thus, O ye Gods, this Ani-
' mal has been the Occaſion of Mens making
' ſome account of us and our Actions, for
' you ſee now, that however mortal they be,
' they know their own Weakneſs, and ex-
' pect to come thro our hands. And if they
' deſpiſe us, if they laugh at our Actions,
' and look on us as Apes and Monkeys,
' what ſhould they have done, if they had
' become immortal like us?'

' *Saturn* has reaſon'd very well, ſaid *Ju-*
' *piter.*' ' Let it remain then, cry'd all the
' Gods.' *Jupiter* anſwer'd, ' But let Envy,
' Evil-ſpeaking, Treachery, Falſhood, Re-
' proach, Contention and Diſcord depart,
' and let the contrary Virtues, with ſerpen-
' tine Sagacity and Caution, remain. But I
' cannot endure that Raven there. There-
' fore let *Apollo* remove that divine and good
' Servant, that ſolicitous Ambaſſador, that
' diligent News-monger and Poſt; which ſo
' well diſcharg'd the Office which the Gods
' entruſted him with, I mean when they ex-
' pected to have quench'd their Thirſt by the
' Sedulity of this Servant.'

' If he would reign, ſaid *Apollo,* let him
' go into *England,* where he will find a thou-
' ſand Legions of his Fellow-Creatures. If
' he would lead a ſolitary Life, let him go to
' *Monte-*

' *Montecorvino* near *Salernum.* If he would
' be where there are many Figs, let him go
' to *Figonia*; that is, where the *Ligustick* Sea
' washes the Shoar, from *Nizza* all the way
' to *Genoa.* If he longs for Carrion, let him
' go and stay in *Campania*, or in the way be-
' tween *Rome* and *Naples*, where so many
' Robbers are quarter'd, for there at every
' pace he will have many sumptuous Ban-
' quets of fresh Flesh, more than any where
' else in the World.'

Jupiter subjoin'd, ' Let us send down with
' him all Filthiness, Derision, Contempt,
' Loquacity, and Imposture; and let Ma-
' gick, Prophecy, all Divination, and Prog-
' nostication of Effects good and useful, suc-
' ceed to that Seat.'

Saul. I should be glad to know your Opinion, *Minerva*, about the Metaphor of the
Raven, which was first found and figur'd in
Egypt, and afterward taken up by the *Hebrews* in form of History; with whom this
Science transmigrated from *Babylon*, and travel'd from *Greece* in form of a Fable, dress'd
up by the Poets. For the *Hebrews* speak of a
Raven sent out of the Ark by a Man whose
Name was *Noah*, to see if the Waters were
dry'd up, at the time when Men had drank
so much that they burst; and this Animal,
charm'd with so many dead Carcasses, remain'd, and never return'd from its Message
and Service: which appears quite contrary
to the Accounts of the *Egyptians* and *Grecians*,

which

which are to this purpofe; That the Raven
was fent from Heaven by one of the Gods
call'd *Apollo*, to try if he could find any Water, at a time when the Gods were ready to
die of Thirft; and that this Animal charm'd
with Figs he found in his way, ftaid away
many days, and at laft came home late without Water; and I believe he loft the Veffel
too.

Soph. I will not at prefent put my felf to
the trouble of explaining to you the learned
Metaphor: I'll only tell you, that the Relation of the *Hebrews* and *Egyptians* anfwers all
to the fame Metaphor; for to fay that the
Raven went out of the Ark that was ten
Cubits above the higheft Mountain on earth,
and to fay that it went from Heaven, is in
my mind all one and the fame. And that
Men in fuch a Place and Region are call'd
Gods, is not very ftrange; for being celeftial, they may with little trouble be Gods.
And that the *Jews* call the principal Man
Noah, and the *Egyptians Apollo*, may be eafily
reconcil'd, becaufe the different Denomina-
tion concurs in the very fame Office of rege-
nerating: for *SOL ET HOMO GENE-*
RANT HOMINEM. And that it happen'd at a time when Men had too much to
drink, and that it was when the Gods were
ready to die of Thirft, is certainly one and
the fame thing, becaufe when the Cataracts
of Heaven were open'd, and the Cifterns of
Heaven broke loofe, it muft neceffarily have
follow'd,

follow'd, that Men had too much Drink, and the Gods died for Thirft. That the Raven was allur'd and charm'd with Figs, and that the fame was attracted by a ftrong Defire to dead Bodies, comes to the fame thing, if you confider the Interpretation of that *Jofeph* who explain'd Dreams. For he prognofticated to *Pottphar*'s Baker (who faid he had had a Vifion, that he carry'd a Basket of Figs on his Head, of which the Birds came to eat) that he was to be hang'd, and that the Ravens and Vultures fhould eat his Flefh. That the Raven return'd, late, and without any advantage to thofe that fent him; and yet was not only faid never to have return'd, but even that he was never fent, nor never went; this is eafily reconcil'd: for one that goes, does, and returns in vain, may be properly enough faid not to go, do, nor return. And we are wont to fay to one that comes late and in vain, altho he brings back fomething: ' You went, ' my Brother, but did not return; I thought ' I faw you at *Lucca*.' You fee then, *Saulinus*, how *Egyptian* Metaphois can agree to other Hiftories, othei Fables, and other figurative Sentiments, without contradiction.

Saul. This Concordance of Texts, if it does not altogether, yet it comes near to fatisfy me. But now go on with your piincipal Story.

Soph. ' What fhall we do now with the ' Cup, faid *Mercury*? What fhall we do ' with that Jar there?' ' Let it be given, ' faid

‘ said *Momus*, to the greateſt Drinker that
‘ *Upper* or *Lower Germany* produces, *jure ſuc-*
‘ *ceſſionis durante vita*, where Gluttony is ex-
‘ alted, magnify’d, celebrated, and glorify’d
‘ amongſt the heroick Virtues, and Drunken-
‘ neſs is number’d among the divine Attri-
‘ butes: where with treink and retreink,
‘ drink and redrink, ſtumble and reſtumble,
‘ belch and rebelch, ſpue and reſpue, *uſque*
‘ *ad egurgitationem utriuſque juris* ; id eſt,
‘ Broth, Pudding, Pottage, Brain, Soul and
‘ Sauſage, *videbitur porcus porcorum in gloria*
‘ *Ciachi.* Let it be gone with Drunkenneſs,
‘ which you ſee there in a *German* Habit,
‘ with a pair of Breeches ſo wide, that they
‘ appear to be the Hood of the begging Ab-
‘ bot of St. *Anthony*; and with that great
‘ Cod-piece, which ſhews it ſelf from the
‘ middle of them, ſo that it appears as if it
‘ would batter Paradiſe. Behold how that
‘ She-Bear goes there, juſtling ſometimes
‘ with one Hip, ſometimes with another,
‘ now at the Noſe, now at the Tail of any
‘ thing, ſo that there is not a Rock, Stone,
‘ Hedge, or Ditch, to which ſhe does not
‘ pay her Reſpects: you ſee with her, her
‘ faithful Companions, Repletion, Indigeſ-
‘ tion, Fumoſity, Sleepineſs, Staggering *alias*
‘ Stumbling, Babbling, Stammering, Pale-
‘ neſs, Deliriouſneſs, Belching, Nauſea, Vo-
‘ miting, Uncleanneſs, and their Followers,
‘ Servants and Attendants. And becauſe ſhe
‘ is not able to walk any longer, you ſee her
                              ‘ mounted

' mounted on her triumphal Chariot, to
' which are tied many good, wife and holy
' Perfonages; the moft celebrated and fa-
' mous of which are *Noah, Lot, Chiaccone,*
' *Vitanzano, Zucavigna,* and *Silenus.* The
' Enfign *Zampaglón* carries the Colours, which
' are made of Scarlet; in which appear two
' Starlings drawn to the Life, with the true
' Colour of their Feathers: and four glorious
' Hogs, join'd in Couples, draw the Pole of
' the Chariot; one white, one red, one
' fpeckled, and one black; the firft of which
' is call'd *Grungargampheftrophiel,* the fecond
' *Sorbillgramphton,* the third *Gluttus,* the
' fourth *Strafocatto.* But of this I will fpeak
' to you more at large another time.'

Let us confider what happen'd, after *Ju-*
piter had order'd Abftinence and Temperance with their Retinue and Servants to
fucceed, which you fhall hear afterwards:
For 'tis now time to difcourfe of the Centaur *Chiron,* who following next in order,
old *Saturn* faid to *Jupiter,* ' My Son and
' Lord, fince you fee 'tis near Sun-fetting,
' let us quickly difpatch thefe four that re-
' main, an't pleafe you.' And *Momus* faid,
' What fhall we do now with this Man that
' is planted in a Beaft, or this Beaft that is
' engrafted on a Man; in which one Perfon
' is made up of two Natures, and two Sub-
' ftances concur in one Hypoftatical Union?
' Here two things are united to make a third
' Entity; and this is as clear as the Sun.

T   ' But

' But the difficulty lies here, *viz.* Whether such
' a third Entity produces a thing better than
' both or any of the two Parts of which it is
' compos'd, or rather more vile? I would
' say, whether the caballine Nature being
' join'd to that of a Man, produces a God
' worthy of a place in Heaven, and not ra-
' ther a Beaft worthy of the Fold or the
' Stable? In fine, (let *Ifis*, and *Jupiter*, and
' the reft fay what they will about the Ex-
' cellence of being a Beaft; and that in or-
' der to be Divine, a Man muft have fome-
' thing of the Beaft; and that when he
' would be efteem'd highly Divine, he muft
' appear with a proportionable Meafure of
' the Beaft) I can never be brought to be-
' lieve, that where there is not an entire and
' perfect Man, nor an entire and perfect
' Beaft, but only a piece of a Beaft with a
' piece of a Man, it can be better, than
' where there is a piece of Breeches with a
' piece of a Doublet, out of which there ne-
' ver can be made a Garment better than a
' Doublet or Breeches, nor fo good as either
' the one or the other.'

' *Momus*, *Momus*, anfwer'd *Jupiter*, the
' Myftery of this thing is great and occult,
' and you cannot comprehend it; and there-
' fore you ought only to believe it as a thing
' too high and great for you.' ' I know very
' well, faid *Momus*, that this is a thing nei-
' ther I nor any body elfe that has the leaft
' grain of Underftanding can comprehend:
' But

'But before I, who am a God, or any other
'who has as much Understanding as a grain
'of Millet, be oblig'd to believe it, I would
'have you after some pretty manner give a
'power to believe it.'

'Momus, said *Jupiter*, you should not de-
'sire to know more than is necessary to be
'known; and believe me, 'tis not necessary
'to know this.' 'This then, said *Momus*, is
'what I would tell you, that in spight of my
'teeth I will know, and to please you, *Ju-*
'piter*, will believe, That a Sleeve and a
'Stockin are better than a pair of Sleeves
'and a pair of Stockins, and a great deal
'more; That a Man is not a Man, that a
'Beast is not a Beast; That the half of a
'Man is not half a Man, and the half of a
'Beast not half a Beast; That half a Man
'and half a Beast, is not an imperfect Man
'and an imperfect Beast, but a God, and
'*pura mente colendus.*'

Here the Gods solicited *Jupiter* to make
quick Dispatch, and declare his Pleasure concerning the Centaur, according to his Will.
Wherefore *Jupiter* enjoin'd *Momus* silence, and
determin'd in this manner : 'Whatever I
'may have said against *Chiron* on another oc-
'casion, I now retract, and say, That *Chiron*
'being a most just Man, who formerly liv'd
'on the Mountain *Pelius*, where he taught
'*Æsculapius* Physick, *Hercules* Astrology, and
'*Achilles* Musick, healing the Sick, teaching
'the way how to mount up to the Stars, and

'how

' how the fonorous Strings fhould be tied to
' Wood, and how manag'd ; he feems to me
' to deferve a place in Heaven. Next, I
' judge him moft worthy of it, becaufe in
' this heavenly Temple, at this Altar where
' he affifts, there is no other Prieft but him-
' felf ; whom you fee with a Beaft in his
' hand ready to be offer'd up, and a Liba-
' tion-Bottle hanging at his girdle : and be-
' caufe an Altar, a Chappel, and an Oratory
' are neceffary (which would be to no pur-
' pofe without one to minifter at them)
' therefore let him here live, here remain,
' and here eternally continue, if Fate has
' not otherwife decreed.'

    Here *Momus* added, ' You have worthily
' and prudently determin'd, *Jupiter*, that he
' fhould be a Prieft at the heavenly Altar
' and Temple ; becaufe when he fhall have
' deftroy'd that Beaft in his hand, yet it is
' impoffible he fhould ever want one : for he
' himfelf being one, he will ferve both for
' Prieft and Sacrifice.'

    ' Well then, faid *Jupiter*, let Beftiality,
' Ignorance, unprofitable and pernicious Fa-
' ble depart from hence : And where the
' Centaur is, let juft Simplicity and moral
' Fable remain. Let Superftition, Infidelity
' and Impiety depart from where the Altar
' is ; and let Religion that is not vain, and
' Faith that is not foolifh, and true and fin-
' cere Piety, fojourn there.'

Then

Then *Apollo* ask'd, what fhould be done
with that *Tiara*; how they would difpofe of
that Crown? ' That, that is the Crown,
' faid *Jupiter*, which by the high Decree of
' Fate, and the Inftinct of the Divine Spirit,
' is defervedly expected by the invincible
' *Henry* III. King of the magnanimous, po-
' tent and warlike *France*, which he pro-
' mifes himfelf after that of *France*, and
' that of *Poland*; as he teftify'd in the be-
' ginning of his Reign, by taking that cele-
' brated Device, where two Crowns below,
' and one more eminent make the Body; and
' this Motto ferves for the Soul, *Tertia Cælo*
' *manet.* This moft Chriftian King, holy,
' religious, and pure, may fecurely fay *Ter-*
' *tia Cælo manet*, becaufe he knows very well
' that it is written, *Bleffed are the Peace-makers,*
' *bleffed are the pure in Heart, for theirs is the*
' *Kingdom of Heaven.* He loves Peace, he
' maintains his People as much as poffible
' in Tranquillity and Devotion: He is not
' pleas'd with the noife of martial Inftru-
' ments, which adminifter to the blind Ac-
' quifition of the unftable Tyrannies, and
' Principalities of the Earth; but with all
' manner of Juftice and Sanctity, which
' fhew the direct Road to the eternal King-
' dom. The fiery, tempeftuous, and turbu-
' lent Spirits of any of his Subjects, don't
' hope that while he lives (the Tranquillity
' of whofe Mind is a ftrong Bar againft war-
' like Fury) they fhall receive any Affiftance
' vainly

' vainly to difturb the Peace of other Coun-
' tries, under pretence of adding other Scep-
' ters and Crowns to his ; for *Tertia Cœlo*
' *manet.*

' In vain fhall the rebellious *French* Forces
' go againft his Will to difquiet the Borders
' and Coafts of others; for the Propofals of
' inftable Counfels, the Hope of changeable
' Fortune, nor the Advantage of foreign Ad-
' miniftrations and Suffrages, will be able,
' under a pretence of invefting him with
' Robes, and adorning him with Crowns, to
' take from him, otherwife than by Neceffi-
' ty, the bleffed Care of Tranquillity of Spi-
' rit; he being more liberal of his own,
' than covetous of what belongs to others.
' Let others endeavour to mount the vacant
' Throne of *Portugal*, and others be folici-
' tous for the *Belgick* Dominion. Why fhould
' you break your Heads, and beat your Brains
' about this and the other Kingdom? Why
' fhould you fufpect and fear, you Kings and
' Princes, that your Neighbours fhould con-
' quer your Forces, and rob you of your
' Crowns? *Tertia Cœlo manet.*' ' Let the
' Crown remain then, added *Jupiter*, till
' fome one comes who fhall be worthy of fo
' magnificent a Poffeffion: And here alfo let
' Victory, Reward, Perfection, Honour and
' Glory have their Throne; which if they
' are not Virtues, they are at leaft the End
' of Virtue.'

Saul.

Saul. What said the Gods to this?

Soph. There was neither great nor small, greater nor leſſer, Male nor Female, neither one ſort nor another, who did not, with one Voice and Conſent, extremely approve the moſt prudent Counſel, and moſt juſt Decree of *Jove.* At which the Almighty Thunderer, being fill'd with Joy and Gladneſs, rais'd himſelf on his Feet, and ſtretch'd out his Right Hand towards the Southern Fiſh, which alone wanted to be diſpatch'd, and ſaid, ' Let that Fiſh remove from thence im- ' mediately, and let nothing remain there ' but its Picture; and let it in ſubſtance be ' catch'd by our Cook; and let it be brought ' the laſt Service of our Supper, part of it ' roaſted on the Grate, part fry'd, part ' pickled, and part dreſs'd any other way you ' pleaſe, prepar'd with *Roman* Sauce: And ' let it be done as ſoon as can be, for having ' gone thro ſo much Buſineſs, I am ready to ' die of Hunger, and I preſume you're not ' very full. Beſides, I think it proper that ' this Purging ſhould be attended with ſome ' Profit to us.' ' Well, well, very well, an- ' ſwer'd all the Gods.' And there were there preſent *Health, Security, Profit, Joy, Repoſe,* and the moſt exalted *Pleaſure,* which are the Reward of Virtue, and the Recompence of Study and Labour. And with this they went merrily and joyfully out of the Con- clave, after having purg'd the Space which

lies

lies beyond the Zodiack, which contains three hundred and fixteen remarkable Stars.

Saul. I'll go to my Supper likewife.

Soph. And I will retire to my nocturnal Contemplations.

T H E   E N D.

Ingram Content Group UK Ltd.
Milton Keynes UK
UKHW022327090623
423211UK00005B/22